Rebels and Rulers, 1500–1660

Volume II

Provincial rebellion
Revolutionary civil wars, 1560–1660

Contemporary or near contemporary engraving of Dutch or German origin of the execution of Charles I: *Most abominable unheard of execution . . . of . . . Charles Stuart King of Great Britain . . . before the palace of Whitehall 30 January . . . 1649 . . . in the afternoon between 2 and 3 . . .* The king's neck remains on the block while the executioner displays his head to the crowd. The portrait insets are the parliamentary generals Fairfax and Cromwell left and right flanking the king in the center (see ch. 12). (Courtesy of the Ashmolean Museum, Oxford.)

Rebels and rulers, 1500–1660

VOLUME II

PROVINCIAL REBELLION
REVOLUTIONARY CIVIL WARS, 1560–1660

PEREZ ZAGORIN

CAMBRIDGE UNIVERSITY PRESS

Cambridge
London   New York   New Rochelle
Melbourne   Sydney

Published by the Press Syndicate of the University of Cambridge
The Pitt Building, Trumpington Street, Cambridge CB2 IRP
32 East 57th Street, New York, NY 10022, USA
296 Beaconsfield Parade, Middle Park, Melbourne 3206, Australia

First published 1982

Printed in the United States of America

Library of Congress Cataloging in Publication Data
Zagorin, Perez.
Rebels and rulers, 1500–1660.
Includes bibliographical references and
indexes.
Contents: v. 1. Society, states, and early
modern revolution – v. 2. Provincial
rebellion.
1. Revolutions – Europe – History – 16th century. 2. Revolutions – Europe – History – 17th
century. 3. Europe – History – 1492–1648.
4. Europe – History – 17th century. I. Title.
D210.Z33 1982 940.2 81–17039
ISBN 0 521 24473 0 (vol.2) hard covers AACR2
ISBN 0 521 28712 X (vol. 2) paperback

Contents

Volume II
PROVINCIAL REBELLION
REVOLUTIONARY CIVIL WARS, 1560–1660

Preface

Volume Two of this work completes the examination of early modern revolution begun in Part III of the preceding volume. Although the two volumes are best used in conjunction with one another, this second volume may also be read relatively independently should need require. Those readers in particular whose primary interest may be limited to the great revolutionary civil wars of the period will find separate accounts of each of them in four successive chapters. The latter are designed, in accordance with the general plan of the book, to provide a synoptic view of these conflicts that explains their inception and overall development and aligns them in comparative perspective.

9

Provincial rebellion

I

Provincial rebellion, the revolts of provinces, regions, and entire subject kingdoms against their monarchical center, were endemic in early modern Europe, evidence of the fierce resistance provoked by the aggressions of royal state builders. To be sure, it might be said that much of the political history of medieval Europe was related to the growth and expanding functions of the state – or, if one prefers, to the emergence and consolidation of the state out of conditions of feudal independence and fragmentation of authority. Nonetheless, the sixteenth and seventeenth centuries witnessed the transition to a new political order in the monarchies of Western Europe.[1] Step by step, late feudal kingships evolved into much more centralized governments of an absolutist character, wielding ever larger bureaucratic resources to perform the tasks of national and imperial rule. Royal power steadily extended its reach in breadth and depth, equipping itself in the process with new administrative means to achieve the political integration of kingdoms, to govern dependent realms and imperial possessions, and to make polity, social order, and economy instrumental to its supreme will and interests. Understandably, contemporary legal and political thought was much preoccupied with rationalizing and facilitating these developments; or else, contrariwise, it set itself to formulate a case against the absolute power of kings. In 1576, in his encyclopedic treatise of comparative politics, *Six books of the commonweal,* Jean Bodin provided one of the most influential justifications for royal absolutism through his examination of the nature and necessity of sovereignty. Seventy-five years later, Thomas Hobbes undertook the same task, when he devised with remorseless logic and none of Bodin's reservations the formidable image of Leviathan as the personification of absolute sovereign power to which

---

[1] See Ch. 4 in this book.

subjects and corporate groups were obliged to render unconditional obedience.

To speak of state building is to cite a fact that loomed large nearly everywhere upon the scene of revolutions in the sixteenth and seventeenth centuries. We have already noticed its importance within the causal background of both agrarian and urban revolt. Whether in its general operation or in its particular effects, no other single factor was of wider significance in contributing directly or indirectly to the preconditions from which the different revolutions of the time arose.

Viewed as a type, however, provincial rebellion represented a specific response to the state-building process. This is easily understood when we call to mind the tenacious localisms and recurring tendencies toward autonomy or separation that preserved a vigorous life in the nations of Western Europe despite the centralizing thrust of early modern absolutisms. It has recently been shown with rich illustration how, even until the mid-nineteenth century, the peasants of France remained differentiated and set apart by their parochial ways and tradition-bound attachments; not until after the establishment of the Third Republic did peasants finally become Frenchmen.[2] We are aware as well of the enduring opposition of peoples like the Basques and Catalans to political and cultural absorption in a monolithic Spanish state. Lately, moreover, we have seen even in a long united country such as Great Britain a revival of Scottish and Welsh nationalism issuing in demands for devolution, autonomy, and even independence. Other similar examples could easily be mentioned. If this is true of the present and recent past, what must have been the strength of provincialism and regionalism within states three and four hundred years ago?

In acknowledging the latter's reality, there is no need to deny the importance of national patriotism coupled with loyalty to kings. England, France, and Spain entered the early modern era with a strong and growing consciousness and pride of nationality among their peoples that attached itself to rulers as its supreme expression. But national consciousness coexisted with and was modified by other sentiments and loyalties. These were planted in the soil of provincial and regional societies and their communities.[3] They reflected the influence of common traditions or religion. They belonged perhaps to older ways of life slow to change. They might be associated with a distinctive political identity and with prescriptive rights and privileges sanctioned by the past. They could be embodied in vertical structures of patronage and deference allying territorial aristocracies and common folk.

Consider one or two terms that illuminate the situation. In France, al-

[2] E. Weber, *Peasants into Frenchmen*, Stanford, 1976. [3] See Chapter 4 in this book.

though men could and did speak of the *patrie* in the large, unrestricted meaning of country or fatherland, more commonly it signified one's province or native place, also called the *pays*. Thus, it was the province, rather than France or the kingdom, that was likely to be thought of as one's *patrie*. Similarly, in England, the word *country* referred either to the county and its community or to the country as a whole. Both senses were current and familiar. So again, one's "country" was the county, the local place of one's home or birth, no less than it was the land or kingdom in which one was a subject.[4]

Thus far I have been referring mainly to provincialism in its internal aspect as it manifested itself within a particular state or kingdom. Here, as related to revolution, it was not a question of opposition to a foreign or external dominion but of resistance to the prince and his government by a province or region politically incorporated within the realm.

There was a further aspect to provincialism, however, reflecting the consequences of dynastic unions. When disparate and independent states, countries, and nations were affiliated through royal marriages, inheritance, or conquest, they usually had no political tie save the same prince. In theory, each was to be ruled separately in accord with its own indigenous institutions. As pointed out in an earlier chapter, however, these dynastic associations caused serious strains and frictions.[5] Absentee kingship itself bred special problems of government and provoked the discontent of subjects who felt themselves neglected or mistreated. On the other hand, the presence of a stranger prince with his entourage aroused fears of undue foreign influence or exploitation. Thus, an English adviser cautioned the future Philip II of Spain upon his marriage in 1554 to Queen Mary Tudor, "It is an extreme grief to men of any nation or province to see other men, foreigners, possess those honors, offices, and dignities which in past times their fathers or predecessors enjoyed."[6] Indeed, the entire burden of this writer's political counsel was the question of how a foreign prince could rule England.

It was inevitable, moreover, that one of the states in a union of crowns should predominate over the rest, despite their formal equality and independence. Under English rule, the kingdom of Ireland practically became a colony, while Scotland, if continuing essentially independent, was nonetheless reduced to an inferior position after its king inherited the English throne in 1603 and removed his seat of government to London. A similar situation developed in the Spanish monarchy, which built supraterritorial

[4] See G. Dupont-Ferrier, "Le Sens des mots 'patria' et 'patrie' en France au moyen age et jusq'au début du XVIIe siècle," *Revue historique 188* (1940); P. Zagorin, "The court and the country: A note on political terminology in the earlier seventeenth century," *English historical review 77*, 303 (1962).

[5] See Chapter 4 in this book.

[6] P. Donaldson (ed.), *A Machiavellian treatise by Stephen Gardiner*, Cambridge, 1975, 133.

institutions to administer an empire dominated by Castilians and Castile, where the king of Spain reigned over his many possessions.

Amid the ambiguous, complicated relationships resulting from an amalgam of kingdoms under the same ruler, diverse patterns were possible. Yet in some measure, at any rate, the less-favored states and countries would resemble provincial dependencies subject to a metropolitan power. At worst, they would be like inferior subject realms under a foreign sovereignty, exploited for its dynastic and imperial needs, as were Spain's Italian states. At best, they would retain their independence and privileges, yet tend to view themselves at times as victims of an external and intrusive government pursuing interests inimical and distant to their own. The same English adviser previously cited took note of the harshness of Spain's rule of Naples and Milan; someday, he opined, the natives might rise and exterminate the Spaniards, as the English once did their Danish masters.[7] If their prince made unaccustomed demands upon such provincial subjects or tried to bind them with a heavier yoke, he risked inciting opposition all the more probable in proportion to the vitality of national patriotism and autonomous liberties. The possible difficulties were described in a nutshell by a Spanish commentator apropos of Catalonia in 1640. There were only three ways, he thought, that a prince could deal with a province of uncertain loyalty: go and live in it, put down its liberties and independence, or leave it with its laws and customs to be governed in its own fashion.[8] Philip IV and his minister, Olivares, precipitated a rebellion in Catalonia because they felt compelled to adopt the second of these alternatives.

Hence, provincialism in this aspect signified primarily a resistance directed against external rule, where a separate state or people opposed itself to alien domination or oppression by another.

II

So ubiquitous and entrenched were localisms and provincialisms in the life of early modern Europe that no revolutionary conflict of the time was ever entirely free of their influence. Even the biggest revolutions, which engulfed entire states and peoples, were crucially affected by them. Tudor and Stuart England, the most politically unified of kingdoms, has nonetheless been pictured (if with some exaggeration) by local historians as a sort of federation of semi-independent county communities;[9] and, certainly, county insularities and loyalties had a considerable effect upon the English revolution of the mid-seventeenth century. In France, where pro-

---

[7] *Ibid.*, 133.   [8] J. H. Elliott, *The revolt of the Catalans*, Cambridge, 1963, 491.
[9] See A. Everitt, *The community of Kent and the Great rebellion, 1640–1660*, Leicester, 1966, 13.

vincialism retained exceptional strength, it ran right through such great internal struggles as the later sixteenth-century civil war and the Fronde. The revolt of the Netherlands was also interwoven with a marked provincialism, which stemmed from the vigor of provincial institutions and the comparatively modest level of political integration that Habsburg sovereignty had achieved in the Low Countries before resistance to its rule began.

We have also seen how much both localism and provincialism entered into the structure of agrarian and urban revolts. The bond between peasant or urban rebels and their particular locale, the inability of nearly all such movements to transcend territorial limits or unite with similar movements elsewhere, and their connection in some instances with the defense of provincial privileges all serve to illustrate this fact. We have seen, too, how in the case of the urban revolution in Naples in 1647 provincialism manifested itself in a short-lived attempt at actual separation and independence from Spanish rule.

Despite the appearance of localism and provincialism in all sorts of revolutions, provincial rebellion must be distinguished nonetheless as a separate type. Here the basic determinant was the presence of provincialism in its fullest, least deflected form so that resistance by the provincial society constituted the core of the revolutionary event. Even from a political standpoint, provincial rebellion was apt to represent not only a polarization against the monarchical center over particular grievances but an elemental affirmation or self-defense of a people's beliefs, liberties, or way of life. Therefore, its social participation tended to be broad and, besides masses, in most cases to include aristocracies in directing roles. Geographically, it centered upon the political space from whose griefs it arose. Its aims and targets of violence reflected the protest of the provincial or dependent society against the encroachments and pressures of central or external authority. The organization of revolt utilized communal structures and indigenous solidarities and institutions. Finally, provincial rebels looked to religion, laws, and custom to justify their demands and their defiance of innovative and oppressive state builders.

These may be considered the constellation of typological traits to which provincial rebellions approximated although, needless to say, also qualified in different ways in particular cases.

The Spanish, French, and English monarchies all knew provincial rebellions in these years of the sixteenth and earlier seventeenth centuries, when royal central power set forth on new conquests over the obstacles that continued to bar its way. Spain's Habsburg sovereigns had to contend with it mainly in its external aspect, which meant the resistance to Madrid's rule by subject realms bent either on preserving autonomy or else on separation. The revolts of Aragon in 1591 and of Catalonia and Portugal in 1640 were all three of this kind. Of provincial revolt of the internal sort, the only significant occurrence was the Morisco insurrection of 1568 in Granada, the once Muslim principality that was part of the kingdom of Castile.[10]

The revolution in the Netherlands, another subject possession of imperial Spain, presents a special case. Although we could liken it in several respects to a provincial rebellion, fundamentally it transcended the latter in its scope, issues, activated forces, and international ramifications. On this account, it is more closely related to the biggest and least common struggles of the age, those I have called revolutionary civil wars.

The French monarchy reigned over a unitary kingdom, a collection of provinces, not of disparate realms. Therefore, its provincial rebellions were all of the internal sort, mirroring the particularist resistance of provincial society to the centralizing and leveling aims of the French crown. Nowhere did provincialism have stronger foundations than in France. The existence of provinces with a distinctive political status and privileges formally recognized by earlier kings, the connection between autonomist tendencies and the possession of hereditary governorships of provinces by members of the high nobility, and the upsurge of a disruptive particularism at every period of royal weakness all hindered the advance of political centralism and were a perennial problem to the royal state.

With provincial protest so easily provoked and widely diffused in France, the line of demarcation between provincial rebellion and other types of revolution is sometimes difficult to establish. In the first half of the sixteenth century, provincial resentment of royal fiscality was occasionally an ingredient of both agrarian and urban revolts like those of 1548 in Guienne. Then, with the advent of the civil war of the later century, the energies of a centrifugal provincialism were taken up in it along with all the other violent differences rending France. Again, in the second decade of the seventeenth century, we should probably recognize an element of provincial discontent behind the intrigues and conspiracies of the prince of Condé, the dukes of Bouillon, Vendôme, and others of the high nobility against the regency of the Queen Mother Marie de Médicis during the minority of Louis XIII. Such *grands*, governors of provinces, where they commanded followings and power, could exploit provincial com-

---

[10] There was an earlier Morisco insurrection in Valencia in 1526, provoked by the mass conversions that the rebels of the Germania attempted to impose on the Moorish population of the region; see J. Lynch, *Spain under the Habsburgs*, 2 v., Oxford, 1965–9, v. 1, 207–8. Of this tragic conflict a historian has remarked, "Religious and popular hatreds found their most authentic manifestations in these forced conversions . . . in the same blow the Germania rebels punished the infidels and the too loyal subjects of the territorial seigneurs" (T. Halperin Donghi, "Les Morisques du royaume de Valence au XVIᵉ siècle," *Annales E. S. C. 11*, 2 [1956], 154).

plaints for their own self-interested ends.[11] Also in the earlier seventeenth century, we see peasant and urban insurrections serving at times as a vehicle for provincial antifiscal grievances, a fact that helps to explain why these popular seditions received elite approval or support.

Besides these cases, however, certain revolts bore a predominantly provincialist character. The Huguenot rebellions of the 1620s belonged to this category. French Protestantism, now reduced in extent and numbers, survived in its political-military form only as a regional-provincial power. It waged its losing battle against the crown to preserve its political immunities from bastions in the southwest. The revolt of the Huguenot fortress city, La Rochelle, was the culminating incident of this conflict. Another manifestation of provincial resistance was the revolt in Languedoc in 1632 by the duke of Montmorency. Lastly, before the Fronde supervened, there was the Nu-pieds rebellion of Normandy in 1639. Although resembling in some ways other *soulèvements populaires* of antifiscal motif such as we have seen in France, this movement contained traits that stamped it primarily as a provincial protest.

All three kingdoms of the English monarchy – England, Ireland, and Scotland after the union of crowns – were alike the scene of provincial rebellions. England itself was immune to the extreme forms of provincialism prevalent in France, but the weight of Tudor government and regime-imposed change upon outlying regions touched off several provincial revolts in the sixteenth century. The most threatening was the Pilgrimage of Grace against Henry VIII in 1536, the biggest English insurrection between the Tudor accession and the revolution of 1640. Another provincial revolt occurred in 1549 under Edward VI, the Prayer Book or Western rebellion in Devon and Cornwall. A third, smaller and more easily suppressed than the others, was the rising in the north in 1569 led by the earls of Westmorland and Northumberland. Along with these, we must also reckon Sir Thomas Wyatt's rebellion in 1554, the result of Mary Tudor's Spanish marriage and English fears of Spanish domination.

Ireland in the sixteenth century passed through perhaps ten insurrections against English rule. All were limited to a particular area or province; all likewise showed the effects of both the traditional division of Irish society between old Irish and old English and of the disunity of a subject population fragmented into rivalrous feudal and tribal units under England's paramountcy. These revolts began with the Kildare rebellion of 1534 under Silken Thomas Fitzgerald, son and heir of the earl of Kildare; they included the insurrection of Shane O'Neill in the 1560s and subsequent outbreaks in this and the following decade; they ended with the

[11] See V. Tapié, *La France de Louis XIII et de Richelieu*, Paris, 1967, 92–100.

rebellion of 1595–1603 in Ulster led by the great native nobleman and clan chief Hugh O'Neill, earl of Tyrone.[12] The latter was Gaelic Ireland's final and strongest stand against the expansion of English power. Its defeat completed England's conquest and exposed the country to total domination and intensified colonization by English Protestant interests. In 1641 a subjugated Ireland rose once more. This attempt at freedom was the nearest approach to a united national resistance the Irish had ever achieved. Although it, too, foundered on internal quarrels, it was among the biggest provincial rebellions of the age.

Finally, in Scotland, English interference and other differences led to the rebellion of 1638, the first in the violent cycle of mid-century revolutions in the possessions of Charles I. It was an irresistible assertion of Scottish independence animated by flaming zeal for religious and political reforms. The Scottish rebellion may be compared with some of the biggest revolutionary movements of the era. Scotland, however, could no longer escape the connection with a more powerful, dominant England, with whose destinies its own were now permanently interlocked. It was, moreover, an ironic consequence of the English revolution that its victory led to the temporary conquest of Scotland and a coerced political union with England. Thus, in view of this overshadowing relationship, the revolt of Scotland is best understood within the context of provincial rebellion.

III

FRANCE: THE LANGUEDOC REVOLT OF 1632 AND THE NU-PIEDS REVOLT IN NORMANDY OF 1639

To achieve a closer understanding of these several provincial rebellions, we shall consider them partly as a whole and partly as they group themselves into those largely of an internal and those largely of an external aspect. Empirically, to be sure, they present many peculiarities and differences. Nonetheless, a comparative view may make it possible to recognize some parallel and common features that relate them similarly to their world.

It is revelatory of provincial rebellion that conjunctural factors ordinarily played a negligible role in its genesis. This was in contrast to peasant and urban revolts, where such factors were in most cases essential. Provincial rebellions were not usually economic conflicts, nor were they outbreaks of a population afflicted beyond endurance by the adversities of

---

[12] For sixteenth-century Irish revolts, which are hard to count because of their diffuseness, see G. Morton, *Elizabethan Ireland*, London, 1971; N. Canny, *The Elizabethan conquest of Ireland*, London, 1976; and R. D. Edwards, *Ireland in the age of the Tudors*, London, 1977.

conjoncture. An exception may be made for the antifiscalism of the Nu-pieds revolt in Normandy, which was preceded by the ravages of plague, the quartering of troops upon the province, and similar burdens.[13] As a rule, however, short-term economic reverses, slump, harvest failure, dearth, and social misery had little to do with the eruption of provincial revolt.

What principally engendered it, rather, was the enmity aroused in the provincial society by commands and rule in contradiction to its privileges, political assumptions, local structures, and basic values. It was a product of the confrontation between an obdurate provincialism in unitary king-doms or inferior realms and the architects of sovereign power set on achieving a more efficient exploitation of subjects, a tighter religiopolitical unity, and a stronger concentration of governmental authority in royal hands.

In France, we see this confrontation in perhaps its clearest form. So ridden was France with irresponsible localisms and a variety of privileges limiting government action that only an aggressive absolutism seemed able to master them. The challenge they posed to central authority became even more acute with the advent of the war years from the later 1620s on: a time when the crown had to mobilize the kingdom's resources for costly combat against France's main European adversaries, the Spanish mon-archy and the Austrian Habsburgs. War has always been a major factor, probably more important in the long run than any other, in extending and fortifying the powers of the state. Under its iron necessities, Louis XIII and Richelieu made a gigantic effort to strengthen royal command over the lives and goods of subjects. To effect this end, a historian has com-mented, the minister "inevitably rode roughshod over many rights, priv-ileges, and immunities that bore the sanction of tradition and, in certain instances, of accepted law." But to Richelieu there seemed to be no other way to achieve control over an insubordinate kingdom except by doing battle with the entrenched interests and collective prerogatives of sub-jects.[14]

Richelieu's opponents accused him of transforming the French mon-archy into an outright tyranny based on sheer coercion. The author of a *Remonstrance* addressed to Louis XIII in 1631 declared that the pretext of the preservation of the state and *lèse-majesté* was used to justify grave in-justices.

If the sovereign courts remonstrate against edicts that oppress the people, if fron-tier provinces point to their privileges . . . if they oppose the introduction of changes

---

[13] See M. Foisil, *La Révolte des Nu-pieds et les révoltes normandes de 1639*, Paris, 1970, pt. 1.
[14] W. F. Church, *Richelieu and reason of state*, Princeton, 1972, 303.

that will ruin them, all are reduced to questions of authority. Petitions are called rebellion; no mention is made of kindness, clemency, or justice, only severity, rigor, and force.[15]

Such statements expose some of the reasons for provincial rebellion. A case in point was Languedoc's revolt in the summer of 1632, incited by the crown's attempt, begun three years earlier, to establish *élus* and by other assorted severities. Its leader was the duke of Montmorency, governor of Languedoc, a dignity hereditary in his family for a century. Montmorency was at once a figurehead of both provincial and aristocratic disaffection. In one of its aspects, his rebellion was connected with the incessant conspiracies and intrigues by the *grands* against Richelieu, of which the focal point was the king's mother and brother, Gaston, duke of Orléans, known as Monsieur. Montmorency allied himself with Monsieur, who claimed to wish to deliver France from Richelieu's tyranny. The rising was nonetheless an authentic expression of Languedoc's grievances. The governor had behind him a clientele of noblemen, clergy, officials, and other followers in the province. "The character of the house of Montmorency is so impressed in Languedoc," Richelieu was informed, "that the people regard the name of the king as imaginary."[16] The assembled Estates of Languedoc, opposed to *élus*, called on Montmorency to unite with them in defense of provincial liberties. Four or five bishops also endorsed the movement. The Parlement of Toulouse, however, condemned it. All the dissidents, of course, denied that they were rebels.

Montmorency took the field with an army of about five thousand men that was defeated in September by royal troops at Castelnaudary. Captured in battle, he was tried by the Parlement of Toulouse and beheaded on October 30, despite many petitions to the king and cardinal to spare his life. Having come to Languedoc to pacify the province, Louis XIII abolished some of the *élections* whose introduction had ignited resistance. But the prompt suppression of the revolt and the ruthless punishment of Montmorency declared the crown's intention to have its will. The conflict was an opposition of right against right, province against crown, local liberties against imperatives of the state.[17]

A similar affirmation of provincialism dominated the Nu-pieds rebellion in Normandy between July and November 1639. The Nu-pieds, or "barefeet," who gave it its name were not so called on account of poverty or wretchedness; they were the saltmakers who worked barefoot on the

[15] M. de Morgues, *Très-humble, très-véritable, et très-importante remonstrance au roy* (1631), cited in *ibid.*, 213.

[16] *Lettres de Richelieu*, v. 4, 365, cited in J. B. Perkins, *France under Mazarin with a review of the administration of Richelieu*, 2 v., New York, 1886, v. 1, 139n.

[17] This account is based on Tapié, *La France de Louis XIII*, 367–75; J. Mariéjol, "Henri IV et Louis XIII, 1598–1643," in *Histoire de France depuis les origines jusqu'à la Révolution*, ed. E. Lavisse, Paris, 1903, v. 1, pt. 2, 286–7; and Church, *Richelieu and reason of state*, 234–5.

sands of the Bay of Mont-Saint-Michel, where they boiled sea water for salt. Antifiscal hatred inspired the revolt, which started in protest against the crown's projected extension of the *gabelle* to exempt areas of the province where peasants and small gentlemen produced and sold salt relatively free of imposts. Normandy was one of the most heavily taxed of provinces, and insurrection was set off by this new action on top of an accumulation of other fiscal grievances. Its main sites lay in the region where the Nu-pieds movement appeared: in lower Normandy, around Avranches, Coutances, and elsewhere in both towns and villages. More distantly, Rouen and Caen were each affected by brief episodes of violent disorders that erupted for one or a few days during August.

In lower Normandy the rebels mustered a force of about five thousand men that bore the suggestive title of the "army of suffering." It had a mysterious leader, Jean Nu-pieds, whom some believed to be a nobleman, others a priest, and still others a fiction. (We meet chiefs in other French revolts of the time with similar popular sobriquets: Captain Boot, Captain Wooden Shoe, Captain Bare-legs, Captain Save-the-grain, Captain Straw.)[18] The insurgents were organized in groups of parishes, which furnished men led by their chosen sergeants; four priests, who collectively may have been Jean Nu-pieds, took a directing part. The army never fought as a body. The rebels' usual tactic was to proceed in small units, adding supporters as they went, to attack tax farmers and finance officials.

Structurally, the revolt was as much urban as rural. Although some communities and parishes in the rebel areas refused to join, country and town were equally involved, the insurgents being mostly peasants and urban *petites gens*. The victims of their violence were tax agents, *élus*, receivers of *tailles*, the oppressors of the province. The phenomenon seen in other antifiscal outbreaks also repeated itself in Normandy, as nobility, officials, and bourgeoisie revealed their sympathy with the protest by their inaction. In Caen and Rouen, the insurrectionary movement was exclusively one of impoverished inferior folk – artisans, laborers, and petty traders; in lower Normandy, though, the Nu-pieds received some support from elites. A few local noblemen participated, like Jean Quetil sieur de Ponthébert, head of the revolt in Avranches. Some priests, bourgeois, lawyers, and minor officials also openly took the rebel side. No one appeared, however, who was remotely similar to the duke of Montmorency or the eminent personages we are apt to find in the leadership of most other provincial rebellions.

With all these characteristics, the Nu-pieds rebellion was essentially a "front of the province against the state."[19] It was far more strongly in-

[18] See Y.-M. Bercé, *Histoire des Croquants: Etude des soulèvements populaires au XVIIe siècle dans la sud-ouest de la France*, 2 v., Geneva, 1974, v. 2, 644.
[19] M. Foisil, *La Révolte des Nu-pieds*, 339.

scribed and animated by provincialist sentiment than were other antifiscal revolts in France. The few fugitive tracts the rebels produced were full of Norman patriotism, imploring both noble and peasant to act in the name of provincial liberty. "To Normandy," a Nu-pieds poem, called the province the *patrie* and invoked its "liberty" in exhorting Normans "to conserve your charter." This last allusion was to Louis X's charter of 1315, become a dead letter, which exempted Normandy from extraordinary taxes. The *Manifesto of Jean Nu-pieds*, disseminated in many copies, condemned the "tyranny" and "oppression" of the "*gabeleurs*" and "outsiders" from which the people suffered. "To Normandy" declared that God had sent Jean Nu-pieds "to place Normandy in perfect liberty." The liberty thus envisioned signified provincial autonomy and particularist freedom from imposts and the excesses of centralized rule.[20]

During November and December, four thousand specially dispatched royal troops put an end to the revolt. They occupied Caen and then took Avranches and the affected areas in lower Normandy, where the Nu-pieds offered little concerted resistance. While repression reigned, the chancellor of France, Pierre Seguier, made an extraordinary visitation lasting from the end of December into late March 1640, armed with special powers to restore the king's authority. The government meant by his formidable presence to teach sedition a cruel lesson. Going in judgment from place to place, Seguier meted out summary executions, ordered rebels' houses razed, and sacked officials for their laxity toward the revolt. In Rouen, Normandy's capital, he punished the provincial *parlement* by interdicting its judges from their functions, a prohibition not withdrawn for nearly two years to the damage of their incomes. The crown displayed the full strength of its anger to the terror of the province.[21]

In the Nu-pieds rebellion, provincial autonomism was the driving force in channeling resentment of fiscality. Probably this accounted for the exceptional rigor Louis XIII and Richelieu used against it. So, at any rate, thought a contemporary political writer, who observed that the cardinal "punished with great severity the sedition of the Nu-pieds in Normandy, because that province has formerly had two sovereigns, because it ranks higher than another province, because it is neighbor to England, and because it has still, perhaps, a certain inclination to having a duke."[22]

---

[20] For these texts, *ibid.*, 188–94.

[21] The main study of the Nu-pieds rebellion is the interesting work by Madeleine Foisil (*ibid.*). I have made use of this as well as the accounts by B. Porchnev (*Les Soulèvements populaires en France de 1623 à 1648*, trans. from the Russian, Paris, 1963, pt. 2) and R. Mousnier (*Fureurs paysannes: Les paysannes dans les révoltes du XVIIe siècle*, Paris, 1968, pt. 1, ch. 5).

[22] G. Tallemant Des Réaux (1619–92), *Portraits and anecdotes (Historiettes)*, London, 1965, 91.

IV

MORISCOS AND HUGUENOTS

The two provincial rebellions just examined were each elicited by the pressures of fiscality. In other cases, those of both an internal and an external aspect, religion was the catalyst to resistance. This is hardly surprising, religion forming one of the strongest of communal ties, embracing beliefs, culture, the practices of worship, and different institutions. When the ruler and central authority imposed religious innovation or persecution upon a provincial society, they risked exciting all its accumulated resentments into violent self-defense.

Consider the Morisco rebellion in Granada, perhaps the most extreme case in which religion lay at the heart of a provincial conflict.

As we have previously seen, Spain's Moorish Christians were a separate people, ethnic community, or nation (a term contemporaries used of them), forever divided from the old Christians among whom they lived.[23] What set them apart was their Islamic heritage and common origin. Settled mainly in Valencia and Granada, they constituted in the latter province a compact minority. "All one can say about 'colonialism,' no matter in what country and at which period," Braudel has observed, "was . . . true in the reconquered kingdom of Granada."[24] As their Christian faith was always suspect, the Moriscos were subject to unremitting oppression by the old Christian population and the Spanish monarchy. To them was relegated the most arduous and menial work. Yet, prior to their revolt, in spite of contempt and injustice, they remained an integral society with its own culture, elites, and customs. Even as late as the middle of the sixteenth century, they were still permitted to take a small share in the administration of the city of Granada.[25]

This situation was drastically altered by Philip II's direct assault upon the Moriscos' existence as a people. Aimed fundamentally at their religion, it reflected the current assumptions of state builders. The goal was unity; the means, the elimination once and for all of the anomaly of a separate community that clung to the ways of its Muslim forebears, at heart disloyal, hating Christianity, and sympathetic to Spain's Berber and Turkish enemies.

In January 1567, following the advice of the cardinal archbishop of Granada and other councillors, the king promulgated a comprehensive

---

[23] For contemporary references to the Moriscos as a *"nación,"* see Halperin Donghi, "Les Morisques," 163, and J. Caro Baroja, *Los Moriscos del reino de Granada*, Madrid, 1957, 205.

[24] F. Braudel, *La Méditerranée et le monde méditerranéan à l'époque de Philippe II*, 2nd rev. ed., 2 v., Paris, 1966, v. 2, 121.

[25] J. Caro Baroja, *Los Moriscos*, 155 ff.

edict against the Moriscos of Granada. They were prohibited from reading, writing, or speaking Arabic after three years; they were to cease wearing their traditional garments and were to dress in the Castilian manner; they were no longer to celebrate Fridays or practice other customs and ceremonies; they were forbidden to take Moorish names or surnames; they were to abandon the use of their baths (among the most beautiful relics of Muslim civilization in Granada), which were ordered destroyed. This law was a condemnation without appeal of a way of life; it signified, one student of the Moriscos has written, "the will to put an end forever to an entire social structure, an entire culture."[26]

Morisco notables made representations to the crown against this decree but in vain, and rebellion inevitably ensued. It had no program, perhaps not even any distinct goal. If anything, it was born of the hot desire for vengeance against Christian persecution and from a last-ditch hope for communal survival. Preceded by secret preparation, the revolt broke out, symbolically enough, on Christmas night of 1568. The Albaicin, the Moorish quarter of the city of Granada, failed to rise in force, and the focus of the insurrection became the mountains of the Alpujarras to the south, where the Morisco inhabitants fought a fierce battle against the stronger royal forces.

The rebellion was imbued by the will to reestablish all the values of traditional Muslim culture. Leadership and authority fell to men of eminent Moorish lineages, and in the mountains the Moriscos elected a king, Aben Humeya, descended from the caliphs of Cordova. The insurgents killed and tortured Christians, destroyed shrines and churches, and enacted sacrilegious parodies of Catholic rites. Conversely, they celebrated Islamic worship, observed religious festivals, and installed their king with all the traditional ceremonies. "The intent," it has been suggested, was "to restore in all its aspects the Moorish civilization after seventy years of precarious existence."[27]

The Morisco revolt lasted until the middle of 1570 and put a heavy strain on the government's resources. It was finally extinguished by troops under the command of Don John of Austria, Philip II's illegitimate half-brother, who invaded the Alpujarras and its villages and starved out, burned out, and defeated the rebels. Suppression was swiftly followed by the expulsion of the Moriscos from Granada. Chained in convoys, they were deported to be resettled in other parts of Spain. At least 150,000 may have been moved in this way. The lands and villages that they abandoned were then thrown open to old Christian colonization.

Yet even this brutal "final solution" failed to dispose of the Morisco problem in Spanish eyes. Scattered as they now were and only a small

[26]*Ibid.*, 154. [27]*Ibid.*, 178.

number in comparison with the old Christians, the Moriscos were still considered to be a danger. The monarchy, fanatically devoted to the unity of faith, repeatedly at war, too, with the Ottomans and with Muslim rulers in North Africa, never ceased to regard them as disloyal. They remained a foreign body that Spanish society could not assimilate. Their total expulsion from Spain by Philip III in 1609 was the conclusive acknowledgment of this failure, the closing episode in the broken history of the Moriscos under the government of the Habsburg kings.[28]

The Morisco rebellion was only one of a number of revolts in which a provincial society's defiance of sovereign authority was refracted through religion. We may see another example in the Huguenot revolts of the 1620s, in this case a confrontation between a Protestant body and its Catholic ruler.

The Huguenot saga in seventeenth-century France contained an event tragically similar to the expulsion of the Spanish Moriscos. For it was in 1685 that Louis XIV, after some preliminary persecutions, revoked the Edict of Nantes, which granted toleration to the Reformed church. The king's Protestant subjects were thereby compelled to become Catholics or leave their country. Between two and three hundred thousand Huguenots, it has been estimated, emigrated in consequence.[29] This act of tyrannous injustice, like the Morisco expulsion, was perpetrated in the name of unity as understood by an absolute sovereign.

Sixty years earlier, however, the French monarchy had also sought to contend with the Huguenot presence, although not yet by such extreme methods. The Reformed church allied with aristocratic power had previously been a prime protagonist in France's civil war, which ended in 1598. It emerged from the conflict with the legal recognition given it by Henry IV, a former Protestant himself, in the Edict of Nantes. The latter, with its secret additional articles, was intended as a pacification of religious strife. It conceded to those of the "Pretended Reformed Religion" freedom of worship in specified places and allowed the Protestants to retain their ecclesiastical and political organization; it also authorized them to fortify a number of their towns as *villes de sûreté* (amounting to about a hundred in 1610) and provided certain other guarantees in addition as security for their religious rights. The Huguenots accordingly possessed a dual character, being at one and the same time a religious community and a politicomilitary organization.[30]

---

[28] See for accounts of the Morisco rebellion, *ibid.*, chs. 5–6; Braudel, *La Méditerranée*, v. 2, 124–6; and Lynch, *Spain under the Habsburgs*, v. 1, 211–18. There is an old-fashioned, interesting narrative in Sir W. Stirling-Maxwell's biography, *Don John of Austria*, 2 v., London, 1883, v. 1, chs. 6–12.

[29] D. Ligou, *Le Protestantisme en France de 1598 à 1715*, Paris, 1968, 253.

[30] See *ibid.*, chs. 1–2, for an account of the Edict of Nantes and its application. Although article 82 of the edict banned political assemblies by the Protestants, the secret articles and

It was to preserve the autonomy embodied in these privileges that the Huguenots waged their rebellions in the 1620s. By this time they had further declined in strength and were by no means united in militancy. Politically, they were led by the high nobility, some of whom had found it expedient to abjure Protestantism and return to the Catholic fold. Of the Huguenot *grands*, there remained, most notably, the duke of Rohan, son-in-law of Henry IV's famous Protestant minister, the duke of Sully, and his younger brother, the duke of Soubise, both absolutely faithful to their creed. Many of the bourgeoisie in the Huguenot towns were reluctant to contest anew with the monarchy even in defense of Protestant interests. Altogether, the "Pretended Reformed Religion" had shrunk to a regional and provincial power. Of perhaps 19 million Frenchmen, about 850,000 were Protestants. Although found in all parts of the realm, three-fourths of them were in the provinces of the southwest and south. North of the Loire they no longer had any fortified towns after 1620. Their main strength lay in Poitou, Saintonge, Guienne, and Languedoc and in the possession of such important places as La Rochelle, Montauban, Nîmes, and Montpellier.[31] The Huguenots professed, moreover, to be loyal subjects: No longer did they proclaim the right of rebellion with which in the sixteenth century they had defended their revolutionary resistance to divinely appointed kings.

The Huguenots took up arms against the Bourbon monarchy in self-defense, to retain the political concessions securing their religious existence. The crown, on the other hand, found its sovereign supremacy compromised by the Huguenots' immunities. Their great fortified towns with Protestant magistracies and garrisons resembled city-states. Some of the Huguenot nobility had also taken part with other *grands* in conspiracies against the crown. Huguenot privileges, political activity and independence, and contacts abroad with Protestant powers were seen as subversive and imperiling the kingdom's unity. In 1625, Richelieu, newly risen to chief minister, addressed to his patron, Louis XIII, the well-known words, "As long as the Huguenots retain their position in France, the king will never be master within the realm, nor will he be able to undertake any glorious action abroad."[32] The monarchy was determined to reduce the Huguenots to the same condition as other subjects, leaving them only

Henry IV's own policy waived this prohibition (*ibid.*, 14). The text of the edict and additional provisions are printed in L. Anquez, *Histoire des assemblées politiques des reformés de France 1573–1622*, Paris, 1859, 456–502.

[31] On Protestant numbers and distribution, see Ligou, *Le Protestantisme*, 122–6; and S. Mours, *Le Protestantisme en France au XVIIᵉ siècle*, Paris, 1967, ch. 3. The total number of Protestant churches at this time was about 690. R. Bonney, *Political change in France under Richelieu and Mazarin, 1624–1661*, Oxford, 1978, ch. 16, contains a good account of the Protestant problem as the government viewed it. The career of the duke of Rohan (1579–1638), the Huguenot leader, is described in J. Clarke, *Huguenot warrior*, The Hague, 1966.

[32] Richelieu, *Lettres*, v. 2, 83, cited in Church, *Richelieu and reason of state*, 189.

their freedom of worship. It was a classic conflict between the state-building absolutism of a Catholic prince and a dissident religious minority politically entrenched in the provincial world.

In October 1620, Louis XIII at the head of twenty-five thousand troops made a swift descent upon the Pyrennean province of Béarn, Protestant for over fifty years, and reestablished Catholicism there. The action had all the signs of a Catholic crusade.

Deeply alarmed by these developments, the Huguenots held a political assembly at La Rochelle in 1620–1 to consider their defense. This institution, in which the Protestant synodal provinces were represented on the basis of estates, was one of the Huguenots' most significant innovations from the time of the civil war and played an important part in the earlier revolutionary conflict. The crown had allowed it to continue in the seventeenth century but only under royal supervision and control.[33] The La Rochelle assembly met, however, without the king's permission, prompted by imminent danger. It decided to divide France into eight circles for military purposes, each with its own commander. But weak as they were except in the west and south, the Huguenots fought their struggle in these provinces, with the duke of Rohan as their chief. Along with Rohan stood the smaller Huguenot *noblesse*, the lower strata in the Huguenot towns and rural regions, part of the bourgeoisie, and the pastors. Despite the abstention of some of the *grands* and urban well-to-do who belonged to the Reformed church, the resistance incorporated a representative configuration of the Protestant communities.

Three successive revolts, whose course it is unnecessary to describe, ensued in the next eight years: one in 1621–2, another in 1625–6, and a last in 1628–9, which ended in the extinction of Huguenot power. The Protestants justified their resort to arms by accusing the king of violating the promises made to them in the Edict of Nantes. The crown condemned them as seditious rebels whom it had to crush once and for all. The war was full of carnage, brutality, and devastation and entailed many sieges. The Huguenots fought not only on land but at sea, where their ships out of La Rochelle and other ports preyed on the king's vessels and maritime commerce.

Gradually, the Huguenots lost many of their fortified places and saw their great cities attacked. In October 1628, La Rochelle, the passionate heart of the revolt, fell after a year's siege personally supervised by the king and cardinal. It had been blockaded from the sea and cut off by land. Out of a population of twenty-seven thousand, contemporaries reckoned, fifteen thousand of the defenders died before the city capitulated, starved into submission. During the siege, the English king, Charles I, intervened

---

[33] For the Protestant political assemblies, see above, n. 30 and Chapter 10 in this book.

on the Protestant side and sent an expedition to relieve La Rochelle that had no success. The Huguenot's acceptance of English help, however, only served to emphasize the dangers posed by their political independence. (External foreign intervention is something we shall see in a number of provincial rebellions.) Louis XIII punished the insurgent Protestant citadel by confiscating all its privileges, abolishing the civic corporation, and razing its walls.

La Rochelle's surrender hastened the conclusion of the revolt. Some months of hard fighting continued in the south, but the Huguenots were divided among themselves and losing heart. England made peace with France, abandoning the cause of the Reformed church to its fate. The Protestant communities in the Cevennes were overrun. In June 1629 at Alès, Rohan submitted, and the Huguenot rebellion ended.

The terms of settlement were embodied in a royal edict. The king permitted the Reformed church freedom of worship as conceded by the Edict of Nantes but otherwise deprived the Huguenots of all their political privileges and guarantees. They were obliged to demolish their fortresses and disband their garrisons. Their political assemblies met no more. Stripped of exceptional liberties and military resources, their cities could no longer resist the crown. The victory of Louis XIII and Richelieu meant the liquidation of Huguenot independence. The coexistence of royal authority with an insubordinate, autonomous Protestantism was terminated. From a power with strong provincial foundations that defiantly challenged the royal state, the Huguenots became a religious denomination only. Henceforth they owed their position to the king's clemency and grace, not to their own politicomilitary strength.[34]

The Huguenots have sometimes been considered as presenting the problem of a "state within a state," or as having stood for federalism, for France's dismemberment, or even for republicanism on the Dutch model.[35] All these are gross exaggerations. Viewed correctly, the Huguenots exemplified a common and perennial fact of life in early modern Europe. They were one of many corporate bodies and institutions that refused to submit their being to the power of kings. By this refusal, of course, they could create disorder, encourage other dissidents, and obstruct governmental uniformity and centralization. Nevertheless, their revolts in the early seventeenth century were essentially defensive; the Huguenots sought not new gains but to keep what they had against the threat of falling at

[34] For an account of the Huguenot revolts, see Ligou, *Le Protestantisme*, ch. 4; Tapié, *La France de Louis XIII, passim;* and A. Lublinskaya, *French absolutism: The crucial phase 1620–1629*, Cambridge, 1968, ch. 4.

[35] Such opinions are expressed both by A. Lublinskaya (*French absolutism*, ch. 4) and R. Mousnier (*Les Institutions de la France sous la monarchie absolue*, Paris, 1974, v. 1, 306–7), different as are their viewpoints in other respects. Both historians identify absolutism with progress, and the former with bourgeois advancement as well.

the mercy of the royal will.[36] If they resisted the crown, they did so because they had not achieved the superior wisdom of those modern historians who know with perfect certitude that the conquests of absolutism marked the inevitable path of progress.

V

ENGLISH PROVINCIAL REBELLIONS

In England, four provincial rebellions took place in the sixteenth century (there were none in the earlier seventeenth), all but one of them focused upon religion. The exception was the revolt of January 1554 against Mary I, a revolt whose "main concern," its historian has said, "was with the threat of Spanish domination."[37] Opposition to a Spanish marriage alliance was quite widespread: In November 1553, the House of Commons petitioned the queen to take a husband within the realm. Some feared that England would become a satellite of the Spanish monarchy, and anti-Spanish propaganda appeared with such titles as "The mourning of Milan" and "The lamentation of Naples."[38] Mary was resolved, though, to have Philip of Spain, and the intended marriage released the dangerous spring of English xenophobic patriotism. The revolt of 1554 was organized and led by aristocratic dissidents, the duke of Suffolk and a group of substantial gentlemen of whom the ablest spirit was the Kentish knight Sir Thomas Wyatt. The rebels appealed to nationalist sentiment against the prospect of control by foreigners. Had they been successful, they would probably have deposed Mary in favor of her sister, Princess Elizabeth. Although risings were planned in the west, in the midlands, and in Kent, only the last came off. Wyatt actually brought three thousand men to the gates of London. A force sent against him on the way deserted to his side, shouting, "We are all Englishmen." Nevertheless, the capital stood firm for Queen Mary, and at this display of Tudor loyalism the revolt disintegrated. Wyatt and nearly a hundred rebels were executed, and most of the rest were pardoned. The marriage was celebrated in July.[39]

This very condensed summary of Wyatt's revolt illustrates how, despite the great diversity of circumstances in different states, provincial rebellion of the external sort might break forth if a realm and its elites felt independence and their position menaced. Such was the response of an insular

[36] See Ligou, *Le Protestantisme*, 74. Ligou also remarks on the weakness of Huguenot political thought and the "intellectual defeatism" of the French Protestants at this period. "Till a late time," he observes, "the Reformed theologians took pride in affirming themselves more royalist than the Catholics" (*ibid.*, 172 and ch. 9).

[37] D. M. Loades, *Two Tudor conspiracies*, Cambridge, 1965, 17.

[38] *Ibid.*, 140. These pamphlets are apparently no longer extant.

[39] The principal account of the revolt is *ibid.*; see also the useful discussion and analysis in A. Fletcher, *Tudor rebellions*, 2nd ed., London, 1973, ch. 7.

England to the queen's Spanish marriage, even though the treaty contained provisions to limit King Philip's powers and prevent Spanish interference. True, there was no general rallying to the revolt, and Mary's rule survived. But the resistance demonstrated the unwisdom of the royal action, of which the succeeding reign of Queen Elizabeth was to see the effect in the increasing anti-Spanish orientation of England's policy. Jean Bodin commented on the adverse consequences of the Spanish marriage as he did on so many other contemporary events. Englishmen, he said, "could not . . . patiently endure the Spaniards to set any foot into England," so that distrust bred "the hatred of the English nation."[40]

The three other provincial rebellions that broke out during the Tudors' reign had their deepest roots in the religious solidarities of a regional society. This did not mean, to be sure, that their genesis necessarily lay in religious grievances alone, but it was religion that kindled the will to resistance and gave to these movements such unity as they possessed. The religion in all three cases was Catholicism, the revolts being a defense of the old church against the changes sponsored by Henry VIII and the Protestants Edward VI and Elizabeth I. At the same time, analogously to other provincial rebellions with a religious core, they were no less a defense of the way of life with which the religion was bound up.

The last of these revolts, chronologically, was the northern insurrection of November–December 1569, centered principally in Durham and extending south into Yorkshire. As the royal government's supremacy was by this time strongly entrenched in the north parts, the revolt attracted only limited support. Its leaders, the earls of Northumberland and Westmorland, heads of the great northern families of Percy and Neville, were genuinely devoted to their Catholic faith. They were followed by relatives and other Catholic gentlemen, retainers, household servants, friends, tenants, and villagers. For the chiefs, the revolt had its high policy aspects; behind it lay the factional politics of the Elizabethan privy council and the court, the disputed question of the royal succession, and the hope of a Catholic restoration through the succession of Mary Queen of Scots as Queen Elizabeth's heir. In its immediate reality, though, far away from the capital, the revolt expressed a local society's twin allegiance to the proscribed Catholic church and to noble blood. The earls summoned all men over sixteen to join them in defense of the Catholic religion, saying that the queen's wicked advisers strove to "put down the ancient nobilitie" and maintain "a new found religion and heresie."[41] For a couple of weeks, while they held the city of Durham, Catholic services were celebrated in the cathedral before large congregations. Even the banner of the Five

[40] J. Bodin, *The six bookes of a commonweal* (1576), trans. Richard Knolles, ed. K. D. McRae (1906; reprint ed., Cambridge, 1962), 749–50.
[41] See the earls' proclamation, Fletcher, *Tudor rebellions*, 150.

Wounds of Christ, used years before in the Pilgrimage of Grace, reappeared. Fear of Tudor central authority, however, inhibited fidelity to magnates. Not even the Percy tenantry rallied in force. With the approach of a royal army, the earls, shunning an engagement, disbanded their followers and fled the kingdom; Northumberland to Scotland, from which he was later handed over to the English government for trial and execution; Westmorland to Flanders, where he lived the rest of his days as a refugee under Spanish protection. About 450 of the rebels were executed by martial law. Incoherent in aim and action, the revolt lasted only five weeks.[42]

More serious than this pathetic event, but equally futile, was the rebellion twenty years earlier in Devon and Cornwall, which registered the impact upon an insular provincial society of an avalanche of religious innovation. In 1536, Henry VIII began the suppression of the monasteries. This mortal blow to Catholic devotion was followed in Edward VI's reign by the dissolution of the chantries and the establishment of Protestantism as the state religion. The Western or Prayer Book rebellion broke out in June 1549 against the attempt to introduce the new Protestant service in the churches. Separate risings started simultaneously at Bodmin in Cornwall and Sampford Courtenay in Devon. The crowd involved in the first then marched to the second, and the whole insurgent mass moved some twenty miles east to lay siege to Exeter, the regional capital, which was largely Protestant in sentiment.

The revolt rested on a rank and file of peasants and villagers. It also included some priests, a couple of town mayors, and a few gentlemen of prominent families. "Certayne gentlemen and yeomen," wrote a witness, "of good countenaunce and credit both in Devon and Cornewall were contented not onlie to be associates of this rebellion, but also . . . to be Capetaynes and guyders."[43] Elite involvement was small in comparison with the majority of provincial insurrections but nonetheless crucial for the leadership it provided. The rebels carried crosses, the banner with the Five Wounds, and the consecrated Host. At Exeter, divided into several camps, they numbered about ten thousand men. They were under the direction of five "chief captaynes" and four "Governours of the Campes," who signed the statement containing their demands.

This statement, intended for Edward VI, was drawn up in the name of

---

[42] For discussions of the revolt of 1569, see W. T. MacCaffrey, *The shaping of the Elizabethan regime*, Princeton, 1968, which places it against its high-policy background and issues; see also M. E. James, "The concept of order and the northern rising of 1569," *Past and present 60* (1973). C. Sharp, *Memorials of the rebellion of 1569*, London, 1840, contains many illustrative documents, including the earl of Northumberland's confession (189–206). There is a brief summary and discussion of the movement in Fletcher, *Tudor rebellions*, ch. 8.

[43] J. Hooker, "The description of the citie of Excester," in *Devon and Cornwall record society*, ed. W. J. Harte, J. Schopp, and H. Tapley-Soper, 3 pts., 1919–47, pt. 2, 67.

"us the Commoners of Devonshire and Cornwall" and consisted of sixteen articles, of which all but one concerned religion. Their tone was peremptory, usually beginning with the imperative phrase "we will." Collectively, they were a demand for the complete restoration of Catholicism – the mass and other sacraments, ceremonies, preaching, belief, and worship. Denouncing heretics, the rebels averred that they would follow only the religion of their forefathers. They specifically repudiated the new Protestant service in English and the English Bible. "We the Cornyshe men," ran one article, "(whereof certen of us understande no Englysh) utterly refuse thys newe Englysh." Another article called for the reinstitution of two monasteries in every county. To explain "the particular grieffes of our Countrye," the rebels demanded a safe conduct for two of their leaders to see the king. It was a sign of some sophistication that they also stipulated that their demands should be granted by the king through Parliament.[44]

The Western rebellion took place in the same summer as Kett's agrarian insurrection in Norfolk, although the two had no connection. Both bore witness to the deep crisis of authority that confronted the Tudor regime under the ascendancy of Edward VI's uncle, Protector Somerset. The government, beset with troubles, was therefore slow in dispatching assistance to relieve Exeter. But the besieged city held out stubbornly from late June till early August, when royal soldiers, including some Italian mercenaries, finally made their appearance. They defeated the insurgents in a battle near Exeter and then launched a wiping-up operation to the west, which ended the revolt. Its extinction was the triumph of Tudor power over provincial subjects whom religion had welded together in resistance to Protestant innovation.[45]

Overshadowing all these English provincial rebellions in magnitude and complexity was the Pilgrimage of Grace of 1536. This revolt was a convulsion of the whole northern society under the shock of religious change. The sudden wave of innovations stemming from Henry VIII's government, enforced by an unprecedented intervention of royal authority, struck the tradition-bound regional order like an earthquake. It incited a massive resistance, essentially defensive, yet voicing too its own positive ideals. Had the rebels not succumbed to the awe of monarchy, they might conceivably have toppled the king's rule.

Scholars have sought to discriminate the secular and religious motiva-

[44] The rebel articles are printed in Fletcher, *Tudor rebellions*, 135–6.
[45] A contemporary description of the revolt of 1549 is given in Hooker, "The description of the citie of Excester." F. Rose-Troup, *The Western rebellion of 1549*, London, 1913, is a detailed study, of which ch. 6 and app. L provide a discussion of the leaders and a list of known insurgents. Other accounts are found in A. L. Rowse, *Tudor Cornwall*, London, 1943, ch. 11; and J. Cornwall, *Revolt of the peasantry 1549*, London, 1977. Fletcher, *Tudor rebellions*, ch. 5, provides a summary.

with death or destruction of their property unless they joined and led the movement, thus providing them with an excuse.[57] To the commons, the cooperation of the aristocratic order was an essential source of legitimacy. The Lincolnshire outbreak fell swiftly under gentry leadership and then collapsed when the latter got cold feet. Gentlemen of the county drew up the list of grievances, which they submitted to the commons for approval. One of the Lincolnshire priests active in the rising testified to gentry initiative: His parishioners, he said, "went forward among the rebels by command of the gentlemen"; the gentlemen armed themselves and ordered the commons to arm.[58]

Although sometimes coerced, and despite mistrust between them and the commons, who feared their superiors might leave them in the lurch, noblemen and gentlemen predominated in the direction of the Pilgrimage. It is clear, too, that on the whole they took their stand from genuine motives of principle. By means of their ascendancy over local institutions, particularly the musters procedure, they were instrumental in mobilizing the plebeian insurgency.[59] A key accession was Lord Darcy, one of the eminent royal servants in the north. After many hesitations, Darcy yielded Pontefract Castle and joined the Pilgrims. He claimed that the castle was too weak to hold out (the town had already risen) and that the rebels had threatened to kill his grandchildren. Nonetheless, as he was fundamentally opposed to Henry VIII's religious and political policy, he became a principal leader. The Pilgrim council itself was largely a body of lords, knights, and gentlemen.[60] Upon Darcy's adherence, Aske offered to resign the chief captaincy to him, but he refused. The earl of Westmorland, while holding aloof himself, let his young son, Lord Neville, join the rebels with his followers. Lords Latimer, Lumley, Scrope, and Conyers also took the Pilgrim oath. The earl of Northumberland, ill, weak, and too terrified of the king, would have nothing to do with the matter, but his brothers, Sir Thomas and Sir Ingram Percy, became rebels. The earl's Yorkshire tenants flocked to his castle at Wressell in the East Riding, crying, "thousands for a Percy." A numerous Percy clientele of gentlemen and common folk threw in their lot with the Pilgrimage.[61]

[57] For some examples, see *ibid.*, v. 1, 201–9, 230–1.
[58] See the statement of the priest, Nicholas Leche, in Fletcher, *Tudor rebellions*, 118–19. M. E. James has advanced an interesting interpretation of the Lincolnshire revolt that makes far too much, however, of its alleged "ritual" features and fails to recognize sufficiently its insurrectionary character ("Obedience and dissent in Henrician England: The Lincolnshire rebellion, 1536," *Past and present 48* (1970).
[59] See Smith, *Land and politics*, 166–7. This study supports the view that the revolt was the work of the nobility and gentry.
[60] See the list of those present at the Pontefract meeting at the beginning of December 1536 (Dodds, *Pilgrimage of Grace*, v. 1, 345).
[61] *Ibid.*, v. 1, 189–90, 226, 227, 228–9, 201, 204, 230, 345; Smith, *Land and politics*, 177, 181–2, 206–7.

tions in the Pilgrimage of Grace, and some have stressed the agrarian discontents that helped to mobilize tenants and villagers. Such an approach, though, is rather artificial. Not surprisingly in view of its size, the revolt gathered up numerous grievances, social and economic as well as religious. Neither its timing, however, nor its structure as a resistance of northern society to central authority, nor its union of aristocracy and common folk would have been possible without the regime's threat to the church, and in particular the monasteries, as the most venerable symbol of tradition. The defense of the church brought the revolt to life and imbued it with a common purpose, at the same time providing an occasion for the airing of various other griefs.[46]

Northern landed society was based in a marked degree on the preeminence under the crown of the great territorial houses, the Percys foremost, and the more distinguished lineages, between and under whom were wide networks joining higher to lower through a variety of ties. Notwithstanding the existence as well of violent family rivalries, economic acquisitiveness, and tenant complaints and resentments, the affinities of kinship, lordship, and patronage tended to foster deferential and integrative relationships within the hierarchic social order.[47]

The northern people, moreover, looked upon the monasteries favorably, or at least with no hostility, as the rebellion itself testified. From a devotional standpoint, they regarded the religious and the life of prayer as indispensable to men's spiritual welfare. Apart from this, they also valued the monastic houses for the different services they performed in the region, whether of charity, hospitality, the provision of tenancies, or other benefits.

The events of Henry VIII's rule that precipitated the revolutionary crisis of 1536 and set the north ablaze occurred in swift succession in the 1530s. They included England's repudiation of papal authority, its schism from the visible Catholic body, and the annexation of religious supremacy by the crown; the king's divorce from Catherine of Aragon and his marriage to Anne Boleyn; the beginning of the royal expropriation of the monasteries and religious shrines; and the political rise of Thomas Cromwell, the minister at the helm who dedicated his formidable talents to a many-

[46] See A. G. Dickens, "Secular and religious motivations in the Pilgrimage of Grace," in *Studies in church history*, ed. G. J. Cuming, v. 4, Leiden, 1967; and the comments by C. S. L. Davies, "The Pilgrimage of Grace reconsidered," *Past and present 41* (1968). Robert Aske, leader of the rebellion, declared that "the suppression of abbeys was the greatest cause of the said insurrection," and that the northern people also grudged at the king's "Supremitie of the Church" (M. Bateson, "Aske's examination," *English historical review 5*, 3 [1890], 556). M. and R. Dodds (*The Pilgrimage of Grace, 1536–1537*, 2 v., Cambridge, 1915), in what is still the fullest study, drew attention to agrarian grievances and their significance for the revolt.
[47] See R. B. Smith, *Land and politics in the England of Henry VIII: The West Riding of Yorkshire 1530–1546*, Oxford, 1970; and M. E. James, *Family, lineage, and civil society*, Oxford, 1974.

sided effort to strengthen and consolidate the power of Tudor government and the royal state over all subjects and institutions.

The north abounded with fears and rumors on the eve of the revolt. Groups of royal commissioners who were simultaneously active in the suppression of the smaller monasteries, the collection of a parliamentary subsidy, and the investigation of clerical morals made the king's authority felt as an intrusive, menacing presence. Reports told of strange new taxes on cattle, marriages, christenings, and burials, of the confiscation of gold for the royal mint, and of the reorganization of parishes for fiscal ends.[48] Religious alteration bred acute suspicion and mistrust toward the center of government. An agitated popular opinion blamed the heretic Cromwell, evil councillors, and mercenary royal agents for the attack upon the church and its wealth.

Revolt erupted first in Lincolnshire at the beginning of October 1536, aimed against the dissolution of monasteries and the activity of the king's commissioners. It subsided in under three weeks, owing to want of leadership and the half-heartedness of the gentry who took part. The terrible proclamation of royal wrath overawed the latter, in spite of their sympathies. But the resistance had already spread to Yorkshire with the insurrection of the East Riding in the second week of October. Here Robert Aske, a gentleman, lawyer, and idealist of fearless honor and commitment took over as chief. The fire then swept rapidly on, over Yorkshire and into Durham, Northumberland, Cumberland, Westmorland, and Lancashire, engulfing nearly the whole northern region, although with Yorkshire as its main center. It was there that Aske at the outset gave the rebellion its name and definition as a pilgrimage, a religious crusade under the banner of the Five Wounds of Christ, aimed at ends both sacred and secular.

Only a detailed account of the revolt could adequately convey the complexity of its events, its poignant human drama, and its sad fate at the hands of Henry VIII, a masterful, supremely self-confident monarch who crushed lives without a scruple.[49] Here I shall merely try to highlight certain features helpful to its general understanding as a revolution.

As has often been observed in the preceding pages, the substantial participation and leadership of elites was nearly always necessary to make an early modern revolution really dangerous to the ruling powers. The Pil-

grimage of Grace achieved this condition to a very high ext ing to the ideal-typical character of provincial rebellion a embracing the entire local society.

The commons of tenants, peasants, villagers, and townsf great numbers. Not only the rural population but most of th cluding York itself, the northern provincial capital, adhered t Sir Thomas Percy, the earl of Northumberland's brother, le thousand men to Pontefract, the Pilgrim headquarters. The P that mustered at Doncaster toward the end of October conta said, the "flower of the north" and amounted at full strengt thirty-six thousand men, far outnumbering the forces the kin able to raise.[50] The bells of the village churches, their peal wards, resounded over the northern countryside, summoning lace to rise.[51] Local patriotism and religious loyalties fused in the revolt. In one Yorkshire parish, when the priest did not Saint Wilfrid's day (October 12) because the king had forbidden ing of it and other feasts, the whole community was roused by on the northern saint. The host of ten thousand men that marche from Durham bore the famous banner of Saint Cuthbert, anot ished northern holy man, which was brought forth only on high f and in time of war.[52] The abbot of Jervaux, a Yorkshire abbey, sa raising of forces, "The king doth cry eighteen pence a day. But I shall have as many men for eight pence a day."[53] The expression ular sentiment was visible not only in the movement's devotional but in some of the names that appeared. A shadowy activist colnshire went by the alias of Captain Cobbler. Four rebel cap Cumberland called themselves Poverty, Charity, Faith, and Pity idea of the pilgrimage and the Pilgrim oath devised by Aske struck chord of religious fervor.[55]

Very striking was the extent of aristocratic participation. This in ment of men in the governing class was crucial; the earl of Shrew who remained loyal, merely uttered a truism when he wrote that "gentlemen" withdraw from the commons then the latter "could do hurt."[56] In numerous instances, communities threatened local gentl

---

[48] See Dodds, *Pilgrimage of Grace*, v. 1, ch. 4; and the discussion of rumors, magic, and prophecies in connection with political disaffection in G. R. Elton, *Policy and police*, Cambridge, 1972, ch. 2.

[49] A detailed account that fully evokes the human meaning of the Pilgrimage is given by Dodds's *Pilgrimage of Grace*, on which I have relied extensively. Nevertheless, there is probably a good deal still to be learned about the Pilgrimage of Grace viewed as a revolution. The examination of Robert Aske and other leaders by the authorities after the suppression of the revolt is interesting both for its facts and the expression of attitudes; see Bateson, "Aske's examination."

[50] Dodds, *Pilgrimage of Grace*, v. 1, 230, 261–2.   [51] *Ibid.*, v. 1, 142, 148.
[52] *Ibid.*, v. 1, 152–3, 205–38.   [53] *Ibid.*, v. 1, 206.   [54] *Ibid.*, v. 1, 92, 133, 220, 221
[55] Aske composed the rebel oath, which stamped the movement as "this our Pilgrim Grace" (*ibid.*, v. 1, 182). The insignia of the Five Wounds had an old history; see for a account and photographic reproduction, Rose-Troup, *Western rebellion*, frontispiece and A. In 1511, Lord Darcy had taken some English soldiers to Spain to fight against the M and they had worn the badge of the Five Wounds. It seems to have appeared spontanee in 1536, and was then taken up by the Pilgrim leaders as their symbol (Dodds, *Pilgrima Grace*, v. 1, 19, 238–9).
[56] Dodds, *Pilgrimage of Grace*, v. 1, 113.

Finally, the clergy of the north parts also played a considerable role. Priests and monks incited popular resistance, and gave it moral support and legitimacy as a crusade. The Pilgrim hymn, which began with the lines,

> Christ crucified,
> For thy wounds wide,
> Us commons guide,

was probably written by the monks of Sawley Abbey in Lancashire, who were reinstated by the rebels after the royal commissioners had dissolved the monastery.[62]

The rebellion achieved its organizational foundation through the military musters of the insurgents by wapentakes, parishes, and towns. At these gatherings, the men of the communities formed companies and named captains by acclamation or impressment. The companies came together over wider areas, and eventually the rebel mobilization converged in the great assemblies of the Pilgrim host at York, Pontefract, and Doncaster. Aske sent messengers with advice, orders, and proclamations to Pilgrim groups all over the north. A suggestion, however, to print the rebel oath and grievance articles was apparently never carried out. It was the Pilgrim oath and the badge of the Five Wounds worn by the rebels that gave the movement its identity and symbolic bond. The Pilgrim council seems to have emerged naturally from the leading men, without any formal institution. Composed of lords, gentlemen, and some representatives of the commons, it received grievances from the rebels, which it then shaped and incorporated in demands to be presented to the king. The council consulted with and reported to the captains and the Pilgrim host. Aske and his fellow chiefs made a genuine effort to have all parts of the north represented. When the Pilgrims held a great meeting at York near the end of November, there were present along with the captains about eight hundred representatives chosen out of wapentakes and parishes. For the final Pilgrim assembly at Pontefract early in December, the shires and wapentakes were asked to send their "discreetest men," bringing with them the grievances of their communities. Aske stressed the importance of an agreement on grievances among commons, lords, and gentlemen. On the occasion of this Pontefract meeting, a number of northern clergy were also summoned to come and advise the Pilgrim council.[63]

The Pilgrim demands ranged over a variety of problems and mirrored

---

[62] Dodds, *Pilgrimage of Grace*, v. 1, 213; see D. Knowles, *The religious orders in England*, 3 v., Cambridge, 1961–2, v. 3, ch. 25, for a vivid description of the involvement of the religious in the revolt.

[63] See Dodds, *Pilgrimage of Grace*, v. 1, 147–8, 261–2, 227, 252, 312, 315, 316, 344, 346, 342–3, for these organizational features; for Aske's emphasis upon agreement over grievances, see his statement in Bateson, "Aske's examination," 556.

the composite interests of diverse groups. This was evident in the final list of twenty-four articles drawn up at Pontefract at the beginning of December for presentation to the king, a statement that expressed most fully the rebellion's grievances and goals.[64] Central in the program, of course, was the matter of religion. On this, the rebels called, among other things, for a return to papal authority, the restoration of the monasteries and their property, and the preservation of the rights, privileges, and liberties of church and clergy. Several articles specifically embodied grievances of the commons, of which the most important dealt with the prevention of enclosures and the regulation of customary tenures and rents to landlords in the north. Of high concern to gentlemen was a demand for the repeal of the Statute of Uses, a recently passed, momentous modification of the land law, which, to secure the crown's feudal rights, severely restricted an owner's freedom to dispose of his land. Other articles struck directly at newly acquired powers of the crown. Besides asking for the annulment of the king's religious supremacy, the rebels wanted the repeal of statutes that made even words treasonable and that authorized the king to determine the royal succession. They also called for Thomas Cromwell and other evil councillors to be punished as heretics and subverters of the law. Particularly striking was the attention they gave to Parliament. They sought a meeting of Parliament in the north at York or Nottingham to effect the changes they desired; convinced, moreover, that the Parliament of Henry VIII, which had enacted the recent religious innovations, was not free, they spoke of a reform of elections to the House of Commons and of the maintenance of customary usage in the House of Lords. Still other articles referred to the redress of legal abuses, relief from taxes, and the maintenance of the common law.

This program makes clear that the Pilgrimage of Grace, embedded though it was in a traditional society, was not merely the vehicle of a simple archaism or nostalgia for the normative past. To be sure, allegiance to the ancient church and Catholic religion lay at the heart of the revolt. But it revealed a distinct political consciousness as well, traceable, doubtless, to its aristocratic leadership. This consciousness was especially manifest in the strong emphasis upon Parliament and the desire for measures to curb the king's power. In a very real sense, the Pilgrimage was a frontal attack upon the structure of absolute rule that Henry VIII and Cromwell were building up.

Behind the rebellion's demands lay also the germ of an ideology. Aske appealed to the commonwealth and its good, as well as to religion, as justification for the revolt. The Pilgrimage, he said in a proclamation, intends "the comyn welthe of this realme" and "the reformacyon of that

---

[64] The Pontefract articles are reprinted in Fletcher, *Tudor rebellions*, 128–30, and are discussed in detail in Dodds, *Pilgrimage of Grace*, v. 1, 346–73.

whyche is amysse."[65] He connected the defense of the church and redress of other grievances with this principle as the main end. The same thought pervaded the Pilgrim oath. In it, rebels swore to enter into this "our Pilgrimage of Grace" not for private profit but "by counsel of the commonwealth" and for the love of God, holy church, and preservation of the king's person.[66]

In regard to the king, the rebels at no time avowed any intention of deposing him. Indeed, they proclaimed their loyalty and addressed their grievance articles as a petition to the monarch. Yet, for all that, they were resolved to correct him in a policy they condemned as deeply wrong and to purge his council of Cromwell and other ministers whom they denounced as evil men of low birth. Having taken arms to this end, they groped for a doctrine that would justify a right of resistance. The official teaching of Henry VIII's reign pronounced rebellion sinful and wicked and asserted the subject's unconditional duty of nonresistance to superiors. At its final Pontefract meeting, however, the Pilgrim council tried to obtain from the attendant clergy a declaration sanctioning the lawfulness of waging war against an unjust sovereign. The archbishop of York, whom it called upon to preach, said flatly that subjects might not wield the sword against the prince. Other clergy apparently gave a more satisfactory reply. Nevertheless, Pilgrim leaders failed to come forth at any time with a statement affirming the legitimacy of rebellion and forcible resistance to the king.[67]

This failure was related to the failure and defeat of the revolt itself. The Pilgrimage produced comparatively little violence and hardly any victims. Aske was determined to maintain discipline, prevent looting, and spare lives. About the strongest positive action the insurgents took was to restore a number of monasteries that had been suppressed. The strategy of the Pilgrim leaders, to the occasional suspicions of the rank and file, was to negotiate with the king in the hope of gaining their demands by a display of power. Yet, they could not bring themselves to impose their will on the king by a test of force. When the Pilgrim host appeared at Doncaster near the end of October in overwhelming strength against a weak royal

---

[65] See the text, Dodds, *Pilgrimage of Grace*, v. 1, 175–6.

[66] Text in Fletcher, *Tudor rebellions*, 122. G. R. Elton (*Reform and renewal: Thomas Cromwell and the common weal*, Cambridge, 1973) has discussed the influence of the idea of the common weal in the 1530s and shown its importance in the aims and policy of Thomas Cromwell. But Professor Elton's addiction to celebrating the advance of Tudor power as a "revolution" has prevented him from realizing that the idea of the commonwealth also played a role in the Pilgrimage of Grace, although doubtless with a different meaning than it had for Cromwell.

[67] See Dodds, *Pilgrimage of Grace*, v. 1, 253, 377–81, 386, for these transactions. Some interesting political advice submitted to the Pilgrim council by one of the rebel leaders, Sir Thomas Tempest, came close to advocating the king's deposition by citing the examples of Edward II and Richard II, both deposed for their evil rule and refusal of good counsel; see the excerpts from this statement in Fletcher, *Tudor rebellions*, 126–7.

army, the council preferred a truce and negotiations to submitting the quarrel with the king to battle. Henry VIII, biding his time, received the Pilgrim petitions and treated with the rebels through his representative, the duke of Norfolk. He had no intention, though, of keeping promises to rebels or of granting concessions damaging to the crown's supremacy or prestige. Above all, he meant to punish the insurgents for their disobedience.

The final phase of the negotiations took place early in December over the twenty-four Pontefract articles. Aske believed the king had agreed to a free pardon of the revolt, the holding of a parliament in the north, and the restoration of the monasteries. He brought these terms to the commons but had trouble overcoming their suspicions. He was finally able to get their acceptance only after the king's herald arrived bringing the royal pardon. Then, on December 8 he proclaimed the end of the Pilgrimage, as gentlemen and commons dispersed to go home. The Pilgrims had torn off their badge of the Five Wounds, saying they would wear no insignia henceforth but that of their sovereign lord the king.

The rest was an epilogue in which the imperious ruler vanquished and wreaked vengeance upon the revolt. Failing to carry out the treaty with the Pilgrims, the king meanwhile propagandized the north against rebellion and skillfully exploited the commons' distrust of the gentlemen. The region remained restive and disturbed, as fear of the government's motives mounted. Aske himself did everything possible to prevent fresh disorders, which would be a violation of the royal pardon. In January and February 1537, small ineffectual outbreaks in Yorkshire and Cumberland gave the king his excuse to annul the pardon. The former Pilgrim forces were scattered, leaderless, and demoralized. Then ensued the inevitable repression, conducted amid an atmosphere of terror by the duke of Norfolk. In various places rank-and-file rebels were executed. During the spring, the main leaders of the Pilgrimage, Aske, Darcy, and some others, were brought to London, tried, and condemned for treason. In June, Darcy was beheaded in London; Aske was hung in chains from the castle tower of York in July. Numerous others, gentlemen, common folk, and monks and secular clergy who had aided the revolt, were put to death as traitors. The toll of executed has been variously estimated at 178 or over 200 – not a very large number, considering the threat that had been posed to the regime. The corpses or heads of the dead were displayed in many parts of the north, a gruesome example of the fate of rebels.[68]

In the aftermath of the Pilgrimage, Tudor government fastened a firmer control upon the northern counties, which for a time were like a con-

---

[68] For estimates of the number executed, see Dodds, *Pilgrimage of Grace*, v. 2, 226; and Elton, *Policy and police*, 388–9.

quered province. Henry VIII's work of state building continued unchecked. The monasteries of England were dissolved and their wealth confiscated by the crown. The breach with Rome was maintained. Never again did the northern social order possess the faith or determination to rise in such a display of massive resistance to the crown's interference with its life. The Pilgrimage of Grace was the biggest, most formidable rebellion any Tudor sovereign faced. Perhaps it could have overthrown the king, had it willed to do so. But its leaders, like most of their contemporaries, could not free themselves from the mystique of monarchy and were divided in mind about obedience. Aske himself sadly acknowledged at his execution that he had greatly offended God by breaking the king's commandments.[69] The higher clergy in the north, whom the Pilgrim council consulted and who might have given moral and intellectual support for the principle of resistance, failed to do so. The leaders therefore stopped short of coercing Henry VIII by arms and would not proclaim the right to resist or depose him. Instead, they chose the suicidal alternative of entering into an agreement without any security or guarantees. For this failure, they paid the price in the destruction of themselves and their cause.

VI

ARAGON, CATALONIA, PORTUGAL, SCOTLAND, AND IRELAND

When James VI of Scotland succeeded in 1603 to the English throne, an English poet hailed the event with a panegyric on the union of the two crowns.

> Therefore
> Shake hands with Union, O thou mighty State!
> Now thou art all Great Britaine and no more,
> No Scot, no English, nor no debate;
> No Borders but the Ocean and the Shore;
> No wall of Adrian serves to separate
> Our mutual love, nor our obedience;
> Being all subiects to one imperiall Prince.[70]

At the time, these fulsome sentiments celebrated an ideal or hope rather than any recognizable reality. Not only did King James fail to achieve the closer political union of the two kingdoms that he desired, but in the reign of his son, Charles I, Scotland rose against its absentee prince and English interference. The Scottish revolution of 1638 introduces a last group of provincial rebellions in which the external aspect was decisive. Despite

[69] Dodds, *Pilgrimage of Grace*, v. 2, 224.
[70] Samuel Daniel, "A panegyrike congratulatorie," *Works*, ed. A. B. Grosart, 4 v., London, 1885, v. 1, 143.

their many differences, all shared the fundamental common property of originating in the grievances of subordinate or provincial kingdoms within dynastic unions. Either the absentee ruler and paramount state were guilty of unaccustomed demands and innovations that violated the autonomous liberties of the provincial kingdom, or they inflicted upon it an increasingly repressive government that finally became intolerable. Whether the one or the other, or some combination of the two, rebellion erupted.

We see such cases in both the Spanish and the English monarchies. The revolt of Aragon in 1591 and the revolutions of Catalonia and Portugal in 1640 were alike a resistance to the pressures and intrusions of the central regime in Madrid. The several revolts of Ireland and the Scottish rebellion of 1638 were directed against subjugation or domination by England.

We need pause for only a brief glance at the revolt of Aragon against Philip II to see how it fits into the picture of provincial rebellion. In its kingdom of Aragon, the Habsburg monarchy was confronted by a Cortes and other indigenous institutions that restricted its powers in considerable ways. With Aragon was also associated the famous (although historically fictitious) oath, according to which subjects were bound to render obedience only if their prince observed their privileges, otherwise not (*si no, no*).[71] These privileges, or *fueros*, often served as a cover for local misgovernment and aristocratic oppression; however, they also stood as a real obstacle to royal absolutism.

Philip II first offended patriotic sentiment in Aragon by appointing a Castilian in 1590 as viceroy, contrary to the privilege that all royal officials should be natives. Shortly after this, the case of Antonio Pérez stirred up further provincial outrage. Pérez, one of the famous men of his time whose writings helped make the revolt of Aragon widely known, was Philip II's former principal secretary, minister, and confidant who, after being disgraced and imprisoned in Madrid, escaped and took refuge in Aragon.[72] There he placed himself in the custody of the Justicia, a high court whose judges controlled royal jurisdiction and stood between the crown and subjects. When the king ordered the seizure of Pérez in defiance of the Justicia's authority, violence broke out in the capital, Zaragoza. These events initiated the rebellion of 1591, which Pérez helped to incite and of which he later wrote, whose aim was the defense of provincial liberties. As Francis Bacon noted of it just a few years later, "Only upon the voice of a

[71] R. Giesey, *If not, not*, Princeton, 1968, gives a detailed account of the oath and contains a discussion in ch. 7 of the revolt of Aragon.

[72] On Antonio Pérez's career, writings, and relation to the revolt of Aragon, see G. Marañon, *Antonio Pérez*, 5th ed., 2 v., Madrid, 1954; *ibid.*, v. 2 chs. 19–24, contains a description of the revolt. G. Ungerer (ed.), *A Spaniard in Elizabethan England: The correspondence of Antonio Pérez's exile*, 2 v., London, 1975–6, is an important contribution to the understanding of Pérez's literary and political activity and influence.

condemned man . . . that cried *Fueros*, which is as much liberties or privileges, there was raised a dangerous rebellion which was suppressed with
difficulty."[73] The movement did not spread widely and apparently centered mainly upon Zaragoza; yet it is interesting that the rebels enter-
tained the idea of separation from the monarchy. By early the next year,
the king had crushed the revolt with an army from Castile, executing the
ringleaders, while Pérez fled to France. Then summoning the Cortes, Philip
was able to remodel Aragon's constitution so as to curtail its privileges and
render the realm far more subservient to the commands of sovereign authority.[74]

The Spanish monarchy was at its zenith when Aragon's revolt occurred; it had sunk dramatically in power when faced with the revolutions
of Catalonia and Portugal in 1640. The latter were quintessential conflicts
of the provincial type whose outbreak threatened the whole imperial
structure. Each of them launched out on the path of separatism in which
Portugal regained its independence, and Catalonia was recovered for
Habsburg sovereignty only after a protracted struggle. Save only that
Catalonia's resistance, starting earlier in May–June, encouraged the same
development in Portugal in December, the two rebellions were unconnected. What related them was their common background of imperial rule
and the similar grievances arising from their subjection to the Spanish
monarchy in this period of its decline as the greatest of European powers.

The elements of this decline are already familiar to us. Staggering imperial burdens, the growing weakness of the Castilian economy, and prolonged war and military reverses against France and the Dutch were
draining Spain's strength. War, above all, was Spain's curse. Because of
it, the monarchy was driven to a heavier exploitation of its possessions,
which in turn made it more oppressive to provincial subjects. We have
already seen the effects in Palermo and Naples in 1647. The events of
1640 in peninsular Spain were only an earlier manifestation of the identical underlying problem.

Since the beginning of Philip IV's reign in 1621, his favorite, the count-
duke of Olivares, had determined Spain's policy. The dynamic minister,
whose big, heavy body and florid face look out at us from Velázquez's
wonderful portraits, had to manage in the steadily worsening circumstances of the time. In 1625, he advised his master in a secret memoran-
dum that he should become king of Spain, meaning, he said,

That Your Majesty should not be content with being king of Portugal, of Aragon,
of Valencia and count of Barcelona, but should secretly plan and work to reduce

[73] F. Bacon, *Works*, ed. J. Spedding et al., 14 v., London, 1857–74, v. 10, 320.
[74] Besides the references already cited, a succinct account of Aragon's constitution and the
revolt of 1591 is given by Lynch, *Spain under the Habsburgs*, v. 1, 337–45.

these kingdoms of which Spain is composed to the style and laws of Castile, with no difference whatsoever. And if your Majesty achieves this, you will be the most powerful prince in the world.[75]

Despite these striking words, it is doubtful that Olivares ever tried to weld the disparate realms of the Iberian peninsula into a unitary state based on Castile. Such an enterprise would have run into insuperable obstacles in Spanish regionalism. But he was clearly determined to bring them closer together in unity of purpose and to make them bear a larger share of the burdens of war and defense as an interest common to them all. Toward this end, he proposed in 1626 his scheme of a Union of Arms, a project occupying the following years that provided for larger contributions and mutual assistance by the provincial states in support of the monarchy's war needs.[76]

This policy led in due course to Catalonia's revolt. The details comprising its preliminaries may be left aside, as they were merely a version of the general phenomenon of conflict between the aspirations of centralizing authority and an independent province.[77] An appendage of the crown of Aragon, the principality of Catalonia possessed a keen spirit of local patriotism and vigorous traditions of autonomy and contractual limitations upon the ruler embodied in its *constitucions*. For the Catalans, it was axiomatic, as a native writer declared in 1622, that "the supreme power and jurisdiction over the province belongs not to His Majesty alone but to His Majesty and the three estates of the province."[78] The nobility and the oligarchy that dominated the great commercial city of Barcelona were in accord in their defense of provincial liberties. Before, the province had been but lightly governed and taxed, and now the monarchy's sudden intensification of demands upon it could only incite rising opposition among the population and governing class. In 1626 and 1632, the Cortes refused to grant the king the financial contributions he required. A deadlock prevailed between provincial interests and imperial needs. How were the two to be reconciled if the Catalans found rule by and from Castile more a liability than an advantage?

After 1635, difficulties multiplied, as Spain entered into full-scale war with France on several fronts. Catalonia, a strategic frontier province, soon became a theater of hostilities, and the crown expected it to cooperate fully in its own defense along with forces from Castile. But even now the Catalans remained obstructive and invoked their liberties, as if the mon-

---

[75] Cited in Elliott, *The revolt of the Catalans*, 200.　[76] *Ibid.*, 204–8.

[77] For Catalonia's rebellion, see *ibid.*, which sets the movement in its full context of Spain's imperial government and problems. I have drawn extensively on this study, which is directed mainly to the origins and beginning of the revolt, while dealing only briefly with the subsequent events up to its end in 1652. R. B. Merriman, *Six contemporaneous revolutions*, Oxford, 1938, 1–10, contains a brief description of the movement in Catalonia.

[78] Cited in Elliott, *The revolt of the Catalans*, 45.

archy's quarrel were not their own. Olivares wrote in despair to the viceroy of Catalonia, "The devil take the constitutions and whoever observes them . . . For no man can observe them who has not been abandoned by God, and who is not an enemy of His Divine Majesty, of his king, and of his fatherland."[79]

At this critical juncture, Olivares was resolved more than ever to reduce the province's independence and compel it to join in sustaining the monarchy's military and financial necessities. In the winter of 1640, the government decided to station an army of nine thousand men in Catalonia, both as a necessary measure against the French and to quash Catalan opposition. This action in violation of provincial liberties and the clashes following between the soldiers and native population proved the catalyst to revolt. Resistance exploded in May with attacks by bands of peasants and town crowds against royal officials and rich citizens. A wild outburst of disorder struck the principality, paralyzing all authority. In Barcelona, mobs reinforced by rural laborers ran riot and murdered the viceroy, the count of Santa Coloma. Viceregal administration collapsed before the popular fury, and Catalonia was given over to anarchy and violence.

Thus far the revolt rather resembled the contemporary French plebeian insurrections against the royal state and its agents such as we have observed in preceding chapters. But then the provincial authorities, themselves alarmed by the dangers of this mass outbreak from below, took over the direction of the movement. The key institution of Catalonia's autonomy was the Deputation (Diputació), a standing committee of the Cortes consisting of six delegates representing the three estates of clergy, nobility, and towns. Its members, the deputies, were the supreme representatives of the Catalan nation and its constitution, responsible for the guardianship of native liberties and laws. Led by its president, the priest Pau Claris, the Deputation in the summer of 1640 placed itself at the head of the resistance. This step revealed the extent of Catalonia's alienation from Madrid and how much anger had been provoked by royal policy in the subject realm. The conflict thereby acquired legitimacy and became a rebellion of the whole provincial society. Despite dissensions, it embraced both the dominant class and the inferior orders – part of the nobility, provincial functionaries, the municipal councils and bourgeoisie of Barcelona and other towns, and the clergy. It was a rebellion, too, that was conducted by Catalonia's own government because the Deputation, an organ of the representative assembly of the province, stood as a dual power that had displaced Madrid and the viceroyalty. Events rapidly advanced to a further denouement. As Madrid showed itself intransigent and Olivares prepared to crush the revolt, the Catalan leaders sought French aid.

[79] Cited in *ibid.*, 375.

Thus, in January 1641, after first declaring Philip IV deposed as count of Barcelona, the Deputation placed Catalonia under the sovereignty of Louis XIII of France.

Before the calamitous year 1640 ended, Portugal also broke free of Madrid's authority. For sixty years, ever since its annexation in 1580 by Philip II, Portugal had been incorporated in the Spanish monarchy. The crown was pledged to respect native autonomy and liberties, and for a period Portugal benefited considerably from its union with Spain. Nevertheless, Castile's preeminence reduced it more and more to the position of an inferior dependency.[80]

From the 1620s the balance of gain and loss from association with Castile turned increasingly negative. Subject to the Spanish monarchy, Portugal had to take part in its wars, yet Spain was unable to defend Portuguese overseas possessions from invasion and conquest by the Dutch. Castilian protectionism in the Americas during a time of growing economic adversity was also injurious to the Portuguese. Although Portugal was less harassed than Catalonia by Olivares' attempts to impose the Union of Arms, it too was roused to opposition against Madrid's policy. The popular resentment of new demands was demonstrated in an outbreak of antifiscal rioting in 1637 in Evora and other towns. In a relationship that was necessarily very complex, the interests of Portugal and the monarchy seemed steadily more divergent. It was this, and the survival of the spirit of independence, that led to the revolution of 1640. Portugal was restive, and considerable estrangement from Spanish rule existed in the governing class, the merchant community, and the mass of the population. The rebellion of Catalonia, by pinning down Spain's forces, gave Portuguese disaffection its opportunity. In December 1640 in Lisbon, following some previous plotting, an influential group of the nobility proclaimed one of their number, the duke of Braganza, king as John IV. This act, which evoked broad support, announced Portugal's secession from the union of crowns and the restoration of its independence under a native sovereign.[81]

The revolutions in the two provincial realms offered tempting possibilities of great power intervention, as France's relation to them showed. In the same way as France later tried to aid the revolt of Naples in 1647, so it also supported the earlier rebellions of Catalonia and Portugal. With the second, it allied itself and sent assistance; with the first, its involvement was even closer. The Catalan leaders turned to the French crown because

[80] See A. H. De Oliveira Marques, *History of Portugal*, 2 v., New York, 1972, v. 1, 306–22, for a discussion of the union of Portugal with the Spanish monarchy and its effects.

[81] For the political and economic background of the rebellion of Portugal, see *ibid.*, v. 1, 318–25; and H. and P. Chaunu, "Autour de 1640: Politiques et économiques atlantiques," *Annales E. S. C. 9*, 1 (1953). There is also a good discussion of the subject by Lynch, *Spain under the Habsburgs*, v. 2, 108–15; and a brief account in Merriman, *Six contemporaneous revolutions*, 10–17.

they felt the province would be unable to survive alone and unaided against the Spanish monarchy's determination to recover its possession. Early in 1641, when a Castilian army attacked Barcelona hoping to end the revolt, the city was successfully defended by a joint force of Catalans and French. In 1642, the French gained further victories and captured Perpignan. Under French sovereignty, however, the Catalans soon discovered that they had only exchanged one bad master for another, and they became increasingly disenchanted. But the French crown profited considerably by its intervention. By accepting Catalonia's rule, it increased its territory and extended the war into a province of the Spanish monarchy, thereby adding greatly to the latter's burdens. The advent of the Fronde undermined France's ability to maintain its involvement in the rebellion, but in the final peace with Spain in 1659, it retained the counties of Rousillon and Cerdagne, which it had acquired in Catalonia during the insurgency.[82]

Amid all the disasters experienced at this period, the Spanish monarchy struggled to regain its rebel provinces. Along with other reverses, the defection of Catalonia and Portugal was responsible for the downfall of Olivares. The favorite was forced to retire in 1643 after his long tenure of power and died, crazed and infirm, two years later. Meanwhile, the two provincial rebellions dragged on, neither one giving rise to any outstanding leaders or heroic achievements. Portugal fought off Spain's attempts at reconquest and eventually won formal recognition of its independence in 1668. The Catalan revolution, having renounced the possibility of independence at its outset, disintegrated into division and strife between the partisans of France and Spain, and the principality endured all the miseries and disorders brought by the war onto its soil. To multiply afflictions came the plague in 1650, the worst of the century and estimated to have caused thirty-six thousand deaths in Barcelona alone. In October 1652, a Spanish army forced Barcelona to surrender after more than a year's siege. Philip IV granted an amnesty and vowed to respect Catalonia's traditional liberties. This was the defeat of provincial secession and the rebellion's finale, and Catalonia, minus the parts that remained permanently in France's possession, returned to its former allegiance.

Closely paralleling the revolutions of Catalonia and Portugal were those of Scotland and Ireland. Besides extending across the same star-crossed decade of the 1640s so fatal to princes, the same general situation, born from the inequalities within unions of crowns, underlay both pairs of rebellions. Castile overshadowed the possessions of imperial Spain in the same way as England did the realms of the Stuart monarchy. Under Span-

---

[82] For France's relation to the Catalonian and Portuguese revolutions, see Merriman, *Six contemporaneous revolutions*, 115–27; and Elliott, *The revolt of the Catalans*, chs. 16–18, *passim*.

ish as under English sovereigns, the discontent and grievances felt by provincial states against government from without ended in resistance. Scotland, though, was like Catalonia and Portugal in that it was Charles I's sudden introduction of novel demands and measures that provoked revolt. Ireland, in contrast, borne down by a much harder rule and long administered by the English as a conquered province, broke into revolt when the strong arm of authority was suddenly removed. In the Scottish and Irish cases, moreover, religious grievances and loyalties played a vital part in revolt, whereas they were completely absent from the contemporaneous outbreaks in the Spanish monarchy.

The Scottish revolution began in 1638 and ended in 1651, when the English republic, which was erected upon the fall of the Stuart monarchy, imposed conquest and union with England upon the Scots. The revolution in Ireland broke out in 1641 and came to an end in 1652, crushed by the army of the English republic. Both rebellions were heavily dependent on, if not satellites of, political conditions and developments in England. Had Charles I not first lost the support and affection of his English subjects in the course of the 1630s, he would have had the power to put down a revolt in Scotland; as it was, the Scottish rebels enjoyed English sympathies for their resistance and were able to triumph over the king. Similarly, had revolution not begun in England itself in 1640 and led to the prompt enfeeblement of English power in Ireland, the Irish rebellion could not have taken place. Even in their assertion of native patriotism and autonomy, the two provincial rebellions could not evade the preponderance of England. And their destinies throughout were fundamentally subordinate to events in the paramount kingdom.

The boreal realm of Scotland was poorer, less civilized, and less developed politically than England. The old Scottish enmity toward England had begun to disappear when both countries became Protestant in the second half of the sixteenth century. The union of crowns in 1603 carried the process still further. Yet mutual animosities persisted despite the closer relation between the two nations, and the Scots remained a people deeply attached to their own traditions and independence.

The Scottish revolution was a national reaction to English rule fired by the policies of Charles I. The latter's father, James VI and I, had built a strong foundation for the Stuart monarchy in Scotland and, upon inheriting the English crown, continued to govern it effectively as an absentee. James had been notably successful in establishing royal ascendancy over the two most powerful elements in Scottish life, while securing the support and loyalty of both: the high nobility, which retained a greater political and territorial independence than England's; and popular Protestantism, which was predominantly Calvinistic, partial to presbyterianism in church polity, and fanatically hostile to anything reminiscent of popery.

Charles I, alienating each of the two by his government, undermined the obedience of Scotland within little more than a decade of his accession in 1625.

The Scottish church was a hybrid of episcopal and presbyterian forms. Onto a system basically presbyterian, with parish discipline maintained by ministers and elders, James I had grafted the superiority of bishops to serve as the instruments of the crown's ecclesiastical supremacy. There was also a general assembly of the church, subject to royal summons, composed of clergy and lay representatives. Charles I, a devout son of the Anglican church who disliked Puritans, wished to bring Scotland's religion into more conformity with England's. Ignoring native sensibilities, he sponsored innovations tending toward ritualism and sacerdotalism. He stimulated antiepiscopal sentiment by adding to the political authority and prestige of the Scottish bishops. When he visited Scotland in 1633 for his coronation, he used the Anglican service in the ceremony and for public worship in the royal chapel.

The nobility's estrangement was due especially to a momentous royal act revoking all grants of crown and church land that had been made since 1542. Although not the only ones, noblemen had been the main beneficiaries of such grants. The chief purpose of this act of revocation, which, although not new in itself, was unprecedented in its scope, was to reform the system of tithes and thus place the provision of clerical stipends on a secure and adequate basis. The crown undertook to indemnify owners for the lands and tithes they would have to surrender. By a series of complex negotiations and laws, the crown achieved the revocation's aim. But the effect was to arouse insecurity and hostility among the magnates and noble landowners, who saw their property and influence threatened. "They fretted," the king later declared, "for being robbed, as they conceived, of the clientele and dependence of the clergy and laity . . . which by that tie of tithes they had enjoyed."[83]

Scotland's simmering discontents came to an explosive head as the result of a further installment of religious innovation. The king in 1629 had authorized the preparation of a new Scottish prayer book more in correspondence with English practice; the work of revision was done jointly by some Scottish in consultation with English bishops and Archbishop Laud of Canterbury. In 1637, the new liturgy was ready, and the king commanded its exclusive use in the Scottish church. Its introduction provoked a storm. The prescribed changes in worship contained departures from tradition in the direction of ceremonialism that gave deep offense. Moreover, they were ordained by the king alone, without the authorization of either the Scottish Parliament or the general assembly of the church.

[83] Cited in W. C. Dickinson, G. Donaldson, and I. Milne (eds.), *A source book of Scottish history*, 3 v., London, 1952–4, v. 3, 77.

In July, the initial attempt to perform the new service in Edinburgh's cathedral started a riot. This was the first episode of violence in a swiftly expanding crisis. It may seem strange that an alteration in worship should have produced such a powerful reaction. But the passions of Scottish Protestants ran far more to religion than to politics. The new prayer book outraged religious sentiment and stirred up a furious spirit of fanaticism. In addition, its imposition declared too clearly the plight of Scotland as victim to the crown's Anglicizing policies. The issue was one to unite religion with patriotism, draw other grievances to itself, and build a coalition of disaffection among the Protestant populace, ministers, and nobility.

During the following months, a massive wave of protest intimidated and immobilized the representatives of royal authority. An outpouring of petitions to the king against the new liturgy was followed by the creation of an organized political center in Edinburgh to direct the opposition; called the Tables, it consisted of commissioners representing each of the four Scottish estates: clergy, burghers, lesser nobility, and greater nobility. The attack upon the liturgy spread to the bishops, condemned as the wicked authors of innovation.

Despite these danger signals, the king remained inflexible and reiterated his command that the new liturgy be used. The Tables rejected it and in February 1638 drew up the National Covenant in justification of Scotland's stand. By now the kingdom was in the midst of upheaval beyond any royal control.

We have seen the influence of oaths and covenants in other early modern revolutions like the German peasant war. There was therefore nothing unique about the National Covenant as such. But in no other revolution did a covenant play so significant a role both as a sacred bond of union and as an ideological banner. Citing many precedents in Scottish law and earlier confessions of faith, the National Covenant repudiated all the recent religious innovations as illegal, subversive of the reformed religion, and tending to restore popery. It stated that no changes in religion could be made without approval of Parliament and the general assembly of the church; and it affirmed that the king was obliged by the fundamental laws that preserved the religion, law, and liberties of the kingdom. The signers bound themselves by a solemn vow to defend true religion, law, liberties, and the king's person and authority.

The covenant was intended for general subscription and spoke in the name of "noblemen, barons, gentlemen, burgesses, ministers, and commons." In form, it was a pledge that the signers made to one another and collectively to God on behalf of the covenant's principles. The document was quickly circulated throughout the country and attained an extensive subscription by all ranks. The exaltation with which it was received in many places demonstrated its symbolic power. Implicitly, it embodied the vision of Scotland as a covenanted nation like the Israelites, enjoying a special relation with God. Even though it appealed to law and promised allegiance to the royal person and authority, it legitimized and laid the groundwork for resistance. A manifesto of rebellion, it voiced the joint religious and political inspiration behind Scotland's defiance of its king. It welded secular to religious radicalism, helping to initiate a revolution that looked to a new religious reformation as well as to political change.[84]

Adherents to the National Covenant became known as the Covenanters; for the moment they were nearly all the Protestants of Scotland. The movement's leadership lay in some of the nobility, most notably one of the greatest of Scottish magnates, the presbyterian earl of Argyll, in zealots among the lesser nobility and lawyers, and in prominent ministers who supplied religious enthusiasm and guidance. Its popular base was the mass of pious folk in the capital, Edinburgh, and the towns and country of southern Scotland. Prior to the inevitable splits that every revolution undergoes given time, a broad array of Scottish society, nobility at the head, middle ranks, lower orders, and clergy, stood against the crown.

Confronted with such an overwhelming defection, Charles I was compelled to temporize and try negotiations. As a concession, he consented to call a general assembly of the church – the first in twenty years – which met in Glasgow in November 1638. The assembly, packed with Covenanters, disdained any compromise; when dissolved by the royal appointee who presided, it continued to sit, as did the French Estates General in 1789, claiming legality for its acts. It then wreaked a wholesale transformation upon the church of Scotland, abolishing at one stroke bishops, the new liturgy, and other obnoxious features; in their place, it instituted an exclusively presbyterian system from bottom to top such as some reformers had long dreamed of. With this act it cut the neck of the king's power over religion and the church.

In England the king now saw that he must deal with his Scottish subjects by force. The Covenanters also raised an army and seized fortresses to maintain their position. As the course of events revealed, however, Charles was militarily weak because he could not count on English support against rebellion in Scotland. England, too, was alienated by his government and therefore friendly to the Scots, who seemed like deliverers to the English opposition. When the issue finally came to battle in August 1640, the royal troops retreated in disorder, and a victorious Scottish army of twenty-five thousand men marched across the English border and occupied the northern counties. This was the momentous emergency that left Charles I no choice but to summon a Parliament in

---

[84] The text of the National Covenant is printed in *ibid.*, v. 3, 95–104.

England, where his opponents took charge and initiated a revolution against his rule.

In Scotland, meanwhile, the National Covenant reigned in triumph. Another meeting of the general assembly of the church had confirmed the destruction of episcopacy and the institution of a national presbyterianism. The Scottish Parliament had also met and thrown off all royal supervision. Among its acts in 1640 was the ratification of the general assembly's work, the abolition of its own clerical estate (which meant the bishops), and a measure to assure its meetings at no longer than three-year intervals. It also took into its own hands the naming of the committee that managed its business, the so-called Committee of the Articles, formerly a body controlled by the crown. Moreover, it provided for a committee of estates to function between sessions as its surrogate. These significant additions to the Parliament of Scotland's powers were crowned in August 1641, when the king in his weakness conceded to it the right to approve the royal appointment of all privy councillors, judges, and officers of state. The Scottish Parliament was thus raised by the revolt to a new position of authority and independence.[85]

The revolution of Scotland, to the point we have followed it, was not in essence anti-English; indeed, we have seen that it was welcomed in England. But it was intensely national, a general uprising of provincial subjects in defense of religion and autonomy. The National Covenant was inscribed with patriotic consciousness and became the charismatic incarnation of Scottish protest as well as the inspiration of an enthusiastic and intolerant spiritual creed. In establishing a full-blown presbyterianism, the Covenanters claimed to draw on and to restore traditions of the Scottish Reformation. They stood, it has been said, "for the Reformation (against Rome), Calvinism (against Arminianism), Presbyterianism (against Prelacy), Constitutionalism (against Tyranny), Scottish independence (against English interference), and Puritanism in morals, art and everything (against the Devil)."[86] The revolution, while it survived, freed religion and the state from domination by the monarchy. What succeeded was a regime based on the domination of the Covenanter nobility in alliance with the Presbyterian church and ministers, supported by the congregations of believers of Calvinist persuasion.[87]

The Irish rebellion of 1641 was akin to Scotland's, even though as a Catholic resistance it was utterly alien to and condemned by the Covenanters.

---

[85] For these changes, see *ibid.*, v. 3, 113–16, 234–47.

[86] G. D. Henderson, *Religious life in seventeenth-century Scotland*, Cambridge, 1937, 169.

[87] A detailed account of the origin and beginning of the Scottish revolution is given by D. Stevenson, *The Scottish revolution 1637–1644*, Newton Abbot, 1973, from which I have profited; *ibid.*, ch. 10 provides a general assessment. See also W. Ferguson, *Scotland's relations*

In fact, it was no less an affirmation of religion and nationality by a provincial society – one far more severely ruled and burdened than Scotland had ever been.

Ireland was not an independent kingdom, like Scotland, but was governed by the English crown as a conquered colony. An army was always indispensable to the maintenance of English power. Irish institutions of law and government had been introduced from England and were based on English models. The crown and the English privy council exercised authority over Irish administration. Despite the fact that the majority old Irish and old English population was Catholic, Ireland's state church was Protestant, in conformity with the established church and religion in England. Toward the old Irish, and especially their aristocracy, the Tudor monarchy had pursued a policy of Anglicization to draw them into loyalty. According to the expert opinion of a high English official in the reign of James I, Ireland would never be safe or peaceful until the Irish "in tongue and heart and everyway else become English, so as there will be no difference or distinction but the Irish sea betwixt us."[88]

Recalcitrant religious, cultural, and national differences, though, obstructed this fusion. Many times and long before Pearse, Connally, and the other Easter rebels of 1916 watered Ireland's rose tree with their blood, there had been rebellions in Ireland. I have alluded earlier to the numerous insurrections of the sixteenth century. All of them were struggles against the extension of English control and colonization, and the men who conducted them, whether old English of Anglo-Norman ancestry or Gaelic Irish, belonged to the highest rank and were the natural leaders of Ireland's resistance.

After the victory of Protestantism in England, English government was always concerned with the danger of foreign aid by Catholic rulers to Irish rebels. And the latter repeatedly sought such aid. As we have seen in a number of cases, provincial disaffection offered a favorable target for external subversion and intervention by hostile great powers. During Queen Elizabeth's time, Irish insurgents looked for help again and again to Philip II. They appealed for the Spanish sovereign's support in the interests of Catholicism and to convert Ireland into a base to bleed England in the same way as the English government supported the Dutch revolt to undermine Spain's power. In 1579, Pope Gregory XIII and the king of Spain gave assistance to rebellion in Munster, which received papal blessing as a crusade. In 1601, a Spanish force of over three thousand men landed at

with England: A survey to 1707, Edinburgh, 1977, for a history and discussion of the Covenanter revolution in the context of the overshadowing relation to England.

[88] See J. C. Beckett, *The making of modern Ireland*, New York, 1966, 33–8. The quotation comes from Sir John Davies, who was attorney-general in Ireland. For the distinctions among the population of Ireland, see Chapter 4 in this book.

Kinsale in Munster in support of Tyrone's rebellion. Both these interventions were defeated by the English.[89]

The rebellion in Ulster by the earl of Tyrone from 1595 to 1603 was the most serious and powerful attempt till that time to halt the relentless penetration of English authority. Its suppression cleared the way to the effective establishment of English government over the whole island, as well as to big new expropriations of land for alien settlement. Tyrone fought for Catholicism and freedom for Ireland under the English crown. In a set of articles compiled in 1599, he indicated his demands, which an English minister contemptuously termed Utopia. In religion, they included the restoration of papal supremacy, complete freedom for priests and religious, and the return of all cathedrals, churches, and religious houses to Catholics. Politically, he stipulated that only Irish should hold offices in Ireland, with noblemen as governors of provinces. Among other provisions were security for land, freedom of trade for Irishmen with England and other countries, and the removal of various forms of discrimination against the Irish. One article called for the creation of a university in Ireland financed by the crown, where all sciences should be taught according to the manner of the Catholic church.[90] These aims mirrored the aspiration to eliminate the effects of colonial status and alien subjection that England had imposed.

During the earlier seventeenth century, the royal policy of promoting colonization through confiscations of Irish land became a major grievance. The first such project was the huge Ulster plantation, extending over six counties that were forfeited by Tyrone and his allies in consequence of their revolt. Others followed. One of the methods for Anglicizing Ireland, its scale posed a serious danger to old English and old Irish proprietors alike. Land titles in Ireland were generally obscure and uncertain, and the crown might always find ways to claim ownership itself. With respect to religion, the government never possessed the means to enforce the prohibition of Catholicism, yet intermittent attempts at persecution fanned Catholic resentment. At the same time, the growth of Protestant settlement through immigration contributed with other factors to the steady erosion of Catholic security.

The rebellion of 1641 sprang from these conditions as well as more directly from the rule of Ireland by the earl of Strafford, whom Charles I appointed governor in 1632. One of the first great English proconsuls of empire, Strafford set out, as had Olivares in Catalonia, to make Ireland pay its own cost and become a source of profit to the crown. His hard and

[89] See J. Silke, *Ireland and Europe 1559–1607*, Dundalk, 1966, and *Kinsale*, New York, 1970.
[90] Printed in E. Curtis and R. B. McDowell (eds.), *Irish historical documents 1172–1922*, London, 1943, 119–20.

unscrupulous methods achieved success, but only at the price of universal hostility. He incurred the hatred of the old English and old Irish landowners victimized or threatened by his confiscations, effected through legal pretexts in the interests of royal finance and to foster plantations. He angered Protestant English and Scotch settlers by his repressive measures against Puritanism. He even alienated the colonial elite of new English landowners and officials in Irish administration, who resented his autocratic ways and his interference with their jobbery and peculation. In Ireland and England alike, he came to be regarded as bent on tyranny in the king's name.

Strafford's government was the prelude to revolt. He advanced the progress of state building to its highest point, reducing Ireland to unprecedented unity, prosperity, and order. Nonetheless, the direct result was to isolate the royal regime from every sector of Irish society. Momentarily, his severity welded the provincial kingdom with its inborn hatreds and its hereditary griefs, its religious divisions and its ancestral distinctions between old Irish, old English, and new English, into a common rancor and opposition.[91]

A rule, if sufficiently repressive, may survive indefinitely, but Strafford's was terminated by the troubles that engulfed Charles I in Scotland and England at the close of the 1630s. After the outbreak of the Scottish rebellion, Strafford was recalled home to help the king against the Covenanters. The onset of revolution in England in the fall of 1640 brought with it an immediate attack upon him by the English Parliament, which ended with his execution in May 1641.

The sudden removal of viceregal power and the simultaneous collapse of Charles I's authority in England caused a dramatic reversal in Ireland. The Irish, previously subservient, promptly began to vocalize their complaints. Strafford and other officials were denounced by the Parliament of Ireland. Even more significantly, the Irish House of Commons advanced the momentous claim that the Irish "are a free People, and to be governed only according to the common law of England, and Statutes made and established by Parliaments in this Kingdom of Ireland, and according to the lawful Custom used in the same."[92] This was a plea not for separation but for association with the crown on terms of independence and emancipation from England's rule.

Political opinion in England, however, could have no sympathy with

[91] See H. Kearney, *Strafford in Ireland 1633–41*, Manchester, 1959, and Beckett, *The making of modern Ireland*, chs. 1–3, for a description of Irish conditions and government in the earlier seventeenth century; and see, as well, the remarks of A. Clarke, "Ireland and the general crisis," *Past and present 48* (1970).

[92] First stated by the Irish House of Commons in February 1641, this claim was formally adopted as a resolution a few months later; see T. L. Coonan, *The Irish Catholic confederacy and the Puritan revolution*, New York, 1954, 79.

Irish grievances once Strafford was gone. To the English Parliament, moreover, which had become the main factor in affairs, to relinquish England's power over Ireland was unthinkable. Such a development must necessarily imperil English interests, reinstate Catholicism, and turn Ireland into a potential base for foreign intervention. Indeed, as the Irish Catholics realized, if the English Parliament consolidated its ascendancy over Charles I, they faced a gloomy future. The Parliament, dominated by Puritans and bitterly opposed to Catholic toleration, would inflict a heavier persecution on them than ever before and threaten even greater expropriations of Irish land.

These were the immediate circumstances in 1641 that gave the impulsion to revolution in Ireland. The general breakdown of authority offered a favorable opportunity. The Irish were also encouraged to act by the example of the Covenanters' success in Scotland, and they feared what the English Parliament would do in Ireland should it gain a free hand.

The rebellion broke out in Ulster in late October 1641, planned and led by prominent old Irish gentry. The natives rose in fury, butchering the English settlers or driving them in thousands from their homes to perish in the weather. These widespread cruelties, due to the stored-up hatred of a subject people, were interpreted in England as signifying a Catholic plot to exterminate the Protestants of Ireland. With the government in Dublin confused and able to do little, the revolt spread beyond Ulster. By early in 1642, it also had been joined by the old English lords and gentry in other parts of the kingdom. Their adhesion turned resistance for the first time in Irish history into a national movement of the Catholic population.

The Irish rebellion was initiated and directed by an aristocracy. Its goal was not complete divorce from the English crown. Indeed, in the conflict between Charles I and the Parliament of England, the rebels professed support for the king and his just prerogatives, seeing Parliament as the main enemy of Irish aspirations. The rebellion aimed at an independent, self-governing Ireland, still affiliated with the English monarchy, in accordance with the principle already proclaimed in the Irish Parliament in 1641. This would have meant, of course, the restoration of Catholicism as the dominant religion. There was the additional hope as well of recovering for the original owners the lands they had lost by confiscation.

The most significant political step in the revolt was the creation of a central governmental authority in place of the English. It grew out of a decision by Catholic prelates, rebel leaders, and nobility and gentry to summon a general assembly to speak for Ireland. This assembly met at Kilkenny in October 1642, composed like a parliament of shire and borough representatives and of spiritual and temporal peers. It established a government that was entitled "the Confederate Catholics of Ireland" and prescribed an oath of union to be taken by all rebels. This oath was very similar in purpose to the Scottish National Covenant and other religious bonds that so often united the insurgents in early modern revolutions.

As instituted by the general assembly, the Confederation government consisted of the assembly itself plus a supreme council of twenty-four to exercise overall political and military authority. The assembly declared the restoration of the Catholic church to all its freedoms. It also affirmed its allegiance to Charles I and his just rights and prerogatives. One of its most striking actions was the disavowal of all "national distinction" among the Catholics of Ireland as "not to be endured in a well-governed commonwealth." In particular, it ordered that no distinction or comparison should be made between the old Irish and old English. It stated its readiness to accept the adherence of all Catholics willing to join in union.[93]

The Irish Confederacy thus assumed a national character as a rival state power to England's. Its motto was, "pro deo, pro rege, pro patria Hibernia unanimis." It stood for the defense of the Catholic church, redress of Ireland's grievances, and independence, along with continued attachment to the crown. These were the grounds on which the rebels justified their resort to arms. The independence they sought would have ended all subjection to the English Parliament and government. Instead, Ireland would be governed by its own Parliament and laws, in obedience only to the crown.[94]

The Irish revolution survived as long as it did largely because disorder and civil war in England hampered succor to Ireland. English forces and authorities in Ireland were also divided between the king and Parliament and thus incapable of common action. The Irish military effort was led by gentlemen who returned from abroad to serve the cause, like Owen Roe O'Neill, the earl of Tyrone's nephew, who had been a soldier for the king of Spain in Flanders. But rivalries between the rebel generals prevented any unified command or strategy, and their peasant troops were poorly disciplined and led. The Irish fighting consisted of scattered sieges and engagements in which the English, despite weakness and inferior numbers, were nearly always the victors. Through the whole course of the war, the rebels won only one important battle, which they were unable to follow up. The Confederation government sent agents to solicit help from Catholic powers, but slight material assistance was forthcoming except from the pope.[95]

---

[93] The plan of government provided by the general assembly for the Irish Catholic Confederation is printed in Curtis and McDowell, *Irish historical documents*, 148–52.

[94] See J. C. Beckett, "The Confederation of Kilkenny reviewed," *Historical studies, Irish conference of historians* (1959), for a discussion of the rebel government and principles.

[95] Beckett, *The making of modern Ireland*, chs. 3–4, gives an account of the background and development of the revolution of Ireland. Coonan, *The Irish Catholic confederacy*, contains a narrative with many valuable details.

We should reap little profit from tracing the remaining events and stages of the Scottish and Irish revolutions. The history of both was one of ever growing confusion due to internal splits and schisms, and inevitably the fate of both was determined by events in England.

The Covenanters established a political and spiritual dictatorship in Scotland that continually narrowed the basis of their power, as one-time supporters were purged or fell away. In 1643 they came to the military rescue of the revolutionary English Parliament, with which they made an alliance in its war against the king, the Solemn League and Covenant. Their purpose was religious and political unity between the two kingdoms, to be achieved by England's acceptance of a presbyterian church system similar to Scotland's. When the English showed themselves averse to a presbyterian state church, the Scots tried to force it on them. In an ironic reversal, they turned royalist, and a party among the Covenanters took up the fight for Charles I and, after his execution, Charles II; they wanted to use the king to install presbyterianism in England. Three times, in 1648, 1650, and 1651, Scottish attempts at military intervention on the royal behalf in England were defeated by an English army. These developments totally destroyed the remaining unity of the Covenanter movement and completed the disintegration of the Scottish revolution. A further nemesis then ensued. In 1651, the English republic, its dominant figure the great rebel general and leader Oliver Cromwell, invaded and conquered Scotland. Conquest was followed by total union and loss of independence: Scotland was incorporated in the English Parliament and governed by English officials backed by the power of an occupying army. This remained the state of affairs until the restoration of the monarchy in England in 1660, which also returned Scotland to Stuart rule and annulled all that the preceding twenty-two years had accomplished.[96]

In Ireland, the Confederated Catholic government fell into quarrels over the policy to be taken toward the Protestant royalist party, and, despite the hope of abolishing national distinctions, acute conflicts also emerged between the old English and the old Irish. After the arrival in 1645 of a papal nuncio, Giovanni Batista Rinuccini, sent by Pope Innocent X with money and supplies for the revolt, discords intensified. The nuncio was primarily concerned with reinstating the rights of the Catholic church and clergy. He opposed any treaty between the Confederation and the royalists in Ireland that did not secure this aim in the highest degree, including the restoration of ecclesiastical property and jurisdiction. He was strongly opposed by the old English, who were willing to ally with the royalists on more moderate terms. Rinuccini's grasp of control split the Confederation

---

[96] For the later history of the Scottish rebellion and the Covenanters, see D. Stevenson, *Revolution and counter-revolution in Scotland 1644–1651*, London, 1977; *ibid.*, ch. 6 gives an illuminating overview.

and rendered it totally ineffectual. Because of these bitter controversies, he was finally obliged to leave Ireland in 1649, but not before the struggle that had begun as national movement of liberation broke down into contending, even warring, elements. In 1649 the Confederation dissolved itself. Later the same year, Oliver Cromwell and an army dispatched by the English republic landed in Ireland. Cromwell defeated the rebels in a swift campaign, which included the storming of Drogheda, where he slaughtered the entire garrison and all the priests, altogether nearly three thousand people. After his departure in 1650, other commanders completed the English reconquest in two more years of bloodshed. Revolt extinguished and the royalists crushed as well, Ireland lay prostrate at the conqueror's feet. The English regime then imposed a new land settlement, the greatest act of confiscation and colonization so far. Vast quantities of Irish land passed permanently into English possession, designated for plantation. The defeat of the revolt meant the destruction of all Irish aspirations for religious and national freedom, establishing Anglo-Protestant ascendancy in an impregnable position for long into the future.[97]

VII

The procession of revolutions we have just surveyed reveals the repeated struggle provincial societies and dependent realms waged to defend or recover their liberties and withstand subjection to overweening central power. Nearly always they failed in this attempt. The only exception was in the Spanish monarchy, whose vulnerability in this regard was acutely pointed out by Francis Bacon. "Some states," he noted in 1592, "are weak through want of means, and some weak through excess of burthen; in which rank I do place the state of Spain, [for] having out-compassed itself in embracing too much." At the moment of the monarchy's supreme weakness, Portugal won its independence, and Catalonia fought a lengthy resistance before returning to obedience, subdued but its privileges confirmed. Of Aragon, Bacon wrote not long after the revolt of 1591 that Spain had "with much difficulty rather smoothed and skinned over than healed and extinguished the commotion."[98] The French and English monarchies both vanquished their provincial rebels. Scotland, moreover, was soon to lose its independence permanently through absorption in a political union with England after 1707. Following the Irish rebellion of 1641, England held Ireland in thrall until after World War I.

Throughout, it was the state in the long run that triumphed over more

[97] See Beckett, *The making of modern Ireland*, chs. 4–5, and Coonan, *The Irish Catholic confederacy*.
[98] F. Bacon, *Certain observations made upon a libel*, in *Works*, v. 8, 169, 163.

circumscribed associations, autonomies, and solidarities. This general process, which provincial rebellion strove to arrest, has been admirably described by the French sociologist, Durkheim:

It is the State that has rescued the child from patriarchal domination and from family tyranny; it is the State that has freed the citizen from feudal groups and later from communal groups; it is the State that has liberated the craftsman and his master from guild tyranny . . . [The State] must . . . permeate all those secondary groups of family, trade . . . Church, regional areas . . . which tend . . . to absorb the personality of their members. It must do this, in order to prevent this absorption and free these individuals, and so as to remind these partial societies that they are not alone and that there is a right that stands above their own rights.[99]

Durkheim's view of this development was celebratory. Ours, by comparison, considering our twentieth-century experience of the monstrous crimes committed by the state in its claim to exclusive loyalty, must be a more reserved view, reckoning losses as well as gains. What is certain, however, is that the conquest of provincial communities by the royal states of the sixteenth and seventeenth centuries was merely the preliminary to a longer and larger conquest that was to give the state powers and control unthought of by early modern sovereigns.

[99]Cited from E. Durkheim in R. Bendix, *Nation-building and citizenship*, new ed., Berkeley, 1977, 61.

10

Revolutionary civil war:
the French civil war

We arrive finally at revolutionary civil war, the rarest type of revolution in the states and society of early modern Europe. It contains the conflicts that stand out from nearly all the others of the sixteenth and seventeenth centuries by their scope and duration and includes what many historians would probably regard as preeminently the "great" revolutions of the age. It was these that plunged states into the lengthiest and severest violence, split their political order the most deeply, and defied and defeated, temporarily or for good, the greatest monarchies.

> But far above and far as sight endures
> Like whips of anger
> With lightning's danger
> There runs the quick perspective of the future.

Whether by their success or failure or by their ultimate fruitfulness or sterility, these struggles loom up to retrospective vision beyond most of the rest. They appear not merely as events of cataclysmic strife but also as symbols that intimate some destiny in their countries' history.

Four revolutions belong to this category: the French civil war, or wars of religion, between 1562 and 1598; the revolt of the Netherlands from 1566 to 1609; the English revolution of 1640–60; and the Fronde in France from 1648 to 1653.

The centrality of at least two of these four events has been generally recognized. The English revolution is usually considered to rank with the greatest revolutions of the Western world, one in a mighty succession that passed from England in the seventeenth century to America in 1776 and thence to France in 1789 and Russia in 1917.[1] With the English revolution is often joined the Netherlands revolt. Among the classics of nineteenth-century narrative historiography is the American J. L. Motley's *Rise of the Dutch republic* (1856), which pictured its subject as a heroic fight for polit-

---

[1] See P. Zagorin, *The court and the country*, London, 1969, 5–6.

ical and religious liberty. The popularity of Motley's highly colored, partisan work helped to canonize the Netherlands' resistance to Spanish rule in Europe's historical consciousness. Marxism placed it with the great bourgeois revolutions, and Lord Acton saw it as contributing, along with the revolutions in England, America, and France, to the creation of the modern world.[2] (Of course, these views were formed at a time when the conception of the revolutionary tradition was still based entirely on European and Western experience, Asia and Africa being beyond its ken.)

The French civil war has occupied a more problematic ground. Many writers have perceived it to be a revolution yet as also overlayed or entangled with contradictory features that render its fundamental character unclear. Still, it engulfed France in a shattering struggle for power for more than thirty years, turning the kingdom, as one of its recent historians has said, into a "battlefield where rival ideologies confronted each other to the detriment of royal power" in a "sanguinary conflict" of "parties . . . with their political and military structures, their compromising alliances, their new and revolutionary doctrines."[3] On this account, France's sixteenth-century civil war has to be included with the biggest revolutionary phenomena of the age.

Similarly, the Fronde has also appeared in a rather problematic light due to uncertainties about its nature and import; it was an event, moreover, that never achieved any standing in the revolutionary tradition of either France or Europe. Yet it is unquestionable that, after the earlier civil war, the Fronde was by far the most serious ordeal the French monarchy ever faced, not only during the seventeenth century but right down to 1789.[4] As a second massive political breakdown and civil war, it rates with the other conflicts discussed here.

Although magnitude is certainly characteristic of revolutionary civil war, this is not what necessarily distinguishes it from the other types of revolution. We have seen already that "great" revolutions need not be limited to a single type. The German peasant war, an agrarian rebellion, and the Comuneros of Castile, an urban rebellion, ought both to be considered as "great" revolutions by any reasonable standard. The same might be said of the provincial rebellions of Scotland and Ireland. For the political and national communities in which they occurred, at any rate, they were all

<hr/>

[2] Lord Acton, *Lectures on modern history*, London, 1930, 205. E. Kuttner reflects the Marxist tradition in calling the Netherlands rebellion "the earliest bourgeois revolution of modern times" (*Het hongerjaar 1566*, Amsterdam, 1949, 208). Since the latter's work, East German historiography in the DDR has become accustomed to speak of the German Reformation and the peasant war as the earliest bourgeois revolution; see the discussion on typology in Chapter 2 of this book.

[3] G. Livet, *Les Guerres de religion*, 3rd ed., Paris, 1970, 5–6.

[4] See R. Bonney, *Political change in France under Richelieu and Mazarin 1624–1661*, Oxford, 1978, 444.

upheavals of the first order and represented the strongest attempt at revolutionary change of which these communities were then capable.

Revolutionary civil war, however, consists of a set of features not conjointly present in other types of revolution, and from their convergence its magnitude results.

First, social participation in it is the broadest we can find in the revolutions of early modern Europe; it not only implants a schism in the body politic but involves to some extent all the estates, strata, and groups that comprise the society of orders. It includes both elites and masses, and the former in such weight and numbers as to signify a large and menacing defection from the royal regime. The main division it embodies, accordingly, is not horizontal, pitting upper and lower against each other. Rather, it is vertical, an alignment fissioning the social structure from top to bottom. Its most noticeable trait, from a social standpoint, is the support of rebellion by significant elements and important members of the dominant class, both nobilities and bureaucratic elites.

Second, the political and geographic space occupied by revolutionary civil war transcends that in other types of revolution. This does not mean, to be sure, that provincialism exercises no influence – we have seen that it does. But the events we are now dealing with surpass local limits and particularism to a considerable degree. Their theater is the kingdom itself, and they project conflict into many parts of the territory of the royal state.

Third, the goals and targets of revolutionary civil war express a massive societal reaction to the forward march of monarchical state building. Whether in the domain of political and administrative institutions, fiscality, or religion, rebels strive to halt, to limit, and to reverse the accretion of power by centralizing absolute governments. They also attempt to restore and revitalize old institutions or to devise new ones in place of those they oppose.

Fourth, revolutionary civil war attains the highest degree of organization to be seen in early modern revolutions. Insurgent leadership and mobilization tend to be national in scale. Rebels form broad parties or movements, create political and military organs to facilitate resistance, and exploit traditional institutions for their political ends.

Finally, revolutionary civil war is accompanied by the fullest development of ideology. Ideas and principles of reform or restoration fuel and intensify revolt, and ideological debate is a vital ingredient in the conflict waged by rebels against regimes. It is no accident that significant works of political theory are most often produced in such revolutions.

Such are the typological elements of which revolutionary civil war consists. To them we may add some further miscellaneous points indicative of the four revolutions in this category that may help us to see their outlines more clearly.

These wide-ranging conflicts were the longest in point of time, rivaled only by several provincial rebellions. The English revolution lasted through its various vicissitudes for twenty years, the French civil war of the sixteenth century for more than thirty, the Fronde for five, and the Netherlands revolt for twenty-five years or longer, depending on when we reckon that the northern provinces finally secured their de facto independence from Spain.

To understand their parallel genesis, we must again disabuse our minds of the Marxist-inspired view that automatically conceives of revolution, both causally and in its substance, as a class conflict. I have already often criticized this erroneous idea. The revolutionary civil wars of the era took place, as we know from earlier discussion, in a society composed of orders or estates, not classes, one whose stratification was determined primarily by status, not economic differentia or productive relations. They became possible only because nobilities and other elites, on whom royal rule crucially depended, ceased to give obedience. In this hierarchic structure, dominated by aristocracies and impregnated with principles of deference and subordination, only the higher orders possessed the political and social authority to legitimize revolt and draw masses of men into resistance against divinely ordained sovereigns. The French civil war began in the disaffection of the Huguenot nobility from the Valois monarchy. The Netherlands rebellion originated in noble opposition to Spanish administration. The English revolution resulted from a wholesale withdrawal of support for Charles I's government within the political nation led by noblemen and gentry. The Fronde started when the highest judicial officials of the monarchy, part of the crown themselves, imposed their reform program upon the government of Cardinal Mazarin, the Queen Regent Anne of Austria, and the boy king, Louis XIV.

These movements also generally went furthest toward erecting a rival dual power against the incumbent regime and toward establishing a new political order. This was perhaps least the case in the French civil war and the Fronde, where rebels in the main wanted to limit and control the monarchy rather than depose it. Yet, the Huguenots forged independent governing institutions, and the Catholic League, in its opposition after 1576 to Henry III and to the succession of the Protestant Henry of Navarre as heir to the throne, did the same. The Frondeurs principally attempted to force the crown to relinquish the powers gained for it by Richelieu and Louis XIII. But the English revolution culminated in the destruction of the Stuart monarchy and the creation of a republic. The Netherlands revolt brought the formation of a federal republic as the government of the seven united provinces that won their freedom from Spanish rule.

Due to their length and the widespread devastation they caused, the potentialities inherent in their ideologies, and the ramifying divisions they engendered, these four revolutions were also more susceptible than most to the emergence of popular and plebeian radicalism. The latter would have carried or turned the conflict toward ends antagonistic to the members of the governing class who began and led it. Each of the revolutions produced something of this kind. The French civil war, for instance, saw the imposition in 1588 of a radical dictatorship upon Paris by the urban cadres of the Catholic League. The Netherlands rebellion led to popular insurrections and reversals of power in some of the towns. The Fronde was accompanied by the movement of the middle and lower orders in Bordeaux known as the Ormée. Most noteworthy of all, the English revolution created an extraordinary efflorescence of radical groups who agitated on behalf of their aims.

The four revolutions also had important bearings upon international great-power rivalries. Most especially was this true of the Netherlands and France. Situated in the strategic heart of northwest Europe, preeminent in commerce, finance, and industry, the Netherlands were a prized possession of the Spanish monarchy. Rebellion turned the provinces into Spain's and Philip II's Vietnam, a morass of apparently endless war. By the same token, it provoked involvement and intervention by both the French and English governments, who aided the revolt in order to profit from Spain's troubles. In a sense, the conflict in the Low Countries was hardly less international than internal. Similarly, Spain intervened in the contemporaneous French civil war to support the Guise and Catholic faction, for it wanted to see the French monarchy weak and the Huguenots defeated. England on its side also intervened in France to sustain the Huguenots and counter Spanish power. A half-century later, when the French and Spanish monarchies were at war in the 1640s, Spain repeated its policy of intervention by the assistance and alliance it extended to some of the rebels in the Fronde.

Every one of these revolutions formed a vastly extended, enormously complex panorama where disorder reached an extreme. Each produced striking personalities and leaders and composed a scene overflowing with incident and accident, battles and negotiations, bloodshed and devastation. In all, the course of events was continually confused by diversions and cross-purposes, new fissions, and shifting alliances. To try to chronicle these struggles or recount their vicissitudes would clearly be impossible. Rather, beginning with the French civil war, we shall attempt by a selective summary to extract from them those aspects and developments that serve to illuminate their character as revolutions.

I

Eight so-called wars of religion were waged in France between 1562 and 1598. They followed a kind of rhythm, each successive round of military operations and assorted hostilities being terminated temporarily by a royally decreed truce or peace that proved too fragile to endure. As they continued, France descended into anarchy, death, and desolation. The monarchy, even though its existence was never put in question, lost control of events and was helpless to repress or to end the strife of parties. The last two Valois kings, the brothers Charles IX (1560–74) and Henry III (1574–89), and their mother, Queen Catherine de Medici, strove desperately to preserve the royal power amid the collapse of political order. At times the accomplice of the conflict, the monarchy was always its victim. In the next to closing stage, driven even from Paris in 1588, its authority and prestige declined to the lowest point, as France itself seemed to be breaking up. Then, following the succession in 1589 of Henry of Navarre, the first Bourbon king, the crown finally regained the strength to subdue the forces of revolt and restore peace.[5]

All these wars were in reality only one war, the connected episodes of a protracted struggle that, albeit "wars of religion," was also nevertheless a revolution.

This revolution grew from a crisis with a threefold core: the politicization of the Reformed church; the formation of an organized Huguenot party led by the house of Bourbon and others of the high nobility; and the competition for power between the latter and the members of the house of Guise–Lorraine, who stood at the head of an intransigent, intolerant Catholicism.[6]

Growing incidents of violence preceded the outbreak of revolt. The audacious conspiracy of Huguenot noblemen to seize the boy king, Charles IX, at Amboise, alarmed the government, which reacted with extreme repression. Widespread acts of Protestant iconoclasm incited Catholic rage.[7] The event that actually triggered the first war was the massacre at Vassy in March 1562, where the duke of Guise slaughtered and wounded many members of a Protestant congregation near Paris.

Looking at the quarrel of Bourbon and Guise, one might want to see the civil war as a neofeudal phenomenon, the recrudescence of conflict between noble dynasts and their clienteles at the moment of a weakened

---

[5] A detailed narrative of the wars of religion is given by J. Mariéjol, *La Réforme et la Ligue*, in *Histoire de France jusqu'à la Révolution*, ed. E. Lavisse, Paris, 1903–11, v. 6, pt. 1. J. H. M. Salmon, *Society in crisis: France in the sixteenth century*, New York, 1975, is a full recent study containing many insights and valuable information. Livet, *Les Guerres de religion*, presents a lucid, short treatment and discussion.

[6] See Chapter 6 in this book.   [7] *Ibid.*

royal authority. This, however, would be a very inadequate, one-sided view. For interacting with the rivalry of great houses was another element: the existence of the Reformed church rejecting Catholic unity, the effects of Huguenot religious and political organization, and the spirit and beliefs that sustained Protestant resistance. This second element was quite novel and of high consequence. It introduced features that appeared for the first time in a revolution. By an odd irony, moreover, what the Huguenots did to organize and maintain their revolt the Catholics subsequently emulated after the Catholic League was formed in 1576 as an aristocratic and popular movement to coerce the monarchy. By the same irony, the Huguenots turned into upholders of royal legitimacy when the Protestant Henry of Navarre, the future Henry IV, became the claimant to the throne as Henry III's heir.

The Huguenots were led by Louis, prince of Condé, the brother of Antoine of Bourbon, king of Navarre; Jeanne D'Albret, queen of Navarre, Antoine's widow; Gaspard de Coligny, admiral of France, and his two brothers, the sons of marshal de Chatillon and nephews of the duke of Montmorency, constable of France. Allied with them were various Protestant *grands* such as La Rochefoucauld, Rohan, Bouillon, and Montgomery. Besides the valiant Jeanne D'Albret, a number of other exceptional women of strong religious faith, the wives and mothers of Huguenot noblemen, made their influence felt in the movement.[8] The Bourbons were cousins of the king and princes of the blood whose leadership in the Protestant cause passed as a legacy to the next generation. After Condé was killed fighting at Jarnac in 1569, his young heir, Henry, took his place as a Huguenot chief. Jeanne D'Albret's son, Henry of Navarre, bred by her for the service of religion, joined Condé in that role and carried on the conflict after his mother's death.

Francis duke of Guise and his brother, Charles cardinal of Lorraine, dominated the ultra-Catholic forces. These ambitious princes sprang from the dukes of Lorraine and were uncles of Mary Queen of Scots, the wife and widow of Francis II (1559–60), Charles IX's older brother and predecessor on the throne of France. Among the Guises, too, the fighting legacy was transmitted. When the duke of Guise fell by assassination in 1563 (a crime of which his family accused Coligny),[9] his son, Henry,

---

[8] See N. Roelker's biography of Jeanne D'Albret, *Queen of Navarre Jeanne D'Albret 1528–1572*, Cambridge, 1968, and her study of these Huguenot women, "Les Femmes de la noblesse huguenot au XVIe siècle," in *Actes du colloque: L'Amiral de Coligny et son temps*, Paris, 1974, and "The appeal of Calvinism to French noblewomen in the sixteenth century," *Journal of interdisciplinary history 2*, 2 (1972). There were strong and determined noblewomen on the Catholic side as well, like some of the princesses of the Guise family.

[9] Coligny was probably not to blame, even though he rejoiced publicly at Guises's death. See N. M. Sutherland's interesting discussion of the Guise family's "vendetta" against Coligny, which culminated in his murder at the hands of the duke of Guise in the Saint Bar-

succeeded to his honors and place in the Catholic party. Other Guise relatives – brothers, cousins, and nephews, like the dukes of Aumale, Mayenne, Mercoeur, and Elboeuf – also figured prominently in the cause, together with a number of Catholic *grands.*

The overriding issues in the first decade of the civil war were the survival of Protestantism, which the Guises were sworn to destroy, and Guise domination of the state and monarchy. The contemporary Huguenot historian, Agrippa d'Aubigné, poignantly related how Admiral Coligny overcame his scruples against resistance as his wife pleaded with him to heed the cries of the murdered Protestant victims of persecution.[10] The prince of Condé and some of the provincial noble adherents probably took up arms as much from ambition as for faith. Nevertheless, the Huguenots fought to gain legal recognition and hoped eventually to make the Reformed church supreme in France. But the Guises were the more powerful in the government most of the time and compelled their adversaries to leave the court. Charles IX, only twelve in 1562, continued to be subject to others' influence even as he grew older. The queen mother, Catherine de Medici, was dedicated solely to the interests of the crown and her sons. She stood in the main for a politics of moderation that would have allowed limited toleration to the Huguenots for the sake of peace. The crown, however, lacked the strength at this juncture to execute an independent policy. Every edict of pacification it issued to stop hostilities conceded the Huguenots some liberty, and all but the last broke down.

Most Catholics, moreover, looked on Protestantism with hatred as a divisive force that should not be permitted in a well-ordered state. It was during the civil war that the famous formula, "one king, one law, one faith," attained its greatest influence.[11] Even those who approved a degree of tolerance for the Huguenots did so mainly as an expedient until religious uniformity could be restored. Caught amid the ruthless clash of contending creeds and aristocratic factions, the monarchy's sovereign authority was undermined, and the powers it had acquired put in jeopardy. As Francis Bacon observed, "The kingdom of France . . . is now fallen into those calamities, that, as the prophet saith, 'From the crown of the head to the sole of the foot, there is no whole place.' "[12]

tholomew massacre in 1572, "The role of Coligny in the French civil wars," in *Actes du colloque: L'Amiral de Coligny et son temps,* Paris, 1974.

[10] See the passage from d'Aubigne (1552–1630), cited in S. Mours, *Le Protestantisme en France au XVIe siècle,* Paris, 1959, 189.

[11] See M. Yardeni, *La Conscience nationale en France pendant les guerres de religion,* Paris, 1971, 77–8. The author of this formula was apparently the humanist scholar Guillaume Postel (1510–81).

[12] F. Bacon, *Certain observations made upon a libel,* in *Works,* ed. J. Spedding et al., 14 v., London, 1857–74, v. 8, 160.

II

The French civil war was the first European revolution wherein the press, the pamphlet, and political propaganda played a vital role in events. Print, to be sure, had contributed immeasurably to the propagation of the Lutheran reform and the spread of Protestantism in Europe; moreover, as we have noted, it had also made possible an extensive distribution of the Twelve Articles in the German peasant war. But it was in France from the 1560s onward that the press became for the first time an important means of combat and propaganda by both rebels and their opponents. The same was presently to be the case in the Netherlands as well, where revolt began four years after the outbreak of the civil war in France.

The French civil war provoked a mass of publications, which served as both the journalism of the time and a weapon of ideological controversy. The Huguenots took up the pamphlet first, and their adversaries replied in kind. The contending forces waged a fierce battle of public opinion, even allowing that the "public" at that period remained quite restricted. Some pamphlets that enjoyed a great success were reissued as many as ten times and reprinted as well in different towns. Propaganda included placards, tracts, and libels thrown about the streets. The crown issued its own declarations, as did leading personalities and the Protestant churches, and pamphleteers were busy on all sides. The Paris press, the greatest concentration of printing in the kingdom, was incessantly active. In the later period of the civil war during the days of the Catholic League, Pierre de l'Estoile, Paris lawyer, book collector, and contemporary memoirist, wrote, "There was no little printer so poor that he did not find the means to make the press turn daily with some defamatory libel." A modern scholar has calculated that the Paris printers who served the League produced more than 1,000 separate publications on its behalf in the decade 1585–94. The highest year, 1589, saw at least 362; 1588, the next highest, 157. These were the years when the League's insurrection against Henry III was at its height, and the press obviously responded to the pulsation of events.[13]

The Huguenots launched their resistance, like so many other insurgents of the age, professing loyalty and obedience to the crown. Vastly outnumbered by the Catholics, they demanded, of course, liberty for their religion but did not yet proclaim rebellion as a principle. They justified themselves, rather, with the plea that they were defending the ancient constitution of the kingdom against the usurpation of the Guises. They asserted the rights of the Bourbons as princes of the blood to a preeminent

[13] M. Yardeni, *La Conscience nationale*, introduction; and D. Pallier, *Recherches sur l'imprimerie à Paris pendant la Ligue (1585–94)*, Paris, 1975, 41–57. The citation from l'Estoile (1546–1611) is in Pallier, *Recherches sur l'imprimerie à Paris,* 56.

place in the government and claimed to be fighting against evil councillors and nefarious influences. Their declarations and pamphlets spoke of opposing tyranny and of maintaining both liberty and true royalty together. Here and there the idea was bruited that an impious or tyrannous prince forfeited his title to rule. There were also mentions of the rights of the Estates General vis-à-vis the crown, as well as stress on the importance of the nobility. Taken as a whole, Huguenot argument in the first decade of the revolutionary struggle relied on a constitutionalism of precedent that entailed a conception of the monarchy as tempered or limited in various ways.[14]

Behind the revolt stood the Huguenot party, composed of nobility, officials, urban magistrates and notables, bourgeois and lesser strata, and towns adhering to the Protestant resistance. An armature to sustain the military effort was built alongside the Protestants' ecclesiastical structure, with the separate congregations and their consistories, the regional colloquies, and the provincial synods helping to raise forces and money. The nobility provided the military cadres, and leadership in the armed struggle fell to the princes and high nobility, who brought their clientage of followers and with whom were joined the provincial *noblesse* and gentlemen affiliated with the Reform. On the threshold of civil war in April 1562, the third national synod of the Reformed church met at Orléans and recognized the prince of Condé as "protector" of all the churches of France.[15] French Calvinism was thus deeply inscribed by the same principle as the society of orders and adapted itself to aristocratic direction in political and military matters. Great noble personages remained at the head of the movement throughout the conflict. In the places where the Huguenots were strongest, such as Guienne, Languedoc, and Dauphiné, the churches also appointed noble "protectors." The contemporary semiofficial *Ecclesiastical history* of the French Reformed church recorded how the synod of upper Guienne in 1562 named two "protectors," one each for the two provinces comprising the respective jurisdictions of the *parlements* of Bordeaux and Toulouse. The colloquies in each province also had a chief or colonel, who in turn had under him captains of the particular churches belonging to the colloquy.[16]

It was to this structure that the Venetian ambassador, Giovanni Michieli, alluded in reporting to his government on the French civil war. He gave a sketch of the Protestant religious organization in the provinces of

[14] G. Weill, *Les Théories sur le pouvoir royal en France pendant les guerres de religion*, Paris, 1891, 34–6, 68–72, 78–80; Salmon, *Society in crisis*, 168–9, 170, 181; V. De Caprariis, *Propaganda e pensiero politico in Francia durante le guerre di religione 1559–1572*, Naples, 1959, passim.

[15] Salmon, *Society in crisis*, 124, 141–3; Livet, *Les Guerres de religion*, 51–2.

[16] *Histoire ecclesiastique des églises réformées au royaume de France*, ed. G. Baum, E. Cunitz, and R. Reuss, 3 v., Paris, 1883–9, v. 2, 888.

France and the lines that ran from the local churches and ministers to the Huguenot heads, whom he named (this was in 1571) as the queen of Navarre and Admiral Coligny. He noted how the Reformed people taxed themselves voluntarily to sustain their fight, even including the laborers, artisans, and domestic servants, paying with "such promptitude and ardor that it is a marvel." "There is such union and understanding between them," he wrote, "and they show such obedience to their chiefs that the Turk could not equal them . . . In sum, the Admiral possesses in the realm a sort of state separate and independent of the King."[17]

Needless to say, the Huguenots attracted malcontents and opportunists as well as committed adherents, and some of their supporters abandoned them for the Catholic and royal side in due course. But the movement and its leadership remained intact and capable of maintaining rebellion from the bases it acquired. The Reformed churches, although spread widely over the kingdom by the 1560s and well represented in such provinces of the north as Normandy, were most numerous and solidly established in the southwest, south, and southeast. In 1562, Coligny estimated their number at 2,150, a figure that long years of war, persecution, and attrition were to reduce considerably by 1598.[18] Paris was always a Catholic bastion and remained strongly partial to the Guises. In the early years of the civil war, however, the Huguenots succeeded, despite reverses, in conquering territory and strongholds in the south. They possessed La Rochelle, which became in effect their capital, Montauban, Nîmes, and other towns with their adjoining regions. They held these places until the final suppression of Protestant political-military independence by Louis XIII and Richelieu in the 1620s.

While the royal–Catholic and the Huguenot armies both made use of foreign mercenaries, the former did so to a considerably greater extent. A majority of the forces raised by the crown and Guises to suppress the Protestant revolt were foreign – Germans, Swiss, Italians, and other hired soldiers. The Huguenots also employed some foreign troops, mainly Germans brought by the Calvinist princes of the Palatinate, but most of their troops were French. The existence of the religious organization made it possible to recruit men from the Huguenot areas on a systematic basis, almost like conscription. The fighting ranks were filled with bourgeois townsmen and many artisans, *"gens mécaniques."* At Jarnac in 1569, the

[17] Cited in P. Erlanger, *Le Massacre de la Saint-Barthélemy*, Paris, 1960, 137–8. On the Huguenot organization, see also the papers by H. Koenigsberger ("The organization of revolutionary parties in France and the Netherlands during the sixteenth century," in *Estates and revolutions*, Ithaca, 1971) and R. Kingdon ("The political resistance of the Calvinists in France and the Low Countries," *Church history 27*, 3 (1958).

[18] There is a survey of the expansion of Protestantism and the distribution of the churches in Mours, *Le Protestantisme en France au XVIe siècle*, ch. 6 and map, 248–9; for Coligny's figure, see L. Romier, *Le royaume de Catherine de Medicis*, 2 v., Paris, 1922, v. 2, 180.

Huguenots numbered about 15,000 against a royal army of 26,000; at Montcontour later in the same year, 18,000 against 28,000.[19] Although they lost both battles, the Protestants were imbued by the sentiment that theirs was not an army like others. The leaders tried to instill it with a religious spirit and moral discipline that, it has been said, foreshadowed that of the Puritan Oliver Cromwell's New Model army during the English revolution.[20]

The ecclesiastical order of the Reformed church, with its consistories, colloquies, and synods, was distinct from the Huguenot military and political organization. In line with the fundamental Calvinist principle separating the domains of the church and the magistrate, the former concerned itself with faith and discipline. Eleven national synods met from the time of the first one in 1559 to the end of the civil war. They were all occupied with the internal religious life of the communities, the church's institutional unity, and doctrine. Among the most important was the seventh national synod, held in 1571 at La Rochelle. This meeting adopted the definitive version of the Huguenot confession of faith. It was also noteworthy for the measures it took to tighten church discipline and government against some populist and democratic tendencies that had arisen which were favorable to the congregational independence of the churches. Present along with the regular delegates, moreover, were the noble leaders of the Huguenot party, the queen of Navarre and her son, Henry, Henry prince of Condé, and Admiral Coligny. Louis of Nassau, brother of the leader of the Netherlands revolt, William of Orange, also attended. Geneva's direct influence was seen in the participation of Theodore Beza, Calvin's successor, who was the moderator of the assembly. All these personages joined in signing the confession of faith. The synod was a striking demonstration of the Reformed church's internationalism and of its existence as an organized power completely independent of the royal states' authority or supervision.[21]

The exigencies of civil war and rebellion also compelled the Huguenots to create a new organ for political, administrative, and financial purposes.

[19] See J. de Pablo, "Gaspard Coligny, chef de guerre," in *Actes du colloque: L'Amiral de Coligny et son temps*, Paris, 1974, and "Contribution a l'étude de l'histoire des institutions militaires Huguenotes: II. L'Armée huguenote entre 1562 et 1573," *Archiv für Reformationsgeschichte 48*, 2 (1957).

[20] See Yardeni, *La Conscience nationale*, 131.

[21] Mours, *Le Protestantisme en France au XVIe siècle*, ch. 8, contains a survey of Protestant synods and church life; for the La Rochelle synod of 1571, see M. Reulos, "Le Synode national de La Rochelle (1571) et la constitution d'un 'parti' protestant," *Actes du colloque: L'Amiral de Coligny et son temps*, Paris, 1974. The conflict over church government and congregational independence or democracy especially associated with the name of the pastor, Jean Morély, is described at length by R. Kingdon, *Geneva and the consolidation of the French Protestant movement 1564–1572*, Madison, 1967, and summarized in Salmon, *Society in crisis*, 179–83.

This was the political assembly, an institution that performed in secular matters a governmental function similar to that of the church synods in religion. It was based, like the ecclesiastical structure, on corporate representation by communities and took the form of an assembly of estates. It was thus an adaptation of the system of French representative assemblies, constituted in this case, however, of, by, and for the Protestants in their political capacity.[22]

The first Huguenot political assembly seems to have been held in 1562 in Nîmes. It referred to itself as a general assembly of the estates of Languedoc and consisted of both noblemen and the consuls and deputies representing a number of the towns. It included no clerical representation, Calvinist Protestantism not recognizing the clergy as a separate estate (although ministers might be chosen as deputies of the *tiers état*). This body appointed the count of Crussol as provincial chief and protector and named some councillors to advise him. It also laid down a number of administrative and financial regulations for the province.[23]

More than forty political assemblies of the Huguenots convened in the course of the civil war; most were of a province or group of provinces, but some were national assemblies.[24] Their structure and competence were elaborated and formalized during the 1570s. It is possible, and even probable, that their development was affected by the progress of Huguenot political ideas, which by this stage had come to articulate a comprehensive opposition to absolutism and to propound theories in favor of popular sovereignty and the control of executive power.

The Huguenot political assembly of Millau in 1573 took order for councils, for elected local assemblies, and for an estates general of Languedoc – the last a broad representative system made up of deputies of the nobility and the third estate. The provincial estates general was directed to meet every three months and charged with the right to levy imposts and exercise other governmental responsibilities.[25]

At another political assembly held at Millau in 1574, the nobility and third estate, speaking as representative of the Reformed church of France, acknowledged the prince of Condé as their chief, governor general, and protector but specified various conditions upon his authority. The assem-

[22] On the subject of Huguenot political assemblies, which still requires further investigation and clarification, see L. Anquez, *Histoire des assemblées politiques des réformés de France 1573–1622*, Paris, 1859; M. Reulos, "Synodes, assemblées politiques des réformés français et théories des états," *Ancien pays et assemblées d'états 24* (1962); and G. Griffiths, *Representative government in Western Europe in the sixteenth century*, Oxford, 1968, 254–97, which contains a discussion and a selection of documents.

[23] See Griffiths, *Representative government in Western Europe*, 265–8; *Histoire ecclésiastique*, v. 3, 202.

[24] For a list of sixteenth-century Huguenot political assemblies, see Griffiths, *Representative government in Western Europe*, 261–2.

[25] *Ibid.*, 280–1; and Anquez, *Histoire des assemblées politiques*, 7–10.

bly warned the prince against "absolute power" (*"puissance absolue"*), which it condemned as a usurpation and abuse unjustly introduced into the realm. It adjured him to conduct himself with justice and moderation, as a godly judge in Israel, not a tyrant, and to govern according to law and the ordinances drawn up by the assembly. He was forbidden to appoint any governors of provinces and towns except by the latter's advice and nomination.[26]

Subsequent political assemblies decreed similar principles in relation to the aristocratic heads of the party. The Montauban assembly of 1581, in declaring its union with Henry of Navarre as protector of the churches, ordained a number of arrangements constraining his authority. After Navarre became heir presumptive to the throne of France, the national political assembly held at La Rochelle in 1588 prescribed a *règlement* of even more elaborate consultative safeguards to the same purpose.[27] It is worth noting that this La Rochelle assembly of 1588 was intended as a counter to the Estates General of France, which Henry III had summoned to meet at Blois, a Catholic, Guise-dominated body to which no Protestant would have been admitted.[28]

The great historian-scholar Jacques-Auguste de Thou, author of one of the main contemporary accounts of the civil war, said of the Huguenot political assemblies and organization that they created in France "a sort of republic . . . separated from the rest of the state, with its laws for religion, civil government, justice, military discipline . . . commerce . . . taxes and the administration of finances."[29] This statement, if doubtless a bit overdrawn, yet pointed to an undeniable fact. Without their ever disavowing France's monarchy or their fidelity to the crown, the Huguenots constructed in the regions under their control an independent political order that rivaled and displaced the king's. This order was antiabsolutist and possessed a distinctly constitutionalist character. The latter was exemplified in the contractual relation of communities to leaders and the place of representative assemblies of estates in ordaining regulations and defining the limits of executive authority. In no previous European revolution had rebels attempted on such a scale to fashion governmental institutions of this kind.

The Huguenot political assemblies survived the end of the civil war for barely more than two decades. Henry IV, the former Protestant who became a Catholic convert, would have liked to abolish them; nevertheless, as a concession he let them continue to meet biennially, although under

---

[26] Griffiths, *Representative government in Western Europe*, 282–4.   [27] *Ibid.*, 288–95.

[28] Reulos, "Synodes, assemblées, politiques," 106; Anquez, *Histoire des assemblées politiques*, 38 and n.

[29] Cited in Anquez, *Histoire des assemblées politiques*, 21; de Thou (1553–1617) was the author of the famous *History of his own time*, which dealt with the civil war.

the presidency of a royally appointed commissioner and with much curtailed functions.[30] They ceased to exist after 1621, when Louis XIII launched his offensive against Huguenot liberties. The political assembly perished with the other institutions that secured Protestant autonomy and provincialism against the Bourbon monarchy's sovereign authority.

III

The Huguenots did not set out on the path of resistance as conscious revolutionaries and were reluctant to be thought rebels. Toward the existing order and its many inequalities their attitude was one of enduring acceptance. They claimed to be fighting, as Coligny said, "not against the King, but against those who have tyrannically forced those of the reformed religion to take up arms in order to defend their lives."[31] What they demanded first and foremost was freedom for their cult with added political safeguards necessitating some limitation on the royal state. In the 1560s, as we have seen, their arguments bore an essentially conservative cast, appealing to precedent and custom to support their case. If intimations of more radical ideas appeared, they remained subordinate to the prevailing themes.

But the force of circumstances soon led to fresh developments in the party's political position, giving rise in consequence to a crop of doctrines that were destined to exert a seminal influence in the European revolutions of the age.

In August 1570, the third war of religion concluded with the peace of Saint-Germain, which granted the Protestants limited freedom of worship plus other concessions as security. Charles IX and the queen mother, abandoning the ultra-Catholic side, now became reconciled with the Huguenot leaders, who returned to the court, their influence momentarily in the ascendancy. They urged the king to renounce his pro-Spanish orientation and to intervene in the Netherlands on behalf of the Dutch rebels, a design they advocated as both in France's interests and a way to unite the kingdom through foreign war. The crown, although at first acceding to this policy, appeared nevertheless more and more fearful that it would provoke an all-out war with Spain. A French invasion of the Netherlands was actually planned, but in August 1572, shortly before the final hour, the king and queen mother, intimidated by Philip II's warnings, decided to halt course and then abruptly turned upon the Huguenots.

[30] See *ibid.*, 213–14.
[31] Cited in De Caprariis, *Propaganda e pensiero politico*, 424, and see the entire discussion of the development of Huguenot thought in pt. 3, ch. 1. J. W. Allen's account, *A history of political thought in the sixteenth century*, 3rd ed., London, 1951, pt. 3, ch. 4, remains essential. Many of the intellectual currents in the background of the Huguenot revolt are discussed by Q. Skinner, *The foundations of modern political thought*, 2 v., Cambridge, 1978, v. 2, ch. 8.

At that particular moment the court was celebrating the marriage, a symbol of reconciliation, between the Huguenot Henry of Navarre and Margaret of Valois, Charles IX's sister. The Huguenot chiefs with many Protestant noblemen and the duke of Guise and other Catholic partisans were all in Paris for the festivities. On August 22, a Catholic assassin shot and wounded Admiral Coligny. In the dangerous atmosphere of incipient violence created by this incident, the king, his mother, and his advisers made the sudden decision to liquidate the leaders of the Huguenot rebellion, sparing only the princes of the blood. Early on the morning of August 24, Coligny was attacked in his lodgings, thrown from a window, and murdered on the street by the duke of Guise and companions. An orgy of killing was set off in Paris, as the mob, the royal guards, and Guisards hunted down Protestant victims. In less than a week two or three thousand people probably perished in the capital as a result. The news of the massacre inspired a similar blood purge in Rouen, Orléans, Bordeaux, Toulouse, Lyon, and other towns, where ten or fifteen thousand more Protestants were slaughtered by the fanaticism of an infuriated Catholic population.

This was the notorious Saint Bartholomew massacre, whose name became proverbial for treachery and crime and which the papacy and most of Catholic Europe greeted with jubilation. Terrible as it was, it did not destroy the Huguenot movement, but it naturally embittered and altered the party's attitude toward the monarchy. It caused, of course, a resumption of the civil war, and the Protestants proceeded to strengthen and consolidate their political autonomy in Languedoc and the south. In its aftermath they moved as well toward an alliance with a newly emerged moderate Catholic faction, the Politiques, who advocated toleration as the sole means to gain peace. Beyond these several practical consequences, the gruesome atrocities of 1572 drove the party to adopt a new and much bolder ideological position.

In the outburst of propaganda following the massacre, many Huguenot writers denounced the court and Guises and voiced their horror at the tragedy. A host of pamphlets spoke of the king as a tyrant. *Le Réveille-matin des françois* (1573), one of the most incendiary Huguenot compositions, called upon all Frenchmen and patriots, "kept in servitude and treated worse than beasts," to rise and remedy their miseries. Some of the attacks upon Catherine de Medici associated her Italian origin with the pernicious principles of Machiavelli. This provided the ground for a wholesale onslaught on the famous author of *The Prince*, who was named as incorporating all the vice and corruption stemming from Italianate influences at the Valois court. The massacre was attributed to his inspiration, and a number of Huguenot works helped to create the legend of Machiavelli as the diabolical advocate of tyranny, faithlessness, and irreligion.[32]

It was in the postmassacre period that party publicists began for the first time to defend the right of rebellion by subjects and to insist that political subjection was based on pactions, consent, and representative institutions. These focal themes received their most authoritative statement in the three works by Huguenot authors that probably had the widest currency and influence: François Hotman's *Francogallia* (1573); Theodore Beza's *The right of magistrates over subjects* (1574); and the pseudonymous (but very likely in whole or larger part by the Huguenot nobleman and intellectual Philippe du Plessis Mornay) *Vindiciae contra tyrannos* (1579). Despite the differences among them – and the first had a historical-antiquarian cast, whereas the other two were in a more abstract-theoretical mode – all three exemplified the Huguenot shift to an overtly revolutionary doctrine.

Huguenot resistance theory had immediately behind it a considerable line of earlier Protestant and Calvinist ideas in defense of rebellion. The German peasant war produced at least one explicit attempt to justify the peasants in taking up arms.[33] Discussions by German Protestant theologians guardedly laid out the circumstances in which communities might resist their ruler; the *Bekenntnis* or *Confession* of Magdeburg of 1550, wherein the Lutheran cities of the Schmalkaldic League vindicated their resistance to Emperor Charles V; the tracts by the English exiles of Catholic Queen Mary's reign, John Ponet's *Shorte treatise of politike power* (1556) and Christopher Goodman's *How superior powers ought to be obeyed* (1558), which maintained the legitimacy of revolt against tyrannous, idolatrous (*read* Catholic) princes; the inflammatory pamphlets and preaching to the same end by the Scottish reformer and rebel John Knox; and, far from least, Calvin's famous discussion of civil government in the *Institute of the Christian religion*, where he allowed for certain circumstances in which lesser magistrates could authorize resistance. All these writings preceded those of the Huguenot publicists in the 1570s, and most if not all were naturally familiar to them.[34] What remains true, however, is that the French civil

---

[32] The citation from *Le Réveille-matin* comes from Yardeni, *La Conscience nationale*, 49. For the postmassacre Huguenot reaction and joint denunciation of Italian influence and Machiavelli, *ibid.*, ch. 4, and the excellent account in D. Kelley, *François Hotman: A revolutionary's ordeal*, Princeton, 1973, 235–8. The classic Huguenot attack upon Machiavelli, a work crucial to the history of his European reputation, was Innocent Gentillet's *Discours contre Machiavel* (1576), now authoritatively edited by A. D'Andrea and P. Stewart, Florence, 1974. Stewart discusses Gentillet's book and its context in *Innocent Gentillet e la sua polemica antimachiavelica*, Florence, 1969.

[33] See Chapter 7 in this book.

[34] There is a considerable literature devoted to the history of resistance theory in the sixteenth century, both specialized and as part of wider studies such as Allen, *Political thought in the sixteenth century*. For some intellectual connections of the Huguenot theorists, see

war was the first revolution to give the defense and legitimation of revolt a massive and fully developed intellectual expression.

The significance of this fact must not be underestimated. The sixteenth century, as a student of resistance theory has remarked, was "sincerely royalist,"[35] and the main contemporary teaching of religion tended to emphasize obedience and submission to superiors as a primary obligation. Against the exaltation of kings and their power as ordained by God, religious people and Protestant dissidents needed to be convinced that rebellion was permissible, not sin, and might even become a duty. This was the purpose of the fighters against kings or monarchomachs, as they were termed, and of the adversaries of absolutism, to whom the Huguenot writers belonged and without whom a revolutionary tradition could hardly have arisen in Europe.

François Hotman, one of the foremost legal scholars of his day, began his *Francogallia* some time before Saint Bartholomew but completed and sharpened it following the massacre, from which he had fled to Geneva. He was a militant Huguenot publicist whom his biographer and editors have dubbed with good reason "a professional revolutionary."[36] His work offered a significant version of a type of revolutionary thinking common to his time, which I have often referred to as the ideology of the normative past. In France's earliest history, and in consequence of the fusion of Franks and Gauls, he discerned a primitive constitution of freedom whereby the people was sovereign and kings were its servants. Even after the emergence of hereditary royal succession, he believed kingship remained an office depending on popular consent, which could therefore be revoked. Hotman devoted some of his formidable if tendentious erudition to a description of the basic component of the ancient constitution, the assembly or "public council" of estates that had been established by ancestral wisdom as the embodiment of the realm and its consent. Its powers included "the appointing and deposing of kings . . . war and peace . . . public laws," the disposal of the highest honors, offices, and regency in the commonwealth, and, generally, "all those issues which in popular speech are now commonly called affairs of state." Hotman cited many examples of the removal of earlier kings for their misconduct. To him the ancient constitution of freedom was at once both a reality and a model, an

---

O. Olson, "Theology of revolution: Magdeburg, 1550–1551," *Sixteenth century journal 3*, 1 (1972); I. Hoess, "Zur Genesis der Widerstandslehre Bezas," *Archiv für Reformationsgeschichte 54* (1963); R. Kingdon, "The first expression of Theodore Beza's political ideas," *Archiv für Reformationsgeschichte 46* (1955); and the introduction to F. Hotman, *Francogallia*, ed. R. Giesey and J. H. Salmon, Cambridge, 1972, 4–5. Significant fresh light is thrown upon Huguenot resistance theory and its antecedents by Skinner (*Foundations*, v. 2, chs. 7, 9), whose discussion in part supersedes preceding general accounts of the subject.

[35] Weill, *Les Théories sur le pouvoir royal*, 289.

[36] Kelley, *François Hotman*, viii; *Francogallia*, introduction, 3.

"is" and an "ought." Although corrupted, it had not ceased to exist; in its original character and principles alone could Frenchmen find their guide.[37]

Whereas Hotman's justification of resistance and popular sovereignty took the form of a treatise on France's history that gave shape to an idealized picture or myth of the past, Beza's *Right of magistrates* and the pseudonymous *Vindiciae* addressed a similar task through a more generalized approach. Of course, the two also cited Biblical and historical arguments, but their position rested mostly on rational and theoretical considerations.

Beza sought to prove from reason and example that the people created kings and instituted them on definite conditions. Thus, if a king becomes a tyrant or breaks the conditions on which he received his authority, the people is no longer bound to obey and may remove him. From explaining the contractual basis of subjection, Beza went on to canvass various questions concerning tyranny and where the right of resistance and deposition lay. He concluded that it could not belong to private individuals, lest "infinite troubles . . . ensue even worse than tyranny itself, and a thousand tyrants . . . arise on the pretext of suppressing one." This right, he held, inhered in lesser magistrates and assemblies of estates, public authorities whom the constitution of kingdoms empowered with the responsibility to restrain and if necessary remove tyrannical rulers.[38]

The *Vindiciae* pursued a similar line, despite divergences in emphasis and detail, and with even greater boldness. It found the rationale and origin of the political order in the covenants and compacts among God, king, and people. The people created kings and, as their superior, may depose them. In the restraint and supervision of the monarchy, the *Vindiciae* assigned a central place to the Parlement of Paris as a "senate" or "court of peers" and "patricians" that had to approve royal acts and prevent illegalities, as well as to the assembly of the three estates. Subject therefore to definite limits, kings are justly resisted if guilty of tyranny or if they violate God's law and persecute His church. Force, said the *Vindiciae*, may definitely be used in the cause of religion. Like Beza, it withheld the right of resistance from private persons, unless specially inspired by God. It assigned this right to the "lesser magistrates," "the principal persons of the kingdom," and assemblies of estates; in short, to constituted

---

[37] *Francogallia* appeared in Latin in 1573, then in 1574 in French, and in an enlarged Latin edition in 1576. For the texts and variations, see the edition by Giesey and Salmon. The quotations come from the latter, 333, beginning of ch. 11 of the first ed. Extracts from *Francogallia* are contained in J. Franklin, *Constitutionalism and resistance in the sixteenth century*, New York, 1969. For a survey of its ideas, context, and influence, see *ibid.*, introduction; the introduction to the edition of Giesey and Salmon; and Kelley, *François Hotman*, 238–47, as well as the references already cited in Skinner, *Foundations*, v. 2, ch. 7.

[38] I have used the selections from Beza's *Du droit des magistrats sur leurs subiets* in English translation in Franklin, *Constitutionalism and resistance*. The quotation comes from *ibid.*, ch. 6, 109; see also the discussion in Franklin's introduction, and Skinner, *Foundations*, v. 2, ch. 9.

authorities who represent the people and have the duty to defend its liberty.[39]

These Huguenot treatises expressed an identical populism, whether rooted in the myth of primitive Frankish freedom or in an explication of the principles of subjection. They expounded an "ascending" thesis of government that affirmed popular sovereignty as the foundation of authority, the origin of political power in covenants, agreements, and consent, and the consequent right of the people to resist and remove kings who became tyrants. They were also all committed to a similar constitutionalism that looked to the continuing controls upon the ruler and the function of representative bodies as means of preserving liberty and preventing tyranny. It would have been only natural for such principles to operate likewise in the formation of the Huguenot political organization, with its reliance on representation by the estates and its adumbration of a constitutional order.[40] The formulation Huguenot theorists gave these ideas contributed to the common stock of revolutionary doctrines available to rebels. Not only were they taken up in the contemporaneous Netherlands revolt, but afterward they were put to use in the English revolution.

But if Huguenot ideology became much more radical than before, it still retained a conservative core. Its avowal of popular sovereignty was always grounded in aristocratic reservations or presuppositions and thus kept free of any democratic tincture. Huguenot theory did not allow the people or ordinary persons to initiate resistance. The people could act only through its superiors, who represented it or possessed responsibility for its defense. These were the lesser magistrates, other kinds of intermediate authorities, and assemblies of estates. The lesser magistrates, who in French terms corresponded primarily to the nobility, a governing class under kings, and to the assembly of estates or Hotman's "public council," composed of noblemen and other elites, were indispensable to Huguenot political doctrine. This was no more than was to be expected in view of the nature of the movement. In fact, Huguenot constitutionalism and resistance theory were usually framed in an aristocratic sense, precisely as aristocratic leadership dominated the Huguenot rebellion. "When we speak of the people collectively," declared the *Vindiciae*,

we mean the magistrates below the king who have been elected by the people or established in some other way. They take the place of the people . . . and are ephors to kings and associates in their rule. And we also mean the assembly of the

[39] Franklin, *Constitutionalism and resistance*, contains adequate selections from the *Vindiciae* in English translation and discusses its ideas in the introduction; see also Skinner, *Foundations*, v. 2, ch. 9. The quotations in the text come from the Third Question, 149, 151, 165.

[40] See the preceding discussion of Huguenot political assemblies in this chapter. It has been suggested that *Le Réveille-matin des françois*, one of the most radical of Huguenot pamphlets in its populism, exercised a direct influence upon Huguenot political organization; Salmon, *Society in crisis*, 189, 191–3, n. 31 on 195.

Estates, which are nothing less than the epitome of a kingdom to which all public matters are referred.

In the Huguenot conception of the polity, it was, as the *Vindiciae* wrote, "the officers of the crown, the peers, the lords, the patricians, the notables" who had "the office . . . to see that no harm is suffered either by the commonwealth or by the Church."[41]

Alongside Huguenot constitutionalism, the civil war also brought a temporary revival of the Estates General of France, a nearly defunct institution to which it gave a further installment of life. Owing to political turmoil and royal weakness, the idea of the estates was "in the air" during these years of revolt.[42]

In 1560 the king convened the Estates General for the first time since 1484. Further meetings were held in 1561, 1576, 1588, and 1593. On all of these occasions the assembled orders made repeated attempts to initiate administrative reforms, set curbs on royal sovereignty, and gain for the Estates a share in government. In 1561, the Estates General of Pontoise demanded biennial assemblies and that the king levy no new taxes or make offensive war without consent. Perhaps the Estates General of Blois in 1576 went furthest in this direction. It tried vainly to appoint a commission of its deputies to the royal council, to assume for itself a legislative power, and to assert the right of consent to taxes. It, too, like its predecessor, tried to provide for the regular convocation of the Estates. In 1593, during the disputed succession of Henry IV, an Estates General held in Paris under the domination of the Guises and the Catholic League presumed to claim that it could elect a king.[43]

It was to refute both current Huguenot justifications of rebellion and claims to the superiority of assemblies of estates that Jean Bodin published his *Six books of the commonweal* in 1576. In that notable work, a theoretical defense of royal absolutism, Bodin contended that sovereign power, including the power to make law, is the defining property of the state, and that in France, where sovereignty is monarchical, the king alone possesses the power to legislate and is not obliged to consult his subjects.

Institutionally, the Estates General suffered from too many inherent weaknesses to make good the pretensions it evinced during the civil war.

[41] *Vindiciae contra tyrannos*, in Franklin, *Constitutionalism and resistance*, 149–50. The basic orientation of Huguenot political ideas toward nobilities and elites is stressed by Weill, *Les Théories sur le pouvoir royal*, 89–90. P. Mesnard, *L'essor de la philosophie politique du XVIe siècle*, 2nd ed., Paris, 1951, 346, 347; and C. Mercier, "Les Théories politiques des Calvinistes en France au cours des guerres de la religion," *Bulletin de la société de l'histoire du Protestantisme français 83*, 2 pts. (1934).

[42] Weill, *Les Théories sur le pouvoir royal*, 146.

[43] See Griffiths, *Representative government in Western Europe*, 118–211, for a discussion of the Estates General in the sixteenth century with illustrative documents; and the account of the Estates General of Blois in 1576 in Salmon, *Society in crisis*, 220–2.

On the one hand, it was too unserviceable to the crown's needs; on the other, it was too lacking in procedures and powers that encouraged collective responsibility and cooperative action by the orders.[44] Beyond this, neither its history nor its function had ever been such as to inspire Frenchmen to look to it much for redress or political leadership. Its period of renewed activity hardly outlasted the civil war. Henry IV would not summon it at all. After being convened once more in 1614 during the troubles of Louis XIII's minority, it did not meet again until 1789. With the defeat of revolution, the monarchy held all the cards, and, as it shaped its absolutist government, it had no use for the Estates General or for any other representative institution that showed signs of independence.

IV

It would be impossible to understand all the revolutionary implications of the Huguenot resistance without taking some account as well of its foreign connections. I have spoken in a previous chapter of the Calvinist "international" and the ties binding the different Reformed churches.[45] French Protestantism did not wage its revolt merely in a national context. The Huguenot party felt itself no less involved in a deadly enmity with external foes: the Counter-Reformation and Catholic reaction; the papacy; and the armed might of Spain, the tangible embodiment of Catholic militancy. To a certain degree, the Huguenots foreshadowed the position of twentieth-century revolutionists who regard "people's war" and the "national liberation struggle" as fraught with international significance both politically and strategically.

In any event, national revolt in France inevitably possessed wide international ramifications. The French monarchy was a major power, Spain's chief adversary (apart from the Turks), with whom until 1559 it had been at war almost continually for half a century. The Franco–Spanish, Valois–Habsburg rivalry had dominated Europe's state relations. Now civil war undermined the French government's ability to carry on an effective foreign policy, and it also created opportune conditions for Spanish intervention. The house of Guise and extremist Catholics aimed to align France with Spain in a joint offensive to eliminate Protestant heresy and rebellion. Philip II became their patron and paymaster. But Spanish rule was vulnerable itself in the neighboring Netherlands, where revolution erupted in 1566 and which offered an obvious target for French troublemaking and territorial ambitions. The Huguenots strove to take advantage of this fact, to join with and aid the Dutch rebels, and to summon foreign Protestant support for their own insurgency. Between France's internal conflict and external forces there was thus a close and constant interplay.

[44] See Chapter 4 in this book. [45] See Chapter 6 in this book.

In 1562, the Huguenot leaders concluded a treaty with the English government, which promised them six thousand men in return for their pledge of aid in securing the restoration of Calais to England.[46] This particular agreement ended after a few months, but throughout the Huguenot rebellion Queen Elizabeth's England involved itself in French affairs to support the Protestant cause and counter Spain's influence. In the final phase, it contributed forces to help Henry IV establish his rule against Spanish military intervention.

The Huguenots also turned to the German Protestant princes, among whom they raised troops. Their strongest allies were the rulers of the Palatinate, who were committed to a Europe-wide, anti-Catholic policy. In the 1560s and subsequent years the Calvinist Palatines sent armies to fight alongside the Huguenots. The Palatine prince, John Casimir, was one of the leading captains in both the French civil war and the Netherlands revolt.[47]

Huguenot ideology contained a justification for this appeal to foreign powers. It was made explicit in the *Vindiciae contra tyrannos*, which framed the issue as follows: "Are neighboring princes permitted or obliged to aid the subjects of another prince who are persecuted for the exercise of true religion or are oppressed by manifest tyranny?" Its reply was decisively in the affirmative. The church, it claimed, is one, and an injury to any part therefore injures the whole. As princes are obliged to defend the church, so they must act against other princes who oppress it and become tyrants. Justice, the law of God, and charity require such action of them.[48]

This was a doctrine with momentous implications. For it internationalized revolutionary civil wars and offered a rationale for foreign intervention and subversion on their behalf. On the plea of religion, it turned the defense of liberty by rebels into a transnational conflict.

It was with the Dutch rebels that the Huguenot movement maintained the closest relations. Calvinist internationalism was evident in the many ties between the Reformed church of France and that of the Netherlands. French Calvinism, being stronger and better organized at an earlier date, made an important contribution to the propagation of the religion in the adjacent southern Netherlands. The first confession of faith prepared for the churches of the Low Countries was based on the Huguenot confession.[49] In ecclesiastical discipline, similarly, the French church provided the example. The synod of Emden in 1571, the first national convocation

---

[46] Calais, a longtime English possession and the only one retained from the Hundred Years war, had been recovered by France in 1559 in the treaty of Cateau-Cambrésis.

[47] The activity of the Palatine princes in the defense of Protestantism is discussed by C.-P. Clasen, *The Palatinate in European history, 1559–1660*, Oxford, 1963. Livet, *Les Guerres de religion*, ch. 5, contains a brief survey of the Protestants' foreign connections.

[48] *Vindiciae*, The fourth question, in Franklin, *Constitutionalism and resistance*, 197–9.

[49] P. Geyl, *The revolt of the Netherlands*, 2nd ed., London, 1958, 81–2.

of the churches of the Netherlands, was cognizant of the disciplinary and other decisions made earlier in the same year by the national synod of the French church at La Rochelle, and it adopted some of them itself. To demonstrate the solidarity between the two churches, the Emden synod also subscribed to the French church's confession of faith drawn up at La Rochelle.[50] There were various other expressions of accord. Both national churches sent deputies to one another's synods and agreed to supply ministers to each other in case of need. The French national synod of 1581 at La Rochelle referred to the "holy Union and Concord established between the Churches of France and those of the Low Countries."[51]

Similar connections linked the two revolutions. Before the outbreak of rebellion in the Netherlands, Philip II's authorities at Brussels felt certain that the Huguenots in France were inciting the king's subjects to resistance. Coligny was known to have considerable "intelligence" in the Low Countries. The confederation of noblemen that was formed in the provinces in 1565 to oppose the government's policies resembled and was probably even inspired by the similar organization of the Huguenot nobility in France on the eve of the civil war.[52] Especially noteworthy was the relationship between the leaders of the two revolts. In 1568, after the Spanish regime had defeated the first upsurge of resistance in the Netherlands, William of Orange made a treaty of alliance with Condé and Coligny. It provided for mutual aid on the ground that their respective princes, guided by evil councillors, were trying to exterminate the true religion, the nobility, and *"gens de bien."*[53] The count of Horne, who was executed with the count of Egmont in 1568 in Brussels as a rebel and traitor to Philip II, was a scion of the Montmorency family and therefore Coligny's cousin. William of Orange himself married Coligny's daughter as his fourth wife. Orange's younger brother, Louis of Nassau, was not only a principal figure in the Dutch revolt but also participated in the leadership of the Huguenots of France and served as an intermediary between the two movements. In 1570–2, during the reconciliation between the French crown and the Huguenots that ended so dramatically with the Saint Bartholomew massacre, Count Louis helped to influence the direction of France's policy toward intervention in the Netherlands. In the summer of 1572, he and several other commanders led small Huguenot invasion forces from

[50] See the preceding discussion of the La Rochelle synod in this chapter and D. Nauta, "Les Réformés aux Pays-Bas et les Huguenots, specialement à propos du synode d'Emden (1571)," in *Actes du colloque: L'Amiral de Coligny et son temps*, Paris, 1974.

[51] See J. Quick (ed.), *Synodicon in Gallia reformata*, 2 v., London, 1692, v. 1, 143–4.

[52] N. Sutherland, *The massacre of St. Bartholomew and the European conflict*, London, 1973, 37–8; C. Mercier, "Les Théories politiques des Calvinistes dans les Pays Bas à la fin du XVIe et au debut du XVIIe siècle," *Revue d'histoire ecclesiastique 29* (1933), 28. Sutherland's work is an indispensable account of the foreign context of France's revolutionary civil war.

[53] Sutherland, *The massacre of St. Bartholomew*, 75.

France into the Netherlands, which were speedily crushed by the superior strength of Spanish arms.[54] Pitted against similar enemies, the revolutions in the two countries repeatedly collaborated with one another, although the Dutch was destined to emerge triumphant after terrible trials and the Huguenot to be defeated in its struggle.

V

Charles IX died in 1574 and was succeeded by his younger brother, Henry III. This prince, a strange, effeminate personality, highly intelligent but mercurial and weak, reigned over a kingdom in increasing dissolution. Four more wars occurred in the decade after Saint Bartholomew. Meanwhile, a third force came into being, the Politiques, a party of royalist and moderate Catholics opposed to the Guises who, to end the fighting, sought a solution based on toleration. Their leader was the king's brother, Catherine de Medici's youngest son, the duke of Anjou. The Huguenots, who could no longer hope to convert France and continued to fight grimly for survival, allied with them. In 1576, the king issued another edict of pacification giving the Protestants the most favorable terms they had thus far received. It permitted their freedom of worship everywhere except Paris and allowed them to hold eight towns as security.

Catholic zealotry, in its determination to stop the crown from pursuing a middle course, coupled with Guise and noble political ambition, now gave their impulsion to the birth of a new insurrectionary movement, the Catholic League. If the Huguenot organization dominated the earlier part of the civil war, the Catholic League dominated the later. It possessed a no less militant spirit and embraced similar populist doctrines of an even more radical complexion. An organ of intransigent political Catholicism that refused any concessions to the Huguenots, the League was equally dangerous to the monarchy's sovereign authority. It was, as one of its earlier historians has said, an insurrection against royalty in the orthodox sense, just as Calvinism was an insurrection in the heretical sense.[55]

The League was first created in 1576 as an association of "princes, seigneurs, and gentlemen," its founders said, to defend the Catholic church. Bound by an oath in the name of the Holy Trinity, it resembled numerous other revolutionary organizations we have met in early modern Europe that came together under the powerful sanction of religion. Its chief was Henry duke of Guise, who published a manifesto stating its aims. The League pledged obedience to the king's authority, but under conditions that included recognition of the rights of the Estates General and the provinces. It called upon Catholics in towns and corporate bodies

[54] *Ibid.*, 46, 74, 146–7, 240–2, 290–1.
[55] C. Labitte, *De la démocratie chez les predicateurs de la Ligue*, Paris, 1841, lxix.

to support it with arms and men. Dedicated to total war on heresy, it exerted an immediate popular appeal.[56]

To counter the threat of an independent body controlled by the Guises, Henry III joined the League, declared himself its head, and reopened hostilities against the Huguenots. For a time, after he commanded in 1577 that all such unions and associations be dissolved, the League fell into abeyance. But it revived in 1584 under more propitious circumstances.

Although married, Henry III seemed unlikely to have children. In the absence of a son, the throne would pass to his brother, the duke of Anjou. With Anjou's untimely death in 1584, however, the heir presumptive became the Huguenot chief Henry of Navarre, head of the house of Bourbon. To prevent the succession of a heretic, the Catholic League reappeared in far greater strength than before. The duke of Guise and his friends and confederates proclaimed a new League, its aims to expel heresy, provide for a Catholic succession, and correct the abuses of Henry III's government. In December 1584, they made the secret treaty of Joinville with Philip II, in which the Spanish monarch agreed to support and subsidize the League in the common enterprise of extirpating heresy in France and the Netherlands. The interference of Spain in French affairs was now greater than ever before.[57]

Independently, an offshoot of the League was also established in Paris as a conspiratorial association through the initiative of some bourgeois, lawyers, officials, and clerics. It had a small council and an organization based on the quarters of the city. Its direction lay in a committee of the Sixteen, consisting of the council and the representatives of the quarters. Secret and mysterious, assuming a surveillance of morals and political expression, the Paris League grew into a feared and formidable movement possessing activists all over the municipality. It kept in touch with the duke of Guise and noble chiefs and also inspired the formation of similar leagues elsewhere by means of emissaries and letters. In this way, a Catholic organization independent of the crown came into existence in many provincial towns, each with its directing group like the Sixteen.[58]

The League was simultaneously an aristocratic and popular organization that evoked wide support among the urban masses. Although the Catholic princes and nobility joined it for aggrandizement as well as religious reasons, the urban orders were actuated also by their material hardships, which had been aggravated by the civil war. The Sixteen spoke of the miseries that oppressed "the poor and common people, nourisher of

[56] See Mariéjol, *La Réforme et la Ligue*, 174–6; and M. Wilkinson, *A history of the League or Sainte Union*, Glasgow, 1929.

[57] Mariéjol, *La Réforme et la Ligue*, 241, 244–5.

[58] For the Paris organization, see the essential study of P. Robiquet, *Paris et la Ligue sous le regne de Henri III*, Paris, 1886; and J. H. Salmon, "The Paris Sixteen, 1589–94: The social analysis of a revolutionary movement," *Journal of modern history 44*, 4 (1972).

all the other estates," and the Paris populace showed acute hostility to Henry III's extravagance and financial demands.[59] The League was thus able simultaneously to exploit both social resentments and religious fanaticism in the prosecution of its goals. Public sentiment was inflamed and guided by the *curés* and preachers in the parish churches of Paris, who carried on a violent propaganda from the pulpit on the League's behalf.[60] No less than the Huguenot pastors, the presbyterian clergy in the Scottish rebellion in 1638, or the Puritan ministry in the English revolution did the clerical adherents of the League exert themselves to harness religion to the political cause. An active press, as we have already seen,[61] also contributed to the success of the League and combined with the pulpit to foment an insurrectional temper among the people of the capital and the sympathizers in the provinces.

To the crown, the League presented a deadly menace. It dissociated Catholicism from royalism and turned its guns as much against the king as against the Huguenots. Henry III's debauchery, his lavish gifts to his male favorites, and his scandalous public behavior brought him hatred and contempt from the extreme Catholics. The League tried to dictate conditions to him and barred any accommodation with Protestantism. Against Henry of Navarre's succession, it advanced the claim of the cardinal of Bourbon, an orthodox Catholic. In the background also lurked the possibility that the duke of Guise, who asserted his descent from Charlemagne, might himself be a suitable candidate for the throne. Immensely popular and a stark contrast in personal qualities to Henry III, Guise was acclaimed as the church's champion. The League challenged the crown by stressing the limits on royal authority. It invoked the rights of the Estates General and claimed to stand for the supremacy of the fundamental law of the kingdom according to which only a Catholic could inherit the throne.[62] It was merely by a short natural progression that the League's publicists were soon to advocate theories of popular sovereignty analogous to those of Huguenot writers.

The advent of the League turned the revolutionary civil war into a conflict among royalism, Catholic rebellion, and the Huguenots. It effected a deep breach within Catholic opinion between the Politiques who, fearing the disintegration of France, magnified the powers of the crown and advocated a compromise peace, and the aristocratic, bourgeois-plebeian, and clericalist forces aligned against the king. Blessed by the pope and backed by Spanish gold, with the armies of Guise and his allies dominating the

[59] Robiquet, *Paris et la Ligue*, 256–9; F. Baumgartner, *Radical reactionaries: The political thought of the French Catholic League*, Geneva, 1975, 30–4.

[60] See Labitte, *De la démocratie*; and Robiquet, *Paris et la Ligue*.

[61] See the preceding discussion in the present chapter of this book.

[62] Baumgartner, *Radical reactionaries*, ch. 3, discusses the earlier political ideas of the League.

provinces of the north and east, a vehicle not only of religious partisanship but also of a provincialism that rejoiced at the debility of central authority, the League disposed for a time of overwhelming power. Although Henry III fought to preserve some freedom of action against it, he was much too weak to succeed.

His struggle with the League came to a showdown in May 1588. Invited by the Sixteen, on May 9 the duke of Guise entered Paris despite an express royal command forbidding his presence. An exultant throng hailed the League chief's arrival. Intending some counterblow, the king ordered his Swiss guards to take up positions in the city. At this move, the disaffected capital rose on May 12, the famous Day of the Barricades. Insurgent Parisians came out in arms as Guise's partisans. They blocked the streets with chains and set up barricades of casks loaded with stones and sand, behind which they defied the outnumbered royal troops. Overpowered by this display and threatened with a mob assault upon the Louvre, Henry III fled Paris the next day. "O ungrateful city," he exclaimed at departing, "I have loved you more than my own wife."[63]

The Day of the Barricades was a great urban revolt, one of the biggest of the era. Some historians have seen it as a rehearsal for 1789 and for the power wielded by the commune of Paris in the days of the Terror. "It transports us," one has commented, "from the closing scenes of the Valois dynasty to the final tragedy of the Bourbons."[64] The bourgeois militia, instead of upholding authority, defected, as the incensed people opposed the king's soldiers. Humiliated and helpless, Henry III lost the allegiance of his own capital, as Charles I was later to do in 1642 and Louis XIV, the queen mother, and Cardinal Mazarin in 1648.

During the following days, the Sixteen and the League, which had engineered the uprising, assumed control over Paris's government. The existing magistrates were removed, and a new Hotel de Ville installed consisting of League sympathizers. This was the first of a succession of changes by which the Sixteen and ultra-Catholics clamped a dictatorship on the municipality, monitoring opinion, whipping up militancy, and intimidating and punishing any opposition. A general council of the Union of Catholics was created to correspond with towns in the League camp, and committees of surveillance were appointed for every quarter of the city. The nucleus of Parisians in and around the Sixteen that carried through this insurrection and shift of power was socially rather composite. It included men who held legal and financial offices, a few rich merchants, a bishop, minor clergy, and lawyers. Members of the legal profession were the most

---

[63] Cited in Robiquet, *Paris et la Ligue*, 352.
[64] E. Armstrong, *The French wars of religion*, 2nd ed., New York, 1971, 60.

numerous component among the League's militants in the capital.[65]

In the same way as the Huguenot party had done earlier, so the Catholic League at the height of its influence also became a separate power rivaling the crown. Its revolutionary character was no less evident in this than in its political doctrines. After the Day of the Barricades, most of France's important cities fell under League control. Provincial councils of the League were established in at least twelve towns, including Dijon, Lyon, Rouen, Poitiers, and Toulouse. Consisting of members of the municipal magistracy, noblemen, officials, clergy, and other local notables, they exercised an authority without check from the central government. Provinces under governors who supported the League passed similarly out of obedience to the king. League towns and provinces frequently witnessed internecine quarrels between provincial governors and municipal administrations, nobility and civic authorities, and popular extremism and elite groups. In some cities the *parlement* split into royalist and League factions with divided loyalties. The League's ascendancy was accompanied by a disruptive anticentralism that threatened to end in political dismemberment.[66]

The League's relation to Spain posed an equally great danger to the monarchy. In 1588, Philip II, who then stood at a climactic phase of his policy, prepared to launch his great invasion fleet, the Armada, against England, while in the Netherlands his governor, the duke of Parma, pressed forward resolutely to put an end to the rebellion. To incapacitate France from any action hostile to Spanish power was highly desirable at such a moment. The League therefore offered Spain a heaven-sent opportunity. In Paris, Philip's ambassador, Don Bernardino de Mendoza, coordinated Spain's diplomacy with the aims of Henry III's enemies. He was in close touch with the duke of Guise, who received Spanish money to support his armies, and he also had his contacts among the Sixteen. Mendoza probably not only helped to persuade Guise to go to Paris but may well have played some kind of part behind the scenes on the Day of the Barricades.[67]

Driven from Paris, Henry III had to capitulate to the League. He named Guise as lieutenant-general of the realm and vowed himself to fight against heresy and a heretical successor. In the fall of 1588, the king summoned the Estates General, a League-dominated assembly that met at the royal chateau of Blois. There, on December 23, to liberate himself from an

---

[65] See Robiquet, *Paris et la Ligue;* and Salmon, "The Paris Sixteen, 1589–94," and *Society in crisis*, 248–51, for details of the League insurrection in Paris and its social composition.

[66] See Salmon, *Society in crisis*, 251–5.

[67] See De Lamar Jensen, *Diplomacy and dogmatism: Bernardino de Mendoza and the French Catholic League*, Cambridge, 1964, ch. 7.

intolerable yoke, he summoned Guise to an interview and had his personal guards assassinate him outside the royal bedchamber. The duke's brother, the cardinal of Guise, was arrested and also murdered the next day.

These bloody events increased the League's hatred of Henry III beyond all measure. Preachers of the cause implored the monarch's death as a murderous and wicked tyrant. The duke of Mayenne, another of Guise's brothers, took over as the League's chief, fixing his headquarters in Paris. Everywhere the Catholic revolt against the monarchy intensified. The king on his side sought a rapprochement with his heir the Huguenot Henry of Navarre, in the common interests of the crown. In August 1589, however, he was killed himself by an assassin's dagger, the act of a fanatic monk whom the League acclaimed as a deliverer. With Henry III's violent demise, the civil war entered its final stage in Navarre's succession struggle for the throne of France.

An ironic and remarkable reversal of roles ensued from the League's rebellion and Navarre's claim to succeed as king. The Huguenots became legitimists, attenuating and abandoning their former revolutionary principles to defend hereditary right and royal authority. They united with the peace-seeking Politiques, royalists who supported Navarre and exalted kingly sovereignty and the necessity of obedience.[68] The League, on the other hand, took up the themes of a right of resistance and popular sovereignty borrowed in part from earlier Huguenot writings.

The Catholic League's political ideology blended papalism, sacerdotalism, and allegiance to the church with monarchomach and populist doctrines. The banner of antiabsolutism passed in the expiring phase of the long revolutionary civil war from the Huguenot to Catholic theorists. Programmatically, the League insisted that no Protestant could inherit the throne and that Catholic succession was an inviolable fundamental law of the kingdom. With this as corollaries aimed at Henry III and Henry of Navarre went a whole battery of arguments upholding the people's and the kingdom's superiority to rulers. The popular origins of power, the right of the people to depose and elect kings, and the defense of tyrannicide were common theses in the League's propaganda. Such views, moreover, received a considerably more extreme expression than Huguenot publicists had generally given them.

One of the most prominent works to expound these ideas was *The just repudiation of Henry III*, published in 1589 by the Sorbonne theologian, Jean Boucher, a mainstay of the Paris League. Boucher held that the right to remove kings inheres in both the people and the church. Averring that the people create kings, he declared that election is superior to heredity and monarchy itself only a mutual contract. He conceived of the people

[68] See Weill, *Les Théories sur le pouvoir royal*, 199–200; C. Mercier, "Les Théories politiques des Calvinistes en France," pt. 1, 259; and Salmon, *Society in crisis*, 235–6.

as the "prudent multitude" and on behalf of it and the *respublica* made out the case for armed resistance and the deposition of Henry III. Boucher's treatise contained clear signs of indebtedness to Huguenot writers, a fact that demonstrates the essential continuity between the Protestant and League rebellions despite their polar opposition.[69] Another work of similar purport on a considerably higher intellectual plane was the pseudonymous *The just authority of a Christian commonwealth over impious and heretical kings* (1590). Written against Henry of Navarre's succession by a Catholic thinker who called himself Rossaeus, it presented a broad philosophic discussion of the principle of popular sovereignty to enforce the conclusion that the people is the superior of kings and retains the right to depose them at will.[70]

These books, composed in Latin for the learned, were merely a small part of the swarm of publications, generally in the vernacular and of a much more popular kind, that disseminated the League's views. Treatises, sermons, racy tracts, and pasquinades alike revealed how vitally the League's revolt was infused by ideological inspiration. One of the major emphases in its propaganda and program was the elevation of representative institutions and the Estates General. In this it paralleled the Huguenots and the ideas previously voiced in Hotman's *Francogallia*.

League authors claimed supremacy for the Estates General and ascribed to it the right to elect and remove kings. Some made the *parlements* responsible for judging the king to prevent tyranny. These notions surfaced at the Estates General of Blois in 1588, where Henry III faced strong League pressure for governmental reforms and far greater power by the estates. The Paris League demanded that the estates be free of royal supervision. A manifesto of the Sixteen prepared for the Blois meeting declared: "Is it not . . . the Estates which have given to the kings the authority and power which they have? Why then is it necessary that what we deal with and decide in this assembly be controlled by the council of the King?" The Sixteen also circulated articles rejecting the crown's absolute sovereignty, calling for sweeping powers to be exercised by the Estates General, and proposing the election of governors of the provinces by the provincial estates.[71] After the death in 1590 of the cardinal of Bourbon, its candidate for the throne, the League wanted the Estates General to elect a Catholic sovereign. This right was advanced on behalf of the Estates General of

[69] J. Boucher, *De justa abdicatione Henrici tertii*, Paris, 1589. For discussions, see Labitte, *De la démocratie*, 90–8; Allen, *Political thought in the sixteenth century*, 349–50; and Baumgartner, *Radical reactionaries*, ch. 6, which points out Boucher's use of the *Vindiciae contra tyrannos* and other Huguenot works.

[70] *The iusta reipublicae Christianae in reges impios et hereticos authoritate*, Paris, 1590. For discussions and the possible identity of Rossaeus, see Baumgartner, *Radical reactionaries*, ch. 7; Allen, *Political thought in the sixteenth century*, 351–2; and Labitte, *De la démocratie*, app.

[71] Baumgartner, *Radical reactionaries*, 97, 93–5, cites and summarizes these documents.

1593, which the duke of Mayenne, the League leader, convoked in Paris. Despite much discussion, however, the Paris assembly failed to elect a monarch because it was divided over candidates and finally uncertain of its power in so great a matter.[72]

The League was a peculiar coalition of clericalism, aristocracy, and cities that had cut free of royal authority. Within the last, revolt against the monarchy released a surge of popular radicalism that was threatening and troublesome to urban elites and the movement's noble directors. Mob disorders and pressures from below were far more pronounced among the Catholic Leaguers than they had ever been among the Huguenots. Social antagonisms and religious zealotry stirred up some of the bourgeois and *menu peuple* to attack traditional oligarchies. Episodes of this kind were numerous in League towns. Moreover, League militants were often at odds with governmental bodies and less ardent supporters in the municipalities, thus creating violent dissensions. In Paris, for example, the Sixteen with their grass-roots organization and cadres stood outside the regular administration yet dominated the city and demanded political conformity from everyone. They had behind them a sort of inchoate democracy – a mass of people of middling and modest condition in the guilds and religious confraternities who were egged on by enthusiastic preachers. Numbers of noblemen, officials, the wealthy, and royalists left the capital for this reason. The Sixteen forced the Parlement of Paris to submit to their authority and exacted an oath from its members. One of their most notorious actions was the hanging of a presiding judge of the Parlement, Barnabé Brisson, and two other officials for disloyalty. When the duke of Mayenne became the League's chief, he first reduced and eventually destroyed the Sixteen's independence. Among his blows against their extremism was to execute the men responsible for Brisson's death.[73]

The liveliest testimonial to the radical side of the League and its mentality appeared in the *Dialogue between the citizen and the courtier*, one of the most remarkable pamphlets of the civil war. It was published in 1593, when the League had begun to crumble and after the Paris organization had been curbed and the Sixteen's ascendancy broken by Mayenne. The Courtier is a royalist and Politique who favors the succession of Navarre, whereas the Citizen, a Parisian, is a convinced and passionate Leaguer.

[72] The importance of the Estates General in League theory and propaganda is shown in *ibid.*, *passim*, which also discusses the Estates of Blois and of Paris. See also Allen, *Political thought in the sixteenth century*, 350, 353; and Giesey and Salmon (eds.), *Francogallia*, 107–9, for Hotman's influence.

[73] See Salmon, *Society in crisis*, 259–66; Robiquet, *Paris et la Ligue*, 505–6; Baumgartner, *Radical reactionaries*, 236–7. The memoirs of Pierre de l'Estoile offer a vivid contemporary view of the sway of the League and the Sixteen in Paris, including an account of Brisson's execution; see the excellent selections from l'Estoile's *Mémoires-journaux* in N. Roelker, *The Paris of Henry Navarre*, Cambridge, 1958, 198–215 and *passim*.

The foundation of the Citizen's attitude is a total devotion to Catholicism and the unity of faith. He affects religion, not the "nation," he says, and loves "le pays de France" only because of its religion; he would rather have a Spanish Catholic as king than accept a heretic Frenchman and lose his soul. The Citizen subscribes to elective kingship and all the other tenets of popular sovereignty the League championed. Coupled with this belief, though, he expresses a keen animosity toward the nobility and *grands* for their selfishness and ambition. It is not they, he declares, but the bourgeois people and the towns who serve the cause of God. Even the Courtier agrees that the princes and nobility care only for their own power; they want, he remarks in a striking phrase, to force the people into "la servitude moderne" lest their greatness and honors be limited. But when the Courtier attacks the Sixteen, the Citizen defends them as zealous "bourgeois catholiques" who together with the ordinary citizens have saved Paris. The Citizen accuses the Parlement of Paris of corruption and condemns the nobility for exploiting "the sweat and blood of the poor people who haven't a piece of bread." The nobility continues and profits by the civil war, and the people must bear the cost. The Citizen also opposes hereditary nobility. Real nobility, he asserts, comes from personal virtue, not descent, and some of the present *noblesse* are monsters of tyranny. Bitterly, he also denounces Mayenne for subjecting the Paris organization and other acts of personal aggrandizement. He foresees that the princes and nobility will betray the League's cause; unlike the people, their sole interest is in the state rather than religion.[74]

The *Dialogue* was a memorial to the hopes, idealism, and eventual disillusionment of the radical League. No parallel to its biting criticism of the nobility and magistrates can be found in the revolutionary literature of the Huguenot movement. We may want to recall, however, that at about the same time as the Citizen voiced his subversive sentiments an analogous hostility to the nobility manifested itself briefly in the agrarian insurrection of the first Croquants in the southwest.[75]

The *Dialogue*'s publication coincided with the League's impending dissolution. For in July 1593 the Huguenot Henry of Navarre abjured Protestantism for the Catholic church. Eight months after his conversion he was crowned at Chartres as Henry IV. These developments proved decisive. The only alternative to the rule of Henry IV was continued anarchy and Spanish interference. Not only was Philip II's own daughter one of

[74] I have used the *Dialogue d'entre le manant and le maheustre* in the version printed with the *Satyre menipée*, 3 v., Ratisbon, 1752, v. 3; the citations are in *ibid.*, v. 3, 561, 564, 421–2, 456, 458, 470. This work, an essential source for the activity and organization of the Paris League, has been ascribed to Cromé, a lawyer and one of the Sixteen. A modern edition by P. Ascoli (Geneva, 1977) contains the two versions of the text and discusses the significance of their differences as well as the author's ideas.

[75] See Chapter 7 in this book.

the League's candidates for the French throne, but after 1590 Spain entered upon open military intervention, sending its armies to fight for the League in defense of Paris and the provinces. To aid Henry IV, Queen Elizabeth's government dispatched English troops to France. Thus once the sovereign was of the same religion as most of his subjects, patriotism and the longing for peace joined with royalism in his behalf.

Gradually, League provinces and towns submitted and recognized the Bourbon as king of France. In March 1594 Henry IV entered Paris almost unopposed. Some of his enemies he subdued by arms; others he bought off with concessions and gifts. The Guise princes and other dissident *grands* received provincial governorships and great sums of money for their allegiance. In 1595, his position better secured, Henry declared war on Spain to drive its forces from French soil. The peace of Vervins with Spain that ensued after three years of fighting secured this objective. At the same time, the last remaining resistance of the League in Brittany was also overcome.

Henry IV's conversion caused considerable tensions and differences with the Huguenots whom he had abandoned. These were allayed by the Edict of Nantes, which the king granted the Protestants in 1598 after lengthy negotiations with their representatives. A measure of secular expediency, it conceded them legal toleration in specified places, Paris being among those excluded. It also endowed them, as we have noted before, with fortified towns and additional guarantees to assure their liberty of conscience. They were by this time greatly reduced in numbers and prepared to live as a tolerated minority. From about three million in 1562, they had shrunk, according to a survey ordered by Henry IV, to perhaps a million and a quarter. The number of public churches, over two thousand in 1562, had fallen to 694.[76]

By this settlement with the Reformed church and the defeat of the Catholic League, the Bourbon succession finally brought peace. An exhausted France received a breathing spell to recover its strength.

VI

What, then, was the balance of the revolution the Huguenots had launched? As one reviews its fierce polarities, its programs, and its aspirations, one is struck by the extent of its failure. Fundamentally, the civil war was a far-flung resistance to absolutism and its strides in state building; rebels fought against a regime whose persistent thrust was the concentration of

[76] See Mours, *Le Protestantisme en France au XVIe siècle*, ch. 6 and map, 248–9; Romier, *Le Royaume de Catherine de Medicis*, v. 2, 180; and Kingdon, *Geneva and the coming of the wars of religion in France*, 79 and n.

power over all subjects and communities in the will of the monarchy and its immediate instruments. The Protestant demand for toleration, one of the durable issues of the conflict, itself entailed a limit upon royal sovereignty in a Catholic kingdom.

Both the Huguenots and the Catholic League created full-blown revolutionary movements in dangerous opposition to the crown. Each proclaimed full-blown revolutionary ideologies in contradiction to the claims of absolute sovereigns. Alike they justified the right of resistance, appealed to principles of constitutionalism that exalted the sovereignty of the people and subjects over kings, and emphasized the paramountcy of representative institutions in controlling rulers and making them accountable. Finally, both built formidable independent organizations exercising political and governmental functions exempt from central authority.

Yet all of these efforts and experiments achieved nothing in the end. The theories of rebellion and popular sovereignty so widely current in France during the civil war turned out to be like water that ran into the sand. The Huguenots forgot their revolutionary doctrines after Henry IV's succession. In their subsequent provincial revolts of the 1620s, when Louis XIII crushed them in their final struggle to preserve their political immunities, they had no ideological weapon to oppose Bourbon absolutism.[77] The radical principles of the Catholic League also did not outlast the civil war. True, fanaticism and the idea of tyrannicide helped to incite the Catholic assassin who murdered Henry IV in 1610.[78] But, as a political tradition, League populism found no future in France and disappeared in the seventeenth century. Equally, despite the efflorescence of concern with the Estates General, the attempts to gain new power for it and entrench it in the monarchical constitution bore no fruit.

The ultimate gainer from the revolution was the monarchy and absolutism. It seems that France, to borrow a graphic term used of it by political scientists in quite another context, in many respects was a *"société bloquée,"* a stalemated society.[79] Many disparate elements in France's life – noble power, provincialism, venal officeholding, institutions of local privilege, the confusion of political authorities – made for deadlock and disruption. Apparently, only an autocratic absolutism at the center sufficed to overcome them and to impose national unity and policies in the common interest. The same factors operated, as we shall see, in the Fronde.

[77] See Chapter 9 in this book.

[78] R. Mousnier (*The assassination of Henry IV*, London, 1973) deals with this topic at length.

[79] The Gaullist premier, J. Chaban-Delmas, used this description, borrowed from the American political scientist Stanley Hoffman in the 1960s. It also became the title of M. Crozier's well-known work on contemporary France, *La Société bloquée*, Paris, 1970; see E. Suleiman, *Politics, power, and bureaucracy in France*, Princeton, 1974, 32, 114, 383. There are compelling reasons for applying it to the *ancien régime* as well, at least at certain periods.

Because of these characteristics, the French nation, despite its repeated rebelliousness and disorders, eventually bowed to the monarchy as sole master.

Royal government was, of course, profoundly weakened by the centrifugal forces of the civil war, and the further path of absolutism remained strewn with obstacles. Bourbon state builders, nevertheless, were to sweep them aside during the following century, although in doing so they provoked an insurrectionary epidemic.

If France's revolutionary civil war of the sixteenth century left any direct legacy, it was not in its own country but in England, where the revolt against Charles I absorbed some of its principles.[80] The later revolution of 1789 in France did not look back to the Huguenots and the League but rather drew most of its inspiration from English political ideas of the seventeenth century and from the varied thought of the Enlightenment.

[80] See J. H. Salmon, *The French religious wars in English political thought*, Oxford, 1959.

I I

Revolutionary civil war: the Netherlands rebellion

I

The Dutch republic was the first new state of modern times whose independence was born and forged in revolution. Not only that. The revolution in the Netherlands that founded a new republican state also led to the creation of a new nation. Contrary to the supposition of recent theorists of modernization, post-1776 America was not the "first new nation."[1] This place must be reserved for the Dutch, although perhaps because the Netherlands rebellion lacked the universalism of the American revolution the fact is easy to overlook. Of course, the Dutch nation and its country were a truncation of a larger body, the seventeen provinces of the Low Countries subject to the Spanish monarchy, which became politically divided in the course of the rebellion itself. One part, often generally called Holland, achieved independence and under the name of the Dutch republic or United Netherlands became the seat of a durable regime. The other part, Belgium, remained under Spanish and later Austrian Habsburg rule. There was nothing inevitable or preordained about this split, as a modern Dutch historian has made it his lifework to show.[2] Nevertheless, it happened, and from the crucible of rebellion an independent Dutch state and nation arose.

Most of the newly independent states that appeared after 1945 began as colonial possessions from a condition of backwardness. To contemporary students of modernization, they exemplify the assorted problems of underdevelopment, poverty, and deficient economic growth. No such paradigm is applicable to the mid–sixteenth-century Netherlands, whose po-

[1] See S. M. Lipset, *The first new nation: The United States in historical and comparative perspective*, New York, 1963.

[2] This is the main thesis of P. Geyl in *The revolt of the Netherlands*, 2nd ed., London, 1958, and other works. For a succinct statement in relation to the Netherlands rebellion, see his "The national state and the writers of Netherlands history," in *Debates with historians*, New York, 1958.

sition in the Spanish empire was not a colony's but formal equality with all the other monarchy's possessions. On the eve of their revolt, the Netherlands were the most economically developed country in Northern Europe.

The Emperor Charles V was a Netherlander by birth who ruled the provinces as the direct descendant of the Valois dukes of Burgundy, the predecessor of the Habsburg dynasty. When Charles partitioned his vast domains at his abdication in 1555, he gave the Netherlands, along with his Spanish and Italian states, to his son, Philip II. Philip was therefore not a foreigner but their native and "natural sovereign," in the parlance of the time, and a prince unchallengeably legitimate. So much was this so that fifteen years of rebellion elapsed before the seven northern provinces, where the most intransigent resistance lay, finally brought themselves to renounce the Habsburg monarch's rule, which they did in 1581 by their Act of Abjuration.

From a material standpoint, the Netherlands, with a population of about three million, were richer and more highly urbanized than any region in Europe save perhaps Italy. Nineteen towns contained over ten thousand people (England then had only three or four); five had more than thirty thousand, and one, Antwerp, maybe a hundred thousand. The provinces in the mid-sixteenth century were equivalent in their economic importance to both Wall Street and Pittsburgh or to the City of London and Manchester. Commercially and industrially, they were foremost in Europe, a great center of trade and finance, the leading manufacturers and exporters of cloth, and the possessors of a flourishing shipping. Their agriculture, based on steady reclamation and improvement, was probably more productive than any other (although the provinces had to import some food to supply their population). The goods of all the world flowed into Antwerp, the principal money market and commercial entrepôt in the West.[3]

Culturally, too, the Netherlands stood in the front of the most significant contemporary developments of European civilization: the Renaissance, humanism, the Reformation, art and scholarship, the spread of lay education and literacy, printing.

Only politically, if we assess development by the degree of centralized unity – which, as a universal proposition, is doubtful – were the Netherlands among the less-developed of the European states. The political association of all the provinces under Habsburg rule was not completed till well into the time of Charles V. Even with the strides the emperor had made, they were still but weakly centralized and loosely integrated. The

---

[3] For some population figures and aspects of the economy, see S. T. Bindoff's account of Antwerp, *New Cambridge modern history*, v. 2, Cambridge, 1958, 50–69, and G. Parker, *The Dutch revolt*, London, 1977, 23.

royal government in Brussels – which, under Charles V and Philip II, was a regency because the prince was usually an absentee – had its council of state and administration for the provinces. The members of the high nobility, with close ties to the dynasty, occupied provincial offices as royal governors and stadholders. There was also a States General of the Netherlands, an assembly that represented and was composed of delegates from the separate provincial estates. Interprovincial institutions, however, were neither numerous nor strong. The beginning of a sense of common fatherland or nationality existed, but it was offset by powerful localisms. The Netherlands were also linguistically divided: The southern fringe of Walloon provinces spoke French; the provinces to the north, Dutch. French, however, was the language of the court and aristocracy. Perhaps the strongest bond of unity among the provinces was the dynasty itself and the loyalty it evoked. At the same time, provincial particularism, a vigorous commitment to privileges restricting ruler sovereignty, and vital traditions of autonomy remained hallmarks of political life. By running afoul of these characteristics, Philip II precipitated a revolution in the Netherlands.

This revolution, like the contemporary civil war in neighboring France, was of lengthy duration, regionally dispersed, and punctuated by intervals of repression and temporary pacification. Not until 1576, ten years after it began, did the revolution become general throughout the provinces. On this account, it has been pictured as a series of separate revolts that followed one another in succession.[4] Although not exactly untrue, this description may mislead, however, unless one also bears in mind that in its sequences the Netherlands rebellion, no less than the French civil war, formed a single continuous phenomenon. For one thing, revolutionary Calvinism was a permanent factor in the conflict. For another, the genie of resistance, once released, could never be eliminated. The revolt of the provinces must be seen and analyzed as a total movement carried forward from its inception by a continuing, unbroken determination to withstand Philip II's government.

One of the questions historians have posed in trying to penetrate the Netherlands rebellion is whether it was a conservative or modern revolution. Some have called it conservative because its actors lacked a conscious will toward progress, change, and innovation and looked more to ideals of the past than to a vision of the future. Others describe it as modern in that

[4] Parker (*The Dutch revolt*, 15 and *passim*) depicts the rebellion as three separate revolts. A similar picture is implicit in P. Geyl, *The revolt of the Netherlands*. For a general account of the revolution of the Netherlands, I have drawn on both of these works. Geyl's classic history was first published in Dutch in 1931. Parker's lively and learned study, a significant contribution which appeared in 1977, incorporates the most recent scholarship and is provided with valuable notes and bibliography. It also has the additional feature of treating the revolt from the standpoint of Spanish imperial problems and policy.

it brought forth a new political order based upon principles foreshadowing later constitutional regimes in Europe. For the first view, it was centralizing, absolutist government that embodied the new forces of the age, whereas the rebels fought to preserve old privileges and medieval liberties. For the second view, resistance to absolutism was itself modern in the sixteenth century and begot a new free state and society in the provinces that won their independence.[5]

Like the similar controversy concerning the Comunero revolution in Castile, on which I have previously commented, this debate is futile, involving as it does an untenable dualism.[6] "Conservative" and "modern" were inextricably interwoven in the events in the Netherlands and cannot be separated. Moreover, even when men appeal to precedents and strive for system restoration or preservation, they inevitably produce some novelties. This was certainly the case in the Dutch revolt.[7] Inexorably, the circumstances and imperatives of a revolutionary civil war drove rebels toward change, much as they may have professed to be defending an inherited order their prince had violated. In the end, they fashioned in the independent provinces of the north a unique federal structure of government that was a combination of old and new. As Sir George Clark has written (and here there is an implicit comparison with the French civil war), "The claim of right against tyrants was vindicated only in the Netherlands, and this was the only resounding victory in the sixteenth century over arbitrary rule."[8]

II

Revolution is always preceded by the premonitory tremblings, the incipient signs of violence and instability, and the feverish departures from routine that indicate an approaching storm or upheaval. Just so in the Netherlands, resistance first flared up out of an accelerating crisis of authority after Philip II's departure for Spain in 1559. We have already made mention of this crisis in an earlier chapter.[9] The government, left in the

[5] Among others, the distinguished Dutch scholars Fruin, Huizinga and Geyl have defended the "conservative" thesis, while H. A. Enno van Gelder has been perhaps the main champion of the "modern" thesis. For a presentation of the debated issues, see the latter's "De opstand tegen Philips II en de Protestantisering der Nederlanden," *Bijdragen voor de geschiedenis der Nederlanden 10*, 1 (1955); the reply by L. Rogier, "Het karakter van de opstand tegen Philips II," *ibid. 10*, 2–4 (1956); and Enno van Gelder's rejoinder, *ibid. 11*, 2 (1956).

[6] See Chapter 8 in this book.

[7] For similar comments on the "conservative" versus "modern" argument regarding the Netherlands revolt, see J. W. Smit, "The Netherlands revolution," in *Preconditions of revolution in early modern Europe*, ed. R. Forster and J. Greene, Baltimore, 1970, 24, 36; and E. H. Kossmann and A. F. Mellink (eds.), *Texts concerning the revolt of the Netherlands*, Cambridge, 1974, 2.

[8] G. N. Clark, "The birth of the Dutch republic," *Proceedings of the British Academy 32* (1946), 195–6.

[9] See Chapter 6 in this book.

hands of Philip's half-sister, Duchess Margaret of Parma, found itself opposed by a movement of the nobility, supported by an aggressive Calvinism and popular sentiment. The decay of obedience culminated in 1566, in the iconoclastic disturbances of the summer followed by the eruption of revolt. The controversy that provoked these events reflected abiding differences, which were to divide the regime from the various adversaries arrayed against it in the course of the long insurgency. At the heart of the conflict lay a resistance to absolutism, its commands and political ambitions. This antinomy was aggravated by the fact that in the Netherlands the regime could not be dissociated from a foreign and Spanish dominion.

Wherever possible, Philip II was an architect of royal sovereign power and bureaucratic concentration of authority. In Spain and Italy he took the rule left by his father and built it over the years into a much firmer, more cohesive, and bureaucratically administered structure closely supervised by the crown.[10] In the Netherlands, given the prevalence of provincialism and autonomism, the monarchy could only aim at the outset at a moderate centralization. Thus, at the beginning of his reign, Philip received papal approval for a long-projected ecclesiastical reorganization in the Netherlands providing for fourteen new bishoprics to supplant the existing three. The new bishops were to be appointed by the crown and endowed from the revenues of a number of monasteries. Philip also wished to avoid consulting the States General, where there was a backlog of grievances over previous taxes. He wanted no less to exclude the high nobility from any policy-making involvement in his government. By his instruction, Margaret of Parma's chief councillor was the prelate, Cardinal Granvelle, who belonged to an official family long in Habsburg service and was slated to be primate of the reorganized church. In the matter of religion, the king was resolved not to relax the punishment of heresy, a policy that led to fears of the introduction of the Spanish in place of the local Inquisition.

It was out of these circumstances that the crisis grew. The nobility's antagonism toward Granvelle's ascendancy and the Brussels administration, the noble and other vested interests threatened by reform of the diocesan structure, the militant temper of an increasingly bold Calvinism, and the general unpopularity of the harsh religious persecution all coalesced in a common opposition.

The animosity became concretized in the conviction that the ruler was guilty of violating provincial liberties. To appease the growing discontent, the government made a few concessions: In 1564 Philip removed Granvelle from the Netherlands, and the regent turned to some of the high

[10] See I. A. Thompson, *War and government in Habsburg Spain 1560–1620*, London, 1976, 4–5.

nobility for assistance. But the absent king refused all pleas to reverse his general policy or accept the advice of the nobility or estates. To petitions for an end to religious repression, he replied in the negative. In October 1565, he sent Duchess Margaret his famous letter dated from the Segovia Wood, which ended all hope of change. In it he ordered her to enforce the heresy laws rigorously and support the activity of the provincial Inquisition. Taking note of the daring liberty of some of his subjects, he instructed her to punish it severely lest dangerous consequences ensue.[11] The Brussels regime, however, had no soldiers to apply coercion and so could do little to arrest the erosion of its authority.

Without the participation of the nobility the opposition would have possessed no focus. Noblemen were the provinces' natural leaders to whom the other orders looked for political direction and action against grievances.[12] First, a group of the high nobility, of whom some were provincial governors, banded together in a league against Cardinal Granvelle and the government's policy. Along with the counts of Egmont and Horne, Baron Brederode, and other magnates, it included William of Nassau, prince of Orange, head of one of the greatest houses in the Netherlands, also the lord of large German possessions and sovereign of the principality of Orange in the south of France, who was destined to become the foremost leader of the revolution. Born in 1533, Orange was attached by many personal and official ties to the Habsburg dynasty yet more and more estranged from Philip II's measures. Although not yet a Protestant, he was of a tolerant disposition and strongly against persecution.

Next, with the encouragement of Orange and his friends, meetings of the lesser nobility took place during the summer and fall of 1565. They resulted in the formation of a noble Confederation probably modeled, as Granvelle believed, on the Huguenot *noblesse*'s organization in France.[13] Although it was by no means predominantly Protestant, it contained a nucleus of Calvinist sympathizers. Protestant and Catholic alike were united at the moment in rejection of the regime's policy.

In January 1566, the Confederation stated its principles in the Compromise, a manifesto that was circulated for subscription. Like the numerous other covenants and alliances we have seen early modern rebels make, this declaration was a sacred pledge of union for mutual defense and aid with God as witness. As such, it was plainly revolutionary in its implications.

[11] Printed in Kossmann and Mellink, *Texts concerning the revolt of the Netherlands*, 53–6. The Segovia Wood ("El Bosque de Segovia") was a country house of the king.

[12] See the discussion by H. A. Enno van Gelder, "De Nederlandse adel en de opstand tegen Spanje 1565–1572," *Tijdschrift voor geschiedenis*, 2 pts., (1928), pt. 1, and *passim*. C. Wilson, *Queen Elizabeth and the revolt of the Netherlands*, Berkeley, 1970, contains many observations on the nobility's centrality to the revolt.

[13] See Chapter 10 in this book; and H. Pirenne, *Histoire de Belgique*, 7 v., Brussels, 1922–32, 3rd rev. ed., v. 3, 455 and n.

It denounced the foreigners who had no care for the prosperity of the Netherlands and condemned the government's religious persecution and the provincial Inquisition, terming the latter "against all human and divine laws, surpassing the worst barbarism ever practiced by tyrants." It spoke of the king's violation of his oath to his subjects through the influence of evil council and warned that religious repression would destroy law and order and do away with the ancient privileges and immunities of the provinces. Denying they were rebels, the Confederates affirmed their intention to maintain the king's greatness and estate. So incendiary was their indictment, however, that it carried an unmistakable threat of revolt.[14]

Within a couple of months the Compromise was subscribed by perhaps as many as two thousand men, mostly belonging to the lesser nobility but also by some merchants and burghers.[15] Subsequent dissidents' meetings followed at Orange's house in Breda, where the question of resistance was certainly considered. A significant sidelight on these consultations is cast by one of the participants, a Calvinist gentleman who asked Orange's brother, Count Louis of Nassau, to bring "a certain treatise . . . on when it is lawful for the inferior magistrate to take arms against the tyranny of his superiors."[16] Thus here, on the threshold of revolution, and with the Huguenots of France already in revolt as an example, we meet one of the principal arguments that sixteenth-century rebels used to justify resistance.

The outcome of these gatherings was a further defiance of the royal government, a petition delivered to the regent in April 1566 by a crowd of about three hundred Confederate noblemen. It was on this memorable occasion that the rebels of the Low Countries got their famous nickname, *les gueux*, the Beggars, when one of the regent's councillors referred contemptuously by this term to the petitioners, who in turn took it up as a badge of honor.

The Confederates' petition called for an end to the edicts of persecution and the Inquisition. So angry are the people, it averred, that "open revolt and universal rebellion are imminent," threatening ruin to all the provinces. It proposed that the States General be summoned to deal with the situation and asked the regent to dispatch an emissary with its requests to the king. In the interim, to avert ruin, it urged her to suspend the edicts and the Inquisition.[17]

These demands expressed a self-fulfilling prophecy. They worried and terrified Margaret of Parma, who in despair yielded to pressure and or-

[14] Text in Kossmann and Mellink, *Texts concerning the revolt of the Netherlands*, 59–62.

[15] J. L. Motley (*The rise of the Dutch republic*, 3 v., London, 1916, v. 1, 409) gives this figure; and see P. Marnix de Sainte Aldegonde, *Oeuvres*, ed. A. Lacroix, Brussels, 1859, 19–22.

[16] Printed in R. Putnam, *William the Silent*, 2 v., New York, 1895, v. 1, 188. The work in question was probably the *Bekenntnis* of Magdeburg, for which see Chapter 10 in the book.

[17] Text in Kossmann and Mellink, *Texts concerning the revolt of the Netherlands*, 62–4.

dered the moderation of heresy prosecution while two noblemen were sent to Madrid to present the case to Philip II. The regent's actions, however, merely hastened the deterioration of authority.

In the Low Countries, Protestantism had its converts among anabaptists, Lutherans, and Calvinists. The last, though, were the most dynamic element, and their clandestine churches had been growing despite repression. In 1563, the first provincial synods met in Flanders, Brabant, and several other southern provinces. Eight of these took place between 1563 and 1565. Now, with the relaxation of persecution, the conventicles and congregations emerged from underground and started to hold open-air assemblies, which drew thousands of listeners. These crowds were frequently armed and created an atmosphere charged with insecurity and threat. During the same spring of 1566, about fifty Calvinist preachers, previously refugees in England, France, Switzerland, and Germany, returned to the Netherlands to contribute their services.[18] It seemed as if the Protestants had launched an offensive against the ancient church. Threads also existed between the Calvinist church organization and the Confederate nobility, or at least its inner core. In July 1566, some of the latter met at Saint Truiden near Brussels with delegates of the consistories, who appealed to them as protectors of the religion. A council was established consisting of six noblemen, six burghers, and six representatives of the churches.[19]

All these developments hastened the process of mobilization and the fusion of political and religious disaffection, which were a necessary precondition of revolt. From the climate of unrest, its tensions heightened by the agitation of sermons and pamphlets, came the immediate prelude, the riot of iconoclasm that engulfed the provinces during August and September.

Notwithstanding the view of certain writers, it is doubtful whether the iconoclastic fury can be traced especially to the preceding miseries due to *conjoncture* – high food prices, scarcity, hunger, and unemployment – or to the social tensions and discontent among the textile workers and other laboring people.[20] It was a *religious* protest and fraught with all the explosive political implications of such a desecration in a society and state immemorially Catholic. Its targets were almost exclusively religious: the buildings and symbols of Catholic worship, which Calvinism held to be idolatrous. There was virtually no looting. Moreover, besides the spontaneous attacks by mobs, there was also apparently a planned, organized

---

[18] See F. Rachfahl, *Wilhelm von Oranien und der Niederländische Aufstand*, 3 v., Halle, 1906–24, v. 2, pt. 2, bk. 9, ch. 1; and P. Mack, *Calvinist preaching and iconoclasm in the Netherlands 1544–1569*, Cambridge, 1978, 1, 41, 64 and n.

[19] Enno van Gelder, "De Nederlandse adel en de opstand tegen Spanje," pt. 1, 8.

[20] See Chapter 5 in this book.

side to the movement. In west Flanders and the southern provinces, bands of fifty to a hundred itinerant image breakers went from place to place doing their work. Some of the iconoclasts were returned exiles and other people recruited and paid by the Calvinist consistories. What was remarkable was that large crowds sometimes watched them committing their destruction but did nothing to stop it. The burgher militias likewise remained inactive for the most part in the presence of the disturbances.

Beginning first in Flanders toward the Feast of the Ascension in mid-August, the explosion of iconoclasm swept the Netherlands from one end to the other during the next five weeks. Without question the movement spread because it was unresisted. Save in a few cities like Bruges, magistrates and officials remained paralyzed and failed to prevent the outbreaks. Great towns and small were struck by turmoil – Ypres, Ghent, Antwerp, Valenciennes, Tournai, Amsterdam, Utrecht, and many others. Several were hit twice by the disorders. Hundreds of churches, convents, and shrines were sacked, to the scandal and horror of pious Catholics. According to the regent, four hundred churches and convents were destroyed in Flanders alone up to August 27. Altars, crucifixes, statues, pictures, baptismal fonts, books, mass articles, monstrances, organs, benches, choir stalls, and tombs were broken or burnt. Not just the lower orders but well-to-do people took part in this destruction. The iconoclastic fury was a contagion of disobedience that testified to a massive breakdown of political authority.[21]

The royal government's first response to these events was sheer panic. Margaret of Parma begged the nobility to help restore order and consented to an accord permitting Protestant worship where it already existed. The Calvinists only treated this as a concession of full toleration and proceeded to take over churches and extend their cult.

But very quickly a vehement backlash asserted itself. Everyone frightened and angered by the popular disturbances, Calvinist extremism, and insults to the Catholic faith began to rally to the regime. With funds received from Spain, the regent was able to levy troops. Many of the noblemen in the Confederation and civic sympathizers now recoiled from the opposition movement. Some of the high nobility stood steady, but the

[21] A large narrative of the iconoclastic fury is given in G. Brandt, *The history of the reformation . . . the Low Countries* (1671), 2 v., London, 1720–2, v. 1, bks. 7–8. Accounts with analytical comments include Rachfahl, *Wilhelm von Oranien*, v. 2, pt. 2, bk. 9, ch. 5; Pirenne, *Histoire de Belgique*, v. 3, 466–9; E. Kuttner, *Het hongerjaar 1566*, Amsterdam, 1914; W. Brulez, "De opstand van het industrie gebied in 1566," *Standen en landen 4* (1954); I. Schöffer, "The Dutch revolt anatomized: Some comments," *Comparative studies in society and history 3, 4* (1961), 471–3; T. Wittman, *Les Gueux dans les "bonnes villes" de Flandres*, Budapest, 1969, 128–35. Mack, *Calvinist preaching*, discusses the role and attitudes of the preachers. Although most writers have seen the iconoclastic riots as largely spontaneous, the treatment of Parker, accompanied by a map, has stressed, in agreement with several recent Dutch scholars, the organized aspect of the movement (*The Dutch revolt*, 75–80 and 288 n. 7).

majority abandoned the cause. In the fall, the government prepared to station garrisons in Valenciennes and several other disaffected towns, and the regent withdrew permission for Protestant preaching and worship. Reports were already current that the king himself would soon be bringing an army to the Netherlands to deal with the troubles.

In these circumstances the Beggar nobility and the Calvinist militants and communities moved forward into open rebellion. The momentum of religiopolitical protest and imminent repression together created a revolutionary situation. In November 1566, a synod in Antwerp, a center of Calvinist strength, decided that it was licit for a part of the vassals and subjects to take up arms against the superior magistrate if he violated their privileges and inflicted wrong upon them. The synod appointed a committee of noblemen and merchants to raise money and soldiers for resistance. Military command was confided to the Beggar lord Baron Brederode. In Flanders the Calvinist communities had already armed themselves and formed associations for mutual aid and defense.[22]

In December, Valenciennes, which was under Calvinist control, closed its gates against the royal troops, and the regent proclaimed the city to be in rebellion. Beggar risings then broke out in Flanders, Brabant, and scattered places elsewhere. But one after another they were put down by the forces commanded by loyalists of the high nobility. The Flemish insurrections were suppressed and rebel fighters annihilated near Antwerp. Valenciennes was taken, Brederode's bands dispersed. A hope of raising soldiers in Germany in time to aid the insurgency did not materialize. By the spring of 1567, the revolt had been extinguished. William of Orange, who had been in Antwerp during the fighting, did not take part in it, to the anger of the Calvinists, convinced that it had no chance. But he had burnt all his bridges to the monarchy, and now he and other Beggar leaders fled the country. Thousands of Netherlanders, noblemen, burghers, and artisans, did the same in expectation of the repression about to come.

Thus expired the first wave of rebellion, of which we may note several general points in summary. First, its main theater of action lay in Flanders and the southern Netherlands. Second, it was not a protest against foreign domination at this stage but a resistance to Philip II's system of government in politics and religion. The king had succeeded in a very short period in alienating many of the nobility and broad public sentiment. He was considered guilty of refusing to heed noble advice or to consult the States General and of maintaining the machinery of heresy prosecution, all contrary to provincial liberties. Third, the rebel organization depended on the Calvinist communities and noble leadership. It had thrown itself recklessly into revolt but commanded too few resources and, in the after-

[22] See Enno van Gelder, "De Nederlandse adel en de opstand tegen Spanje," pt. 1, 15–16; and Brulez, "De opstand van het industrie gebied in 1566."

math of the iconoclastic fury, too little support, to hold out for long in an armed confrontation with the regime.

III

In August 1567 the awaited Spanish army commanded by the duke of Alva arrived in the Netherlands. This event inaugurated a massive counterrevolution and "white" terror by the regime to wipe out all signs of dissidence. Yet, in spite of it, the revolution remained alive, although sustained largely from abroad, until suddenly, against all expectation, it won a territorial base in Holland and Zeeland from which a new wave of resistance sprang.

If not for other imperial priorities, Philip II would have acted sooner than he did to deal with the situation in the provinces. He considered the nobility's behavior and the failure of authorities to prevent the iconoclastic fury as serious faults betokening a shaky loyalty and had become convinced that drastic measures were needed to reestablish obedience.[23]

Conceivably the king might have made some concessions to the wishes of his subjects. But he had seen Calvinism breed the spirit of revolt; moreover, he was a devout Catholic who could not separate religion from obedience. He was determined, he told the pope in 1566, to settle the religious problem in the Netherlands by force if necessary, even if it meant their ruin.[24]

On top of this, always to be considered by the regime was the possible effect of resistance in the Netherlands upon other imperial possessions. Habsburg Spain, it has been pointed out, "was perhaps the first European power . . . to justify a war abroad with sophisticated 'arguments' of global strategy."[25] Should rebellion gain a foothold in the Netherlands, it could endanger the entire structure of the monarchy. Thus a proto-version of the "domino" theory took possession of the minds of Spanish statesmen. "All Italy says clearly," wrote Cardinal Granvelle to the king from Rome in June 1566, "that if the insurrection of Flanders continues, Milan and Naples will follow." Doubtless it was not forgotten that the city of Naples had revolted in 1547 partly because of the viceregal government's attempt to introduce the Inquisition.[26] Similarly, in September 1566, the council of state in Madrid decided that "if the Netherlands situation is not remedied, it will bring about the loss of Spain and all the rest."[27] This was among the premises that brought Alva's troops in 1567; it was also part of

[23] For Spanish policy and imperial priorities, see Parker, *The Dutch revolt*, 84–90, and *The army of Flanders and the Spanish road 1567–1659*, Cambridge, 1972, 231–2.
[24] Parker, *The army of Flanders*, 132.   [25] *Ibid.*, 127.
[26] Cited in *ibid.*, 128 n; for the revolt of Naples in 1547, see Chapter 8 in this book.
[27] Cited in Parker, *The Dutch revolt*, 88.

the rationale that mired Spain in an interminable war to hold onto the provinces.

Although Philip II had fully intended to come to the Netherlands himself, his councillors persuaded him to put off the journey as unsafe. Then the duke of Alva, a renowned Castilian warrior and royal servant, was dispatched at the head of ten thousand Spanish veterans who marched along the military corridor, the famous "Spanish road," running from Lombardy across the Alps, through Piedmont, Savoy, Franche-Comté, Lorraine (all territories of the king of Spain or his allies), and thence into Luxembourg, the first of the Low Countries. Within five years, this army of occupation was to swell to nearly seventy thousand men because of the tenacity of revolt.[28]

Soon after his arrival, Alva also took over as governor when Margaret of Parma resigned her office. The advocate of a policy of ruthlessness, his mission was to pacify the provinces and entrench royal absolutism. The duke established a special tribunal, the Council of Troubles, headquartered in Brussels with provincial branches, to mete out punishment for the recent insurrection as well as to deal with heresy. Its methods and number of victims caused it to become known to the population as the Council of Blood. Over twelve thousand people were tried before it, more than a thousand of whom were condemned to death and another nine thousand to complete or partial loss of property.[29] Many towns and magistrates were charged for complicity or failure to act during the iconoclasm. More than a score of noblemen were executed, including the counts of Egmont and Horne, who in June 1568 were publicly beheaded in Brussels. The burgomaster of Antwerp also suffered execution. William of Orange and other Beggar leaders outside the country were found guilty of treason in absentia, and their property confiscated.

Philip II's program for the Netherlands entailed financial independence for the central government and maintenance of a permanent military establishment at the provinces' own expense. With this in view, Alva demanded new taxes, of which one was the Tenth Penny, a permanent levy of 10 percent on every sale of merchandise, to be administered by royal officials. In March 1569 he assembled the States General of the Netherlands to approve these exactions. The States General refused the Tenth Penny. Had it consented, it would have relinquished its prerogatives in the introduction and collection of taxes. Although it later offered a large single money grant, it would never agree to a permanent tax. Alva resorted to intimidation, quartered troops on communities, and tried to im-

---

[28] See Parker, *The army of Flanders*, 26. This work provides an extraordinarily interesting treatment of Spanish military organization and of the character of the warfare in the Netherlands.

[29] Parker, *The Dutch revolt*, 108.

pose the Tenth Penny on his own authority. He was met nearly every-where, however, by protest and obstruction. The cry went up all over the country that the tax would destroy the trade of the Netherlands and im-poverish the people. Several provincial estates sent deputations against the impost to Spain. In the end, despite all threats and efforts, it had to be relinquished as impossible to enforce.

Alva's methods of *Shrecklichheit* aroused widespread hatred and indig-nation, even though the population feared to show any active resistance to his yoke. The Spanish troops, often insolent and brutal, were generally resented. The Tenth Penny provoked additional bitter complaint as a bla-tant illegality. It was from this period that an anti-Spanish aspect became part of the Netherlands revolt. The Spaniards' and Alva's tyranny was heavily stressed in rebel propaganda, a theme inevitable in view of the nationality of the governor and most of his advisers and of the weight of the Spanish armed presence on the country.[30]

With the imposition of a Spanish military despotism, only the strongest dedication to provincial freedoms and Protestant existence could survive. The burden of resistance fell on forces outside the provinces, the refugee Calvinist communities and dissident nobility. The Netherlands rebellion is a case of revolution in which exiles played an absolutely decisive role. Up to 1566, the monarchy's religious repression had compelled about thirty thousand people to emigrate. Possibly twenty thousand more fled from Alva's Council of Troubles. During the sixteenth and seventeenth centu-ries, only the Huguenot exodus from France following the revocation in 1685 of the Edict of Nantes exceeded the number that left the Netherlands in these dark years.[31] The Calvinist congregations abroad, most of which were in England and Germany, maintained relations with one another and stayed in contact with their persecuted brethren suffering "under the cross" at home. They contributed money for revolt and helped keep alive the spirit of resistance. In October 1571, the Reformed church of the Neth-erlands was able to hold its first national synod in Emden, in East Fries-land on neighboring German territory. Attended by representatives of the refugee and underground churches, the Emden synod laid the foundations of the Calvinist ecclesiastical organization and discipline for the Low Countries. It also, as we have previously seen, expressed its solidarity in a common cause with the Huguenots of France, whose national synod at La Rochelle had met a few months earlier.[32]

[30] K. Swart, "The Black Legend during the Eighty Years war," *Britain and the Netherlands* 5 (1975), 47–8.
[31] See Chapter 6 in this book. H. Schilling (*Niederländische Exulanten im 16. Jahrhundert*, Gütersloh, 1972, 13) makes the comparison with the Huguenot emigration after 1685.
[32] On the synod of Emden, see Chapter 10 in this book; and Parker, *The Dutch revolt*, 119–20. For a glimpse of the collapse of the Calvinist community in the province of Holland during Alva's regime and the survival of underground conventicles, see A. Duke and R.

The chief rebel now by his personal stature and dynastic resources was William of Orange. From his family principality of Nassau on German soil, Orange exerted all his strength to continue the struggle in the Netherlands. Although accepting Protestantism formally in 1568,[33] he was as opposed to Calvinist as to Catholic intolerance and fanaticism. His desire was coexistence of both Protestant and Catholic in order to build a general union of resistance to Philip II's government. Around him rallied fighting noblemen, advisers, publicists, and Protestant clergy. He had extensive connections among the Protestant princes of Germany and with the Huguenot leaders of France from whom he could seek support. From his circle emanated some of the main propaganda against Alva's rule. Orange's political line refrained from attacking the king, to whom he continued to avow loyalty, and concentrated on the liberties of the provinces and the wrongs done by the Spanish authorities. He directed his call in the name of patriotism to all the subjects of the Netherlands. Addressing them in manifestos in the fall of 1568, he condemned Alva's oppression, violence, and massacres and urged them to rise against such tyranny. The king was bound by oath and compacts, he declared, to respect the privileges of "our dear fatherland." If the ruler breaks the conditions and promises upon which the Netherlanders have received him, then they no longer owe him obedience. Orange denied that those fighting the regime were rebels; he called them "liberators," rather, who seek the true service of the king and the deliverance of the "fatherland."[34]

During 1568 Orange organized several attempts to invade the Netherlands in order to gain a base against Alva's power. For soldiers, apart from some exiles, he was largely dependent on the hire of German mercenaries and the help supplied by his Huguenot allies in France. Three invasion forces, including one from France into Flanders and another in the north into the province of Groningen commanded by Louis of Nassau, were all routed by Alva's troops. Orange himself led a fourth army of thirty thousand men into Brabant that disintegrated through indiscipline and lack of pay. Despite his appeals to the population, not a town rose to support the invaders. These defeats left the revolt at its lowest ebb. The Spanish regime seemed invincible.

The only remaining theater of resistance was at sea. In the North Sea and on the Atlantic were the Sea Beggars, the privateers empowered by the prince of Orange's commission. They did considerable damage against Spanish and Netherlands commerce and made lightning raids on the provinces' coasts, where they spread terror by their atrocities. Their com-

Jones, "Towards a reformed polity in Holland, 1572–1578," *Tijdschrift voor geschiedenis 89*, 3 (1976), 375.

[33] Putnam, *William the Silent*, v. 1, 292.

[34] Texts in Kossmann and Mellink, *Texts concerning the revolt of the Netherlands*, 84–8.

manders were exiled noblemen who bore a violent hatred toward papists and Alva's government. In 1570, they had expanded to about thirty vessels, which used the Huguenot port of La Rochelle, Emden, and English havens for their piratical activity.[35]

The revolt was already becoming a major point of contending great-power interests and potential international conflict. As a matter of *realpolitik*, Queen Elizabeth's Protestant government did not want to see the provincial liberties of the Netherlands annihilated and the Spanish monarchy established in unchallengeable new strength on the North Sea and Channel shore, where Philip II's power would pose a direct threat to England's safety. Hence, it sympathized with Orange's cause and looked the other way when the Sea Beggars sheltered in English harbors. On the other hand, English policy was also concerned that France would exploit the situation to acquire part of the provinces. England's vital security was thus bound up with the survival of the revolt or else its conclusion on terms that did not change the balance of power or increase the danger from Spain. This was the goal that English statecraft pursued, despite its frequent zigzags and retreats. As one of Queen Elizabeth's ministers declared in 1572, "To suffer [Orange] to miscarry knowing our own danger were to lack both policy and magnanimity." Orange was an instrument of God "to entertain" Spain, without whom "a dangerous fire ere this time had been kindled in our own home."[36]

As for France, Orange, as we have previously seen, possessed close relations with the chiefs of the Huguenot party, who were as anti-Spanish as he. In 1568, he concluded a treaty with Condé and Coligny that proclaimed the unity of their respective struggles. His brother, Louis of Nassau, who enjoyed the Huguenots' confidence, fought as a commander in their ranks and acted as a liaison between the two revolutionary movements.[37] One of the cardinal objectives of Huguenot policy, as we have also observed, was to convince the French monarchy to break with Spain, assist the Dutch rebels, and intervene in the Netherlands. In 1570–2, during the temporary reconciliation between the Huguenot leaders and Charles IX of France, this policy nearly succeeded, only to be shattered by the Saint Bartholomew massacre.[38]

Yet the Spanish monarchy could never overlook the possible consequences to its hegemony from France's territorial ambitions in the Netherlands. Neither could it ever ignore the chances for diplomatic meddling and foreign involvement offered by the insurgency. With such momen-

[35] Parker, *The Dutch revolt*, 121.

[36] Quoted in Sutherland, *The massacre of St. Bartholomew*, 303. R. B. Wernham ("English policy and the revolt of the Netherlands," *Britain and the Netherlands 1* [1960]) gives a summary of England's relation to the revolt.

[39] See Chapter 9 in this book.   [38] *Ibid.*

tous interests at stake, it was no wonder that the revolt was profoundly affected by great-power rivalries and proved in the long run to be nearly as much an international as an internal conflict.

IV

The lesson of the defeat of 1568 was that the rebellion had no future without foreign military help and the seizure of a *place d'armes* in the provinces. In 1572 William of Orange was actively pursuing both ends: contriving with his Huguenot allies for French intervention, and expending all his credit and resources to mount another invasion attack from Germany.

Unexpectedly, these plans were anticipated by an event that initiated the second stage of the revolution in the Netherlands.

In April 1572, the Sea Beggars captured Brill and Flushing, small ports in Holland and Zeeland that were crucially located for the maintenance of sea communication with the provinces. Held by the rebels, they began to receive a flow of exiles, ships, local partisans, and soon companies of foreign volunteer troops. From Flushing and Brill as bridgeheads, the Beggars during the summer of 1572 took over most of the towns of Holland and Zeeland. In the northeastern provinces (Overyssel, Gelderland, Friesland), some towns likewise joined the insurgency. Alva at the moment was unable to defend the north, as he was compelled to withdraw nearly all his available power into the southern provinces. There a Huguenot force under Louis of Nassau had occupied Mons in Hainaut, and invasions from France and Germany were also shortly expected.

With the crucial exception of some rebel positions in Holland and Zeeland, the Spanish regime succeeded in also crushing this new wave of revolt. The most calamitous blow to Orange's hopes was the failure of France's military intervention to materialize owing to the French crown's sudden switch of policy and Saint Bartholomew. His own invasion of Brabant and Hainaut with an army of German mercenaries turned out a total failure. Alva, whose army in 1572 rose to almost seventy thousand men by the addition of Netherlands and German troops, enjoyed overwhelming superiority both quantitatively and qualitatively. First, the government retook Mons and eliminated the vestiges of resistance in the south. Then, its forces advanced northward for an offensive against the towns that had defected to the Orangist and Beggar side.

The ensuing fighting in the Low Countries was terrible and cruel. Towns retaken by the government armies were victims of the most brutal atrocities. Zutphen and Mechlin were sacked, and Naarden's whole population massacred; Haarlem, occupied in July 1573 after a seven-month siege, saw its two-thousand-man garrison slaughtered and its magistrates executed.

The Beggars retaliated with savage reprisals of their own. Exhausted by his mission and also in Philip II's displeasure because the provinces were still unpacified, the duke of Alva left the country in 1573, to be replaced as governor by Don Luis de Requesens. Spain had many troubles at this period. The Morisco revolt in Granada, which broke out in December 1568,[39] devoured resources, and the renewal of Turkish pressure during the 1570s in the Mediterranean created further costs and strategic problems for the monarchy.

Everywhere but in some thirty towns of Holland and Zeeland the reconquest triumphed. Thus, the revolutionary civil war in its second stage became a struggle localized within these two provinces, where the enemies of Philip II's rule held out with stubborn heroism. Merely for resistance to survive against the Spanish *tercios*, the finest fighting units in Europe, was in itself a victory. This was possible mainly for two reasons. First, the Beggars kept control of the sea, which lay open to bring them supply and help. Second, the geography of Holland and Zeeland, a low-lying, watery landscape of marshes, lakes, streams, estuaries, and dikes built against the sea, protected by the big rivers that formed the provinces' delta, gave the towns a strong defensive situation and created unfavorable conditions for military operations.[40] Alva told Philip II, "You cannot conceive the great number of troops that is required to invest a position in this country. There is no place, great or small, not even the most wretched village, that has not a water-filled ditch that requires bridging for its passage."[41] To deal with such obstacles, difficult sieges were needed. One of the most desperate fights was Leyden's, which lay under siege from May to October 1574 and refused to surrender even though reduced almost to starvation. It was saved only because the rescuers opened the dikes between it and the sea. Over the flooded land the relieving ships were able to arrive, and the Spanish troops withdrew for fear of being cut off and drowning.

Here, while still isolated in Holland and Zeeland, it is possible to see the evolving structure of the Netherlands revolution and the political order it adumbrated.

The expansion of revolutionary power following the capture of Brill and Flushing was less a spontaneous movement of the whole population than the work of an activist minority. Urban magistracies and elites generally submitted with little or no resistance to detachments of Beggar forces supported by part of the local inhabitants. Here and there weak Spanish garrisons were driven out. In this way, the towns, often alienated anyway

---

[39] See Chapter 9 in this book.

[40] See D. Caldecott-Baird, *The expedition in Holland 1572–1574*, London, 1976, pt. 2, ch. 4.

[41] Cited in *ibid.*, 38.

by Alva's administration, were won for the revolt. Some refused to join the rebel side: Amsterdam, the most important of Holland's cities, remained loyal to the Brussels regime till 1578. The political consolidation of rebel authority was gradually carried out. Exiles returned home to participate in the affairs of their communities, and pro-Spanish and disloyal elements were purged from offices to be replaced by more reliable men. No democratization, however, nor any radical reversal of urban power occurred. The municipal polities continued to be oligarchic and dominated as before by patrician strata of the urban orders.[42]

Socially, the revolt depended on a heterogeneous alignment. Most of the high nobility of the Netherlands, which stemmed from the southern provinces and belonged to great Walloon houses, had separated itself from the opposition to Philip II's rule after the iconoclastic fury. But the revolutionary front in the north was headed by the prince of Orange and embraced a broad segment of society: lesser noblemen, Calvinist militants, urban elites and notables, bourgeois and petty bourgeois, and many artisans, fishermen, sailors, and miscellaneous laboring folk.

Revolution also brought in Protestantism and gave religious supremacy to the Reformed church. The Calvinists were only a small minority of the population in the two insurgent provinces, yet theirs became the state religion; they were the leaven in the resistance who considered themselves an elect people of God, and they would accept nothing less. Notwithstanding Orange's instructions for a modus vivendi between confessions, and despite Beggar promises to the towns at the time of their *overgang* to maintain Catholic freedom, this was not done. The rebels committed fresh acts of iconoclasm, killed some monks and priests, and appropriated Catholic churches. In due course, instead of religious coexistence, the mass was banned, and Catholic public worship suppressed. Catholics, of course, remained – they were indeed a large majority – but without legal toleration. At the same time the Calvinists extended their efforts at Protestantization and built up their own ecclesiastical organization and discipline, as they were now free to do.[43]

All these changes signified the beginnings of a new politicoreligious order. The same process also occurred at a higher level as the insurrectionary provinces established their own provisional government, a revolutionary power independent of the king. This may be seen from what happened in Holland.

In July 1572, the provincial estates or States of Holland convened on

[42] See Geyl, *The revolt of the Netherlands*, 127, and *History of the Low Countries: Episodes and problems*, London, 1964, 9–10; and Parker, *The Dutch revolt*, 146–7.

[43] Duke and Jones, "Towards a reformed polity in Holland," give an illuminating account of these religious changes, which are also summarized by Geyl, *The revolt of the Netherlands*, 127–8, 130–1; and Parker, *The Dutch revolt*, 150–5.

their own authority in Dort, with deputies from twelve of their eighteen regular towns in attendance, as well as representatives of Orange and the nobility. Propositions from Orange were presented and approved. In accordance with them, the States recognized the prince as governor-general and stadholder of Holland, Zeeland, Friesland, and Utrecht, offices once bestowed on him by Philip II and never formally revoked. They also agreed to raise money to pay for the ships and men that were fighting in the defense of provincial liberty. Orange was empowered to appoint various officials but bound himself not to undertake or command anything without the advice and consent of the States or their majority. The States swore fidelity to Orange, pledging not to desert him and to help him in every way, and he in turn gave his oath to protect them. Nothing was said to impugn Philip II's formal supremacy, the fiction being maintained that Orange's offices as governor and stadholder derived from the king. What existed in reality, though, was a contractual, representative regime of Orange and the provincial States. The latter also undertook to establish good relations with the towns of Flanders, Brabant, and the other provinces. The purpose of all these arrangements was declared to be the restoration in full vigor of provincial rights and liberties and the protection of the country "from foreign tyrants and oppressors according to its old rights and privileges."[44]

A regular combat of ideas and propaganda accompanied the conflict in the Low Countries, as it did other great revolutions of early modern Europe. Philip II complained to the regent about "the lampoons that are continually spread abroad and posted up in the Netherlands without the offenders being punished."[45] The printed word in seditious pamphlets helped sow the seeds for the first outburst of resistance. "It proved impossible to stop the flood of publications," wrote an agent of Orange concerning the year 1566, "for the more the court issued edicts against them, the more the number of such booklets and writings increased."[46] Orange himself took a strong interest in the press from the outset. He had publicists in his service like the Calvinist nobleman, Philip Marnix de Saint Aldegonde, and resorted frequently to print to justify his own actions and to exhort the Netherlanders to rally to his side. As the revolt continued, hundreds of libels, pamphlets, and broadsides appeared in a comment upon events and a debate of principles.[47]

[44] The text of the propositions is printed in Kossmann and Mellink, *Texts concerning the revolt of the Netherlands*, 98–101; and see Parker, *The Dutch revolt*, 144–5, for a description of the new regime.

[45] Kossmann and Mellink, *Texts concerning the revolt of the Netherlands*, 54.

[46] *Ibid.*, 68. The author of this statement was Jacobus van Wesenbeke, an Antwerp legal official who joined Orange.

[47] See P. Geurts, *De Nederlandse opstand in de pamfletten 1566–1584*, Nijmegen, 1956, for a discussion of the pamphlet literature and its ideas. Part 1 surveys the pamphlet in relation to

Rebel and Orangist political doctrines did not contain any striking features or novel theoretical claims. Early defenses of resistance included the argument about the duty of inferior magistrates to prevent the tyranny of superiors.[48] The appearance of this theme, drawn from the common reservoir of Protestant resistance theory, suggests that the revolt was probably not specially influenced at its inception by neighboring Huguenot ideas. Later, though, the Huguenot works that were published after the Saint Bartholomew massacre did exercise a marked influence upon Dutch rebels. Hotman's *Francogallia*, Beza's *The right of magistrates*, and the *Vindiciae contra tyrannos* were all known and read in the Netherlands. Marnix de Saint Aldegonde possessed copies of them, and the *Vindiciae* was reprinted in the Netherlands.[49] Given the continual interconnection between the revolutionary movements in the two countries and the much fuller development of Huguenot political ideology, some influence of the latter upon the Netherlands revolution was inevitable.

Orange aimed his propaganda chiefly against the Spanish tyranny. He professed to be fighting not Philip II but an illicit regime imposed in the name of the unwitting king by his wicked ministers and councillors. He attacked Alva in unmeasured terms with the names of legendary tyrants – "that effeminate Sardanapalus, that cruel Phalaris . . . hated by God and mankind alike."[50] Orange summoned the people to restore their freedom from the domination of hired foreigners. A recurrent note of his statements was his patriotic emphasis upon the Netherlands as a whole, the "*commune patrie*" or fatherland, striving to overcome the provincial particularism and religious division that were a barrier to united resistance. In a remonstrance of 1572, he justified his appeal by "the loyalty you and I owe to the dearest fatherland."[51] The same ideal was evoked by the rebel States of Holland when in 1573 they called on all the provinces to cooperate "in chasing these foreign tyrants and rulers out of the country" in order to "restore our oppressed fatherland to its former prosperity."[52]

Orange stated the objectives of the revolt in his remonstrance of 1572 already mentioned, which was published soon after the Beggars began

the course of events. W. Knuttel, *Catalogus van de pamfletten-verzameling . . . in de Koninklijke Bibliotheek*, The Hague, 8 v., 1889–1916, v. 1, lists the pamphlets published during the revolt. From 1566 through 1584, 594 are listed, of which some, of course, are official statements and declarations. For other catalogs of pamphlets and supplements to Knuttel, see Kossmann and Mellink, *Texts concerning the revolt of the Netherlands*, 286.

[48] See Chapter 10 in this book.

[49] See A. De Vrankrijker, *De motiviering van onzen opstand: De Theorieen van het verzet der Nederlandsche opstandelingen tegen Spanje in de jaren 1565–1581*, Nijmegen, 1933, for a review of the arguments advanced by the Dutch rebels. Vrankrijker unduly minimizes the influence of Huguenot ideas on the revolt. On Huguenot writings known in the Netherlands, *ibid.*, 158–9; *ibid.*, chs. 4, 8, deal with the French civil war and its parallels.

[50] Kossmann and Mellink, *Texts concerning the revolt of the Netherlands*, 94.

[51] *Ibid.*, 97.   [52] *Ibid.*, 102.

their entrenchment in Holland and Zeeland. They included the revocation of the edicts of religious persecution and an end to the Inquisition; the annulment of sentences passed by the Council of Troubles; the expulsion of foreigners from positions of authority; the trial of Alva in the Netherlands for robbing their freedom; and the reference of political matters to the provincial estates and the States General for transaction with the king.[53]

The chief legitimation for these aims, which meant a veto on absolutist government, was found in provincial privileges and inherited liberties. The latter formed the basic principle on which the Netherlands rebellion took its stand and were cited repeatedly in declarations and political negotiations. As the provinces and towns of the Low Countries possessed a mass of privileges and immunities, this appeal to provincial privileges necessarily bore a selective and normative character. It involved both a myth of the past and a justification in positive law. When rebels spoke of privileges, they meant such things as the administration of justice and government in accord with traditional local forms that restricted ruler power and protected autonomy.[54] It was on this ground that the procedures of heresy prosecution, the Inquisition, and the Council of Troubles were all condemned as illegal. Moreover, in 1549 the future Philip II had solemnly sworn before the assembled estates of Brabant to observe the Joyeuse Entrée, the famous fourteenth-century charter of provincial liberties.[55] It was to this act that the noble Confederation's Compromise of 1566 consequently alluded when it accused the king of violating his oath.[56] The Joyeuse Entrée was continually regarded as a standard by which to decide if the ruler was guilty of tyranny or not, and its breach considered as giving justification for resistance.[57] By privileges, rebels also meant the ruler's obligation to consult his provincial estates and the States General of the Netherlands. The estates and the practice of consent occupied a central place in rebel ideology and programs. The Confederates in their Compromise and petition of 1566 requested the king to seek the advice and consent of the States General and demanded freedom of expression on the assembly's behalf.[58] One of the Beggars' first actions in 1572, as we have seen, was to convene the States of Holland. In 1576 Orange declared, "My object has never been anything else than to see these countries governed,

[53]*Ibid.*, 96–7.

[54]See on this subject J. Woltjer, "Dutch privileges, real and imaginary," *Britain and the Netherlands 5* (1975), 22, and the entire discussion.

[55]G. Griffiths, *Representative government in Western Europe in the sixteenth century*, Oxford, 1968, 302; see Chapter 4 in this book.

[56]Kossmann and Mellink, *Texts concerning the revolt of the Netherlands*, 59.

[57]Griffiths, *Representative government in Western Europe*, 303; Geurts, "Het beroep op de Blijde Inkomste."

[58]Kossmann and Mellink, *Texts concerning the revolt of the Netherlands*, 64, 60.

as they always used to be, by the States General, consisting of three Estates: the clergy, the nobility and the cities . . . in legal obedience to their natural prince."[59] It was also through and by act of the estates that the insurgent provinces eventually severed their association with Philip II and the Spanish monarchy. It is probably no exaggeration to say that for the Netherlands rebellion the estates were the institution in which the principle of provincial privileges and freedoms found its supreme embodiment.

One tension within the revolt, from whose complication it was never to be free, revealed itself clearly in this period of its establishment in Holland and Zeeland. This was the tension between liberty and religion or Reformation. The first was specially linked to privileges; it also offered the only ground for hope of an alliance of all the provinces against the central government. Necessarily it involved Catholic–Protestant toleration. The second, on the other hand, signified to the Reformed churches and stricter Calvinists their own exclusive dominion and the deference of secular to ecclesiastical authority. William of Orange was himself received into the Calvinist church in October 1573. Attaching little importance to confessional differences, he took this step to solidify his relations with the most militant elements of the revolt.[60] In attitude he remained strongly tolerant, opposed to all bigotry and dogmatism, and essentially a *politique* who wanted to subordinate religious quarrels to overriding political needs. The same latitudinarian view predominated among the urban governing class of regents, as they were called, who formed the chief element in the provincial estates.

This contrast inevitably made for an uneasy relationship between religion and magistrate and for church–state conflicts. Although the Reformed church became recognized in the revolutionary provinces as the state church, it contained only a minority of the population, with a membership drawn mainly from the middle and lower orders. Secular authorities and magisterial elites consented to its religious supremacy but nonetheless refused to be its instrument or sanction its influence in state affairs. Their policy, which favored toleration for all peaceable religious bodies, was to circumscribe its powers and deny it compulsive force. The resulting frictions between *politiques* and zealots, political authority and Calvinist orthodoxy, liberty and Reformation, affected the entire course of the Netherlands rebellion.[61] We shall witness the same problem in an even more acute form in the English revolution of the 1640s.

[59] Cited in Griffiths, *Representative government in Western Europe*, 308.
[60] Putnam, *William the Silent*, v. 2, 39–40.
[61] For comments on this subject, see Geyl, *The revolt of the Netherlands*, 204–5; and I. Schöfer, "Protestantism in flux during the revolt of the Netherlands," *Britain and the Netherlands* 2 (1964), 74–6.

V

The Dutch rebels clung courageously to their strongholds in Holland and Zeeland and even made some further conquests there after 1572, but they still faced overwhelming odds in their isolated struggle. Hemmed in as they were by superior Spanish power, foreign help was essential to their survival, yet slow and inadequate in coming. Queen Elizabeth, because she was wary of worsening relations with Spain, refused to extend outright support or pledge any responsibility for the revolt. In 1572, as part of an attempted détente with Philip II, her government even ordered the Sea Beggars to leave English harbors. It was this step, compelling the Beggars to seek other bases, that fortuitously resulted in their seizure of Brill and Flushing. Although the Queen sent Orange money and permitted English volunteers to serve with him, such aid was too slight to affect the military balance. In Germany, Orange also continued his efforts to obtain help. In the spring of 1574, Louis of Nassau led a futile invasion with German mercenaries in which he himself was killed along with another of Orange's brothers and one of the Calvinist Palatine princes fighting on the rebel side.

What eventually turned the tide was the Spanish monarchy's own internal problems. Requesens, succeeding the duke of Alva as governor at the end of 1573, was constantly harassed by a shortage of money. In 1574, at the time of Louis of Nassau's invasion, the army of Flanders had expanded to over eighty thousand men.[62] Most of the cost of these troops needed to fight the revolt was not provided by the Netherlands. It had to be supplied by Spain, that is, Castile, as the failure of the Tenth Penny only underscored. But other needs as well claimed the monarchy's resources. Philip II could not abandon the defense of the Mediterranean where, despite the famous naval victory at Lepanto in 1571, the Ottoman Turks in 1574 recaptured Tunis from Spain. Nor was the king willing to make peace with his rebellious Dutch subjects. In 1575 an informal negotiation took place at Breda between the government's and Orange's representatives. It came to nothing because intractable religious and political differences prevented any compromise.[63]

Starved for funds, the Netherlands government was continually hard pressed to pay its troops. In turn, the soldiers mutinied, plundering the natives and holding towns for ransom until they received their back wages. These military mutinies resembled nothing so much as big strikes over

---

[62] Parker (*The army of Flanders*, app. A) gives the size and composition of the occupying army at different dates. Spanish troops were always only a small proportion of the total, the great majority being German and Netherlands fighting men.

[63] Parker (*The Dutch revolt*, 160–8) provides an analysis of the monarchy's problems at this juncture and their effect upon the Netherlands situation.

pay and harsh conditions, which followed a consistent pattern. Discontented regiments or garrisons, once they had decided to mutiny, would expel their officers and elect their own representatives to speak in their behalf. The latter, with a sort of common soldiers' democracy behind them, then bargained with the commanders, and only when their demands and grievances were met would the troops return to duty.[64] Three major mutinies of this kind, involving thousands of men, occurred between 1573 and 1575. Besides creating huge expenses for the Brussels government, which had to find the money for arrears promptly, they seriously hampered military operations. Worst of all, these disorders by the soldiers enraged and terrified the local inhabitants with the result that the loyal provinces became increasingly restive and alienated from the regime.

In September 1575, the Spanish monarchy, for the second time during the king's reign, was forced by its insupportable financial burdens to declare bankruptcy in Castile and stop payment on its debts. The shock of this crisis produced serious repercussions in the Netherlands, where money or credit to pay the army of Flanders was no longer available. In March 1576 the governor, Requesens, died, despairing to the last over the disastrous situation of his men. Again mutinies broke out. Like a wandering juggernaut, bodies of insubordinate troops moved from place to place, exacting contributions, plundering, and mistreating the population. Philip II was informed by a Spanish councillor in Brussels that the country would no longer support the war and was on the point of revolt; the people were arming themselves against his soldiers amid a general outcry of "death to the Spaniards."[65] The king presently appointed a new governor of the provinces, his own half-brother, Don John of Austria, the victor of the Morisco revolt. But before this young prince ever arrived in the Netherlands, affairs had taken a new turn and passed out of the monarchy's control.

The loyal provinces were impelled by the mutinous troops to look to their own self-defense. The States of Brabant, invoking the Joyeuse Entrée and provincial liberties, demanded from Madrid the withdrawal of all foreign forces. This now became the cry of the whole country. Other provincial estates in Flanders, Hainaut, and Gelderland joined the protest and called for the meeting of the States General of the Netherlands. The royal council of state found itself discredited and deprived of authority. In September 1576, at the bidding of the States of Brabant, the States General of the Netherlands took the decisive step of assembling in Brussels on its own initiative. It then entered into negotiations with the prince of Orange for the purpose of freeing the country from military occupation and making a reconciliation with the rebel provinces of Holland and Zee-

---

[64] See Parker, *The army of Flanders*, 185–206, for a detailed account of these army mutinies.
[65] Cited by Pirenne, *Histoire de Belgique*, v. 4, 62–3.

land. The urgency of these objectives was evidenced by the increasing menace of the Spanish troops, who early in November crowned their atrocities with an assault upon Antwerp. For several days the "Spanish fury" subjected the great metropolis of the Netherlands to a riot of pillage, arson, and slaughter, destroying untold property and leaving eight thousand dead.

Shortly after this outrage, the provinces represented in the States General concluded a peace with Orange and the States of Holland and Zeeland. This agreement, the Pacification of Ghent made in November 1576, provided in its main terms for the expulsion of the Spanish and other foreign troops from the country; the recognition of Orange in all his offices; the maintenance of the religious status quo in all the provinces and suspension of the heresy laws; and, perhaps most important, the referral of all the affairs of the Netherlands, including religion, to the States General for settlement.[66]

Despite the fact that it didn't last, the Pacification of Ghent was a major milestone marking a new, third stage of the Netherlands rebellion. It ended the isolation of the revolt and transformed it for a while into a general resistance of the Low Countries to Spain's government. Ten years after the struggle began, and four years after the Beggars implanted themselves in Holland and Zeeland, the revolution finally embraced all the provinces in a united front. For William of Orange this development was a victory that signified his emergence as the country's foremost political spokesman and champion. With it went the provisional recognition of Protestantism and the key position allotted to the States General in determining the Netherlands' future. In essence, the Pacification of Ghent stood for the leading role of the States General over against royal absolutism; for the primacy of the interests of the Seventeen Provinces over against imperial Spain's world policy; and for the freedom of Protestantism over against the absolute and exclusive sway of the Catholic church.[67]

Yet the Pacification of Ghent resulted from an unstable combination of forces that had little chance of holding together. Holland and Zeeland were led by people who came to power by conquest and imposed their will in a trial of fire against the might of Spain. There Calvinist Protestantism also reigned supreme. The southern provinces, on the other hand, were led into alliance with the revolutionary provinces by their own estab-

---

[66] The Pacification of Ghent is printed in Kossmann and Mellink, *Texts concerning the revolt of the Netherlands*, 126–32. The events leading up to it are well summarized by Geyl, *The revolt of the Netherlands*, 145–50; Parker, *The Dutch revolt*, 172–8; and with additional interesting details by Pirenne, *Histoire de Belgique*, v. 4, 61–82.

[67] W. Blockmans and P. Van Peteghem, "De Pacificatie van Gent als uiting van kontinuiteit in de politieke opvattingen van de standenvertegenwoordiging," *Tijdschrift voor geschiedenis 89*, 3, (1976), 325; see also the discussion in H. A. Enno van Gelder's essay, "De vrede von Gent (8 November 1576)," in *Van beeldenstorm tot pacificatie*, Amsterdam, 1964.

lished authorities, the governing elites among the cities and nobility. Not only were these elites Catholic; they were fundamentally conservative and moderate, dreading the insurrectionary spirit that the revolt released. For this reason they had abandoned the opposition movement in 1566 and only joined the revolt in 1576 on account of the unendurable presence of the foreign troops. Although hostile to absolutism and centralization, they were nevertheless unhappy at finding themselves at odds with the monarchy and certainly indisposed to withstand it to extremes. The position of the high nobility in the southern Netherlands was especially significant. "The struggle to possess the bodies and souls of the nobility," so an English scholar has commented, "is the essence of the Revolt in the crucial 1570s."[68] But the great Walloon magnates such as the duke of Aerschot, head of the house of Croy, who acted a prominent part in the events ending in the pacification, still felt their fortunes bound to the Habsburg dynasty. They felt no allegiance to a national ideal, as did the prince of Orange, who was exceptional in this respect, and thought more of their particularist interests than of the Netherlands as a whole. Moreover, they were keenly jealous of being eclipsed by Orange's preeminence. In addition, the strength of provincial particularism on all sides, plus the potentiality of religious conflict at any provocation, further militated against unity.[69] With such discordant elements blended together in the revolutionary camp, that the Pacification of Ghent would last was highly unlikely.[70]

In this third stage of the revolt, supreme authority devolved upon the States General as the precarious focus of the Netherlands community. This institution, composed as it was of delegates of the autonomous provincial estates, was more suited by its character to bridle power than to exercise it. The universal reaction against the Spanish regime, however, obliged it to act as a government to replace the king's. Once again, revolution had given birth to a de facto rival sovereignty. To be sure, the States General did not disavow loyalty or obedience to Philip II. Nevertheless, it took over governmental functions: raised money and soldiers, made war and peace, directed orders to the royal council of state, negotiated with foreign rulers, and appointed military and civil officials – all, of course, with the consent and agreement of the provincial estates.[71]

[68] Wilson, *Queen Elizabeth and the revolt of the Netherlands*, 15.

[69] For the importance and attitude of the Walloon nobility and the wider political effects of particularism, see G. Malengreau, *L'Esprit particulariste et la révolution des Pays-Bas du XVIe siècle*, Louvain, 1936, 91–106 and *passim*.

[70] The unstable balance of forces in the Pacification of Ghent is described by Geyl, *The revolt of the Netherlands*, 148–9; and see also the illuminating discussion of J. Woltjer, "De vrede-makers," *Tijdschrift voor geschiedenis 89*, 3 (1976).

[71] See T. Juste, *Histoire des Etats généraux des Pays-Bas (1465–1790)*, 2 v., Brussels, 1864, v. 1, 140–2, 155; and Griffiths, *Representative government in Western Europe*, 308–9.

Don John of Austria, the king's newly designated governor, was forced to face the changed situation when he reached the Netherlands. The States General refused to recognize him unless he first agreed to the withdrawal of foreign troops and the Pacification of Ghent. He finally consented to these demands in January 1577, in the misnamed Perpetual Edict. On its side, the States General undertook to maintain the Catholic religion in all the provinces. This commitment was unacceptable to Holland and Zeeland, which accordingly declined to acknowledge the Perpetual Edict or Don John. Orange and his supporters put no faith in Spanish promises and did not believe Philip II would ever tolerate Protestantism. Nor did most of the Dutch rebels intend to restore Catholicism where they held power. Such dissensions were emblematic of the frictions existing in the States General, where the Catholic provinces were the majority.

In the spring of 1577, the Spanish troops actually left the country, and the new governor was then received in Brussels. Yet, after this beginning, the next three years witnessed the breakdown of the coalition of provinces in the Pacification of Ghent. The revolution, so recently become general, disintegrated into a confusion of religious and political strife that ended in the division of the Netherlands. Amid the welter of events leading to this outcome, two factors were especially important.

On the one side was Don John of Austria's renewal of the war. In bitter frustration at his powerlessness under the new dispensation, he suddenly seized the citadel of Namur and recalled the Spanish troops. At this breach of the Perpetual Edict, the States General recruited soldiers and looked abroad for help. It called in the Austrian Habsburg, Archduke Mathias, to replace Don John as governor and solicited French support through Henry III's brother, the duke of Anjou. England also provided subsidies to pay the Palatine prince, John Casimir, and his German mercenaries. Thus the Netherlands were once more overrun with destructive armies and again a battleground for Spanish reconquest.

This was Philip II's will. Only with the greatest reluctance did the king concede the States General's demands and his governor's humiliation. During 1577–8, however, Spain's fortunes improved. In the Mediterranean the prospect appeared of a truce with the Turks, and big treasure imports from America eased the financial stringency and allowed the monarchy to float new loans. It also became possible thereby to maintain the army of Flanders.[72] In January 1578, Spanish troops inflicted an overwhelming defeat upon the States General's forces at Gembloux in Brabant. Later that year Don John, only thirty-three years old, died unexpectedly, and his successor was the victorious commander at Gembloux,

---

[72] Parker (*The Dutch revolt*, 187–9) summarizes the circumstances of the monarchy's policy at this juncture.

Alexander Farnese, prince of Parma, the former regent Margaret of Parma's son and Philip II's nephew. Of all the Netherlands' governors, Parma was the most brilliant as a military leader, diplomat, and civil administrator. With his advent, Spanish power began its revival, creating the danger afresh that the whole revolt might go down before it.

On the other side was the manifestation of popular radicalism and Calvinist extremism in the southern provinces. This has been characterized by some writers as the "radical" or "democratic" phase of the Netherlands revolution.[73] Brussels, Ghent, Arras, and other towns recalled the earlier traditions of urban rebellion in the Low Countries by popular movements that challenged the civic oligarchies and their political domination. In Brussels after August 1577, the Eighteen, a committee recruited from the guilds, captured the municipal government. Representing rank-and-file burghers and the lower orders, they championed the "patriotic cause" against the partisans of Spain. Of course, they were Orangist supporters, but they went well beyond what Orange himself would have sanctioned. The Eighteen and "*bons bourgeois*" of Brussels insisted on the consent of the bourgeois commonalty to municipal acts "head by head." They threatened the moderate nobility and imposed their demands on the States General. The situation, as Pirenne noted, was analogous to the confrontation during the French revolution between the commune of Paris and the legislative assembly.[74]

In Ghent, an even more militant movement subjected the city to the rule of the Calvinists and guilds in October 1577. The former urban constitution, abolished by Charles V after Ghent's rebellion in 1539, was restored, with the Eighteen, an organ of the artisans and guilds, exercising power.[75] In the name of the patriot cause, the new regime attacked and terrorized civic notables, nobility, the provincial estates of Flanders, and Catholic clergy for their pro-Spanish leanings. Ghent became a hotbed of Calvinist zealotry. In flagrant violation of the Pacification of Ghent, which preserved the religious status quo, the Calvinist minority, led by rich

---

[73] Such is the view, for example, of H. A. Enno van Gelder, who in an attempted stage-by-stage parallel between the Netherlands revolt and the English revolution has pictured this period as the former's radical phase corresponding in England to 1648–55, the republic and Cromwellian protectorate (*De Nederlandse Staten en het Engels Parlement in verzet tegen vorstenmacht en gevestigde kerk*, Brussels, 1960, app., 73–4). See also G. Griffiths, "The revolutionary character of the revolt of the Netherlands," *Comparative studies in society and history* 2, 4 (1960), 464–5; and I. Schöffer, "The Dutch revolt anatomized: Some comments," *ibid.* 3, 4 (1961). Wittman has consecrated his study, *Les Gueux dans les "bonnes villes" de Flandres*, to this "democratic" phase.

[74] Pirenne, *Histoire de Belgique*, v. 4, 101–2. *Ibid.*, v. 4, bk. 2, chs. 1–3, contains an account of these urban insurgencies; see also the interesting discussion in Wittman, *Les Gueux dans les "bonnes villes" de Flandres*, 189–207.

[75] For Ghent's revolt in 1539, see Chapter 8 in this book.

bourgeois but mostly belonging to the middle and plebeian strata, forced a dictatorship on the city. Popery and Spain were seen as a single enemy, and Calvinist violence suppressed Catholic worship. Albeit in a reverse direction, these developments in Ghent resembled those in Paris in 1588, when urban revolt after the Day of the Barricades brought the Catholic League to power.[76] Calvinist and Catholic popular radicalism exhibited an identical seditious character.

With Ghent's help or example, similar revolts erupted in other towns. During the spring and summer of 1578, many communities of Flanders, Artois, and Hainaut fell under the sway of revolutionary committees like Ghent's, which deposed the Catholic magistrates and opened the way to Calvinist ascendancy. To the Catholic ruling orders in the southern provinces, these upheavals were nothing less than religious and social war instigated by Beggar partisans. A patrician of Arras, who experienced the insurgency of his city, recorded his opinion that it was the work of the "vile populace," which supported the prince of Orange. He blamed the Calvinists for overthrowing "*l'estat publique*" to establish their religion and described the seditious elements as "have-nothings" consisting of weavers, shoemakers, and other lowly artisans, who were bent on pillaging the churches, rich bourgeoisie, and gentlemen.[77]

Little as he liked them, William of Orange could not prevent these insurrections, which only attested to the uncontrollable forces the revolution gathered up and to the passionate desire of the lower orders for a voice. Indeed, by his disapproval Orange incurred the criticism and animosity of the Calvinists of Ghent. But in Holland as well, the heartland of the rebellion, the Calvinists' aggression undermined the Pacification of Ghent. This was demonstrated, for example, by what took place in Amsterdam. Despite the Beggar conquests, Amsterdam had remained a fortress of royalism and Catholicism, which held out against the revolution until 1578. Finally, the city yielded to the States of Holland on condition of the maintenance of Catholicism as the sole religion. The Calvinists flouted this agreement, though, and within three months it was torn up by the decisive Alteratie, which drove out Amsterdam's Catholic magistrates and clergy, installed exiles and Calvinists in power, and gave the Reformed church exclusive domination. The like happened in other towns of the northern provinces, which had received promises of toleration from the Beggars. This sequence of events contained its own logic, for the ministers of the Reformed church were no more willing to suffer the public

---

[76] See Chapter 10 in this book.

[77] P. Payen, "Discours véritable de ce quy s'est passé en la ville de Arras," in *Mémoires de Pontus Payen*, ed. A. Henne, 2 v., Brussels, 1860–1, v. 2, 47, 58–9, 72. Payen was a lawyer and royalist ennobled by Philip II in 1582.

exercise of Catholicism than the Jewish prophets of old would tolerate the worship of Baal.[78]

Under the pervasive pressure of these two factors – the renewal of Spain's efforts to crush the rebellion and the cumulative effects of popular radicalism and urban insurrection, Calvinist extremism, and religious animosities – the fragile alliance of the provinces in the Pacification of Ghent broke down. The sentiments of a common fatherland and Netherlands nationhood were too weak to withstand these disruptive stresses. Alienated by the Calvinists' excesses, a party of Malcontents appeared among the Catholic high nobility and civic governors and moved toward a reconciliation with Philip II's rule. The secession from the Pacification of Ghent was signaled by the formation of separate provincial unions in January 1579. In the south, the estates of Hainaut, Artois, and part of Flanders established the Catholic Union of Arras as the nucleus of the provinces that in due course came to terms with Spain. In the north, the Calvinist Union of Utrecht was formed, joining Holland and Zeeland with Utrecht, Groningen, and presently with Gelderland, Overyssel and Friesland as well. To it were also affiliated, till Spanish power overwhelmed them, the great rebel-dominated cities of Flanders and Brabant, Ghent, Bruges, Antwerp, and some others. The members of the Utrecht union bound themselves to fight the king's servants and Spaniards, pledging "to hold together . . . as if they were but one province," although saving all the particular privileges of the constituent towns and provinces.[79]

These events and their sequel put an end to the rebellion as a united resistance of the Low Countries. The States General carried on but with the gradual withdrawal of the provinces and towns that returned to obedience to the king. Before long it became only an assembly of the revolutionary provinces. While Alexander of Parma set out on a course of reconquest that reaped increasing success, the latter continued their struggle. No likelihood existed of their reconciliation with Philip II. They had resisted too long and bitterly and remained divided from the king by a gulf of differences that left them no alternative but to go on fighting.[80]

VI

In March 1580 Philip II proclaimed William of Orange a traitor with a price on his head, to which the prince responded with his *Apology*. A year

[78] On the Alteration in Amsterdam, see Geyl, *The revolt of the Netherlands*, 170–2; and Duke and Jones, "Towards a reformed polity in Holland," 392–3.

[79] The Union of Utrecht is printed in Kossmann and Mellink, *Texts concerning the revolt of the Netherlands*, 165–73. Accounts of two unions are given in all the standard authorities.

[80] During the summer of 1579, the Habsburg Emperor Rudolf II sponsored a conference at Cologne among representatives of Philip II, the States General, and Orange in the hope of mediating the revolt. It failed because the differences were too great.

afterward, in July 1581, the States General declared Philip II's deposition. The two statements, Orange's *Apology* and the Act of Abjuration, gave exemplary expression to the political ideology of the Netherlands revolt just at the juncture when its burden was to be borne once more by only a minority of the provinces in the wake of the dissolution of the revolutionary coalition.

Orange's *Apology*, which was addressed to the States General, was a personal defense of both himself and the revolt.[81] In part, it was noteworthy for its high strain of aristocratic consciousness, as the prince spoke of his honor, his former loyalty, and the greatness of his house and ancestry. In part, it was noteworthy too for its terrible charges against Philip II as a murderer and tyrant, charges that helped to shape the long-lasting "Black Legend" of the wicked king's and Spanish cruelty. Among its indictments of Spain as "a country which is naturally the enemie of the lowe countrey," the Spanish slaughter of the Indians was duly mentioned.[82] On the more purely political side, its predominant theme was the commitment to the estates, consent, and the right of resistance.

The ruler's power, according to the *Apology*, was always restricted by provincial privileges and the Joyeuse Entrée, which Philip II had sworn to uphold. Nevertheless, the latter and his Spaniards aimed to subject the Low Countries "to a certain simple and absolute bondage, which they call a ful and whole obedience, depriving you altogether of your auncient . . . liberties, that they may dispose of you . . . as his officers have done the poore Indians [and] the people of Calabria, Sicilia, Naples, and Millaine."[83] To prevent this attempt, said the *Apology*, the estates must teach the tyrant the limits of his power. The king hated and wanted to suppress the estates as the tree of privileges and spring of liberty; but to what end have the people privileges "if by the meane of the Estates those priviledges be not maintained and so men feele the effects thereof?"[84] The *Apology* also referred to the nobility's duty in resisting absolutism. As duke of Brabant, Philip II could not tax, introduce soldiers, or do other acts except by consent; having transgressed the conditions of his authority, the nobility and vassals stood to him as did the Spartan ephors to their kings, "to keepe the Kingdome sure" and force the ruler to yield equity.[85]

Apropos of religion, the *Apology* combined firm Protestant conviction with a declared opposition to intolerance and persecution. Nevertheless, it made the pregnant observation to the States General about the Re-

---

[81] The *Apology* was presented to the States General at Delft in December 1580. For the original French text, see *Apologie ou defense de tresillustre Prince, par la grace de Dieu, prince d'Orange*, ed. P. Lacroix, Brussels, 1858, which also includes helpful supplementary documents. It was "ghosted" by others, although obviously expressing Orange's convictions. I cite the *Apology* from the contemporary English translation of 1581, ed. H. Wansink, Leiden, 1969.

[82] *Apology*, 48, 50.   [83] *Ibid.*, 54–5.   [84] *Ibid.*, 96–7.   [85] *Ibid.*, 76–7, 79.

formed churches and their religion: "Such is the state of your countrey, that without the exercise and free use of the sayd Religion, it cannot stand three dayes."[86]

The Act of Abjuration, the edict in which the States General pronounced Philip II's deposition in the name of the revolutionary provinces, contained a similar set of ideas. Interwoven with its historical recital of Spanish lawlessness, violence, and tyranny went a statement of the classic theses of sixteenth-century resistance theory. Thus, princes, said the States General's edict, are made for subjects, not subjects for princes; when the prince molests and oppresses his subjects, aiming at absolute power and at making them slaves, they need no longer obey. Right and reason then require that they renounce him, especially if the estates of a country so decide. In the Netherlands, moreover, the prince's power has always been conditional and based on contracts and agreements to govern in conformity with ancient privileges and liberties. Having violated these conditions, he has legally forfeited his sovereignty. The edict appealed to all of these considerations, as well as to the law of nature and necessity, to conclude that "the king of Spain has by right forfeited his lordship, jurisdiction and inheritance of these provinces."[87]

These significant formulations of the ideology of the Netherlands rebellion obviously owed something to contemporary Huguenot political thought. In the same way as the latter, they blended their revolutionary populism with aristocratic qualifications that stressed the importance and historic role of the estates and nobility in acting for the people or community. Duplessis Mornay, the probable author of the *Vindiciae contra tyrannos*, may well have had a hand in Orange's *Apology*. So also may Hubert Languet, another French Calvinist politician to whom *Vindiciae* has sometimes been ascribed. Both men were friends of Orange and his associates and were with the prince in the Netherlands at the time the *Apology* was written. Their relation to him was still another of the bonds connecting the Huguenot and Dutch revolts. Echoes of the *Vindiciae* appeared too in the Act of Abjuration. Besides employing arguments based on their own historical traditions of ruler limitation, Dutch rebels clearly made use as well of Huguenot monarchomach theories, which, as we have noted, were widely dispersed in the Netherlands.[88]

---

[86] *Ibid.*, 142.

[87] The Act of Abjuration is printed in Kossmann and Mellink, *Texts concerning the revolt of the Netherlands*, 216–28. It was adopted by deputies of Brabant, Gelderland, Zutphen, Flanders, Holland, Zeeland, Utrecht, Friesland, Overyseel, and Mechlin; see Juste, *Histoire des Etats généraux des Pays-Bas*, v. 1, 214–16.

[88] See the preceding discussion in this chapter, and for Mornay's and Languet's relation to William of Orange, Putnam, *William the Silent*, v. 2, 318, 442–8; and C. V. Wedgwood, *William the Silent*, New Haven, 1944, 252. The aristocratic dimension of Dutch resistance theory and the influence of Huguenot thought are stressed in both R. N. C. Hunt, "Some pamphlets of the revolt of the Netherlands against Spain," *English historical review 44*, 175

In contrast to these arguments for resistance, which were the common property of the revolt, the latter's "democratic" phase found scarcely any articulation in political theory or programs. Rebels against Philip II's government were preoccupied with collective rights and liberties, not with individual rights or political equality. Thus there was little appearance in the ideological domain of any formulated democratic aspiration and nothing at all comparable to the English revolution or even to the expressions of radical populism in Paris at the time of the Catholic League's supremacy. One of the few declarations of democratic consciousness in the Netherlands rebellion was a pamphlet in 1581 by a Calvinist who urged that town magistrates be chosen from the entire community of godly people, not just from patricians and notables.[89]

With the disintegration of the Pacification of Ghent, the revolution of the Netherlands passed into its fourth and final stage. Although again forced to fight for its existence, it did so now at least from its base in the provinces, where it was already supreme and which were soon to emerge as an independent republican state in the northern Netherlands. At this point, therefore, the end of the revolution was in sight. More and more in the next few years it became transformed into a military conflict to defend the nascent state's embryonic independence against Spanish reconquest; at the same time, it also became more and more an arena for intervention by Spain's enemies.

While preparing to disavow Philip II, however, Orange and the States General did not believe the rebel provinces could exist without a head or stand alone against the might of Spain. So they turned to France and invited Francis duke of Anjou, Henry III's brother, to assume their rule as means of getting French support. Anjou had already been involved in the Netherlands. An ambitious *politique*, he took on this new venture, aspiring to secure himself a kingdom.

The agreement between him and the States General, concluded in September 1580, was remarkable for the restrictions it imposed. It outlined a constitutional order, embodying the centrality of the estates, consent, and ruler accountability that was the goal of the revolt in its denial of absolutism. Anjou as their prince was obliged to take an oath to the States General and the provinces, pledging to maintain all their privileges, rights, and liberties. He was to convoke the States General annually, although the latter could also meet on its own initiative if necessary. The duke's council of state was to be chosen by the provinces, and he would appoint

(1929), and C. Mercier, "Les Théories politiques des Calvinistes dans les Pays Bas à la fin du XVIᵉ et au début du XVIIᵉ siècle," *Revue d'histoire ecclesiastique 29* (1933).

[89] *A fraternal warning to all Christian brethren* (1581), in Kossmann and Mellink, *Texts concerning the revolt of the Netherlands*, 231–4. The author would also have denied political rights to Catholics, contending that "a man cannot be both a good patriot and a papist."

provincial governors and other officers from a list presented by the provinces. Anjou, one of whose councillors was the philosopher Jean Bodin, pressed to have the name *sovereign* added to the other titles of *prince* and *lord* by which he would be recognized. But the States General adamantly refused, responding that, insofar as *souverain* signified absolute power, it was inconsistent with their government.[90]

Anjou had a short and disastrous career in the liberated provinces. Received in 1582, he resented the limits of his position and quarreled with his subjects, and his French troops abused the local population. That he was a Catholic only added to the Calvinists' suspicion of him. In 1583, he seized some towns in a desperate coup but failed to capture Antwerp. Thoroughly discredited after this, he quit the Netherlands and died soon afterward. The hoped-for assistance from the French crown itself never appeared because Henry III had his hands full with the troubles of the civil war and the defiance of the duke of Guise and ultra-Catholics.

The fiasco of Anjou's intervention emphasized the most serious problem of the revolt: As they moved gradually toward republican independence, the revolutionary provinces affiliated in the Union of Utrecht had no efficient central government or executive body to direct and coordinate their action. The States General performed this function very badly or not at all, for it was much more a mirror of particularist interests and autonomism than an organ of central leadership. In some measure, Orange's prestige and offices offset this lack, but he was constantly troubled by the consequences of weakness and confusion at the center. He remonstrated to the States General on this score, complaining of the absence of unity and the need of a power to take binding decisions for the whole country. Again and again, he warned of the danger of particularist interests to the common cause. "Everyone in his own province or town," he declared, "acts as he thinks is beneficial to himself and his particular affairs without realizing that when some town or province is under attack, it may be useful to help it . . . so that in the end the whole country, including these towns and provinces, may be saved."[91] Under these circumstances, for the provinces to maintain an army and assure its pay, to frame and carry out a policy, and to deal with all the other political and military problems incident to a war of survival was extraordinarily difficult.

<hr>

[90] On the treaty of Plessis-les-Tours whereby Anjou was accepted as prince by the States General, see the documents and discussion in Griffiths, *Representative government in Western Europe*, 492–504, 313–15; and the comments in Mercier, "Les Théories politiques des Calvinistes des Pays Bas à la fin du XVIe et au début du XVIIe siècle." In 1577, at the time of the Pacification of Ghent, when the States General called in Archduke Mathias to replace Don John of Austria, it also imposed considerable restrictions on his authority.

[91] See Orange's Remonstrances to the States General in 1580 and 1581, in Kossmann and Mellink, *Texts concerning the revolt of the Netherlands*, 200–3, 234–6. The quotation is in *ibid.*, 201.

Meanwhile, Spanish power expanded, and the split widened between north and south. Alexander of Parma did not repeat his predecessor's methods of terror. Instead, he used blandishments as well as military force and strove successfully to gain the confidence of the ruling orders. He won back the Catholic nobility of the southern provinces with large bribes of money and offices. He was also authorized to promise the observance of their privileges to the provinces that returned to obedience. In 1579, in accord with the terms of peace with Arras, Hainaut, Artois, and part of Flanders, he dismissed his Spanish troops. Then, in 1581, at the request of the loyal provinces themselves, he recalled them to carry on the war. The army of Flanders increased its strength to over sixty thousand men, and, even though money problems did not vanish, for a time Philip II made adequate provision for pay.[92]

In the period after 1580, Parma achieved a continuous string of victories, as one after another nearly all the rebel-held cities of Flanders and Brabant succumbed. In 1584, Ghent, controlled by the Calvinists since 1577 – "energetic, opulent, powerful, passionate, unruly Ghent," as Motley called the town – surrendered. Brussels, Mechlin, and Bruges were captured, and, in August 1585, Antwerp itself fell to the army of Flanders after a year's siege. These successes restored the southern provinces to the monarchy's possession, while several conquests of towns in Holland and the northeast had already begun the circumscription of the heartland of the revolution.

Along with this series of reverses occurred the calamitous death in July 1584 of William of Orange, murdered in his mansion at Delft by the shots of a Catholic assassin. The prince's dying words were, "My God, have pity on my soul and this poor people." He was fifty-one years old. Orange stood in the highest rank among the revolutionary leaders of his time, an age when men were apt to become rebels inadvertently and in spite of themselves rather than by vocation. Despite being born to a most eminent place in the governing class, circumstances and conviction brought him into resistance to the Spanish monarchy. Once committed, he displayed rare qualities of self-mastery and courage to endure trials, as well as exceptional gifts of political intelligence and leadership. Far more than most men in his situation, he was capable of genuine disinterestedness. In particular, he knew how to respect and cooperate with the spirit and institutions of autonomy that signified liberty in the Low Countries. He resembled those other strong, religious personalities who took a chief part in the

---

[92] For Spanish policy and the progress of reconquest under Parma, see Parker, *The army of Flanders*, 236–43. Between 1580 and 1582, the royal forces increased from forty-five thousand to sixty-one thousand men, of which less than five thousand were Spanish and the rest German and Netherlands troops (*ibid.*, app. A). Maps of Parma's reconquest with dates are given in Parker, *The Dutch revolt*, 210–12.

revolutionary civil wars of early modern Europe, the Huguenot Admiral Coligny and the Puritan Oliver Cromwell, all of them aristocrats whose faith and political creed made them enemies of kingly absolutism.

In the critical situation after Anjou's and Orange's passing, the States General once more sought foreign assistance. Despite many misgivings, it offered the rule of the revolutionary provinces to Henry III of France, who refused from fear of Spain. Then it turned to England. Thus far in her tortuous oscillations of policy, Queen Elizabeth had refrained from open, direct involvement in the revolt and had given it only intermittent support through proxies whom she helped to subsidize. Her purpose, it has been said, concerned primarily with national security, "was to get the Spanish army out of the Netherlands without letting the French in."[93] But now that Parma's advance threatened Spanish reconquest, the English government took the final step. In August 1585, just as Antwerp was about to fall, the queen concluded a treaty with the States General for immediate help to the revolt. She rejected an offer to become the provinces' sovereign but undertook to send and maintain six thousand troops and a great nobleman, the earl of Leicester, as her representative. The latter was to exercise the government in consultation with a council of state.

The Anglo–Dutch treaty intensified the international character of the Netherlands revolution. For England it entailed, despite some further hesitations, an all-out war with Spain. As much as anything, it was the efficient cause of the Spanish Armada three years later, when Philip II launched his great invasion fleet to eliminate once for all the English Protestant ally of his Dutch rebels. The English military intervention in the Low Countries, the Anglo–Spanish war, and the closing phase of the French civil war, when Henry III and his successor Henry of Navarre fought Spain and the pro-Spanish Catholic League, were all interlocking pieces of a single gigantic conflict both national and European in its consequences.

The English alliance, although welcomed as salvation by the Dutch, was quickly engulfed in mistrust and quarrels. The earl of Leicester, an incompetent statesman, bungled his delicate mission badly. Accorded extensive powers by the States General following the treaty, he used them with little regard for provincial autonomy or rights. He became deeply

---

[93] R. B. Wernham, "English policy and the revolt of the Netherlands," 30. This essay discusses the Anglo-Dutch treaty and presents a general defense of Queen Elizabeth's policy. Wilson, *Queen Elizabeth and the revolt of the Netherlands*, "Conclusion" and *passim*, takes the opposite view and passes a severe judgment on the queen's caution, indecision, and half-measures, which he blames for contributing to the division of the Netherlands. An illuminating discussion of the international setting and problems for the English government's policy during the period is found in J. R. Seeley, *The growth of British policy*, 2 v., Cambridge, 1895, v. 1, chs. 6–8.

involved in internal factional divisions on the side of the adversaries of Holland, the wealthiest and most powerful of the provinces, which made the largest contribution to the war. Behind him rallied the supporters of centralism, the lower orders in some of the towns, and the rigid Calvinists, all of whom resented the Holland oligarchs' preponderance and their rejection of the Reformed church's interference in state affairs. By this policy, Leicester converted the States of Holland, the province's representative assembly, dominated by the municipal oligarchies, into a determined opponent of his government. Problems of central authority and of the balance between central power and provincial autonomy remained acute within the revolt, and Leicester's actions only intensified frictions.

One of his bones of contention with the States of Holland was over Dutch trading with the enemy. Such trade was periodically embargoed and regulated by a complicated system of licenses. Leicester, naturally, was opposed to it, seeing no reason why the Hollanders should sell to the enemy. Holland's prosperity, however, depended on trade, part of which went in food and other exports to the Spanish monarchy's subjects in the southern Netherlands as well as to Spain itself. The Hollanders maintained that, if they did not supply this demand, it would turn to other sources and the enemy would remain unharmed anyway. Meanwhile they would lose their trade, whose revenues enabled the province to bear the major cost of the war. Over the years, the Holland regents and merchants stood firmly by this position, which happily combined profits with patriotism.

Militarily, although the beginning of English intervention helped to slow Parma's advance, it achieved no striking victories at first. Indeed, relations with the Dutch were further strained in 1587 after two English commanders betrayed their towns to the Spaniards. Queen Elizabeth did not help matters either by holding back on money and, even worse, by urging the irritated rebels to negotiate with Philip II for a reconciliation. Owing to these and other circumstances, Leicester found himself so hampered and discredited that at the end of 1587 he gave up his post.[94]

The painful experience of Leicester's government finally convinced the revolutionary provinces that they must rule themselves and look no more for a foreign sovereign. It is difficult to identify the exact moment when the new republican state of the United Netherlands, free and independent, actually came into existence. This did not yet happen even after the provinces disavowed Philip II in 1581. First they took the duke of Anjou as their prince, who failed them; next they vainly offered themselves to Henry III of France; then they turned to Queen Elizabeth as their pro-

---

[94] The conflicts, problems, and issues connected with Leicester's tenure as governor are treated in detail in J. den Tex, *Oldenbarnevelt*, 2 v., Cambridge, 1973, v. 1, chs. 1–3.

tector, who declined their sovereignty but sent them Leicester to endure. Only after all these disappointments did they finally opt for self-governing independence.[95]

The emergence of the new state in the northern Netherlands reflected the prepotency of Holland and was accomplished in the decade after 1585. It was mainly the work of John van Oldenbarnevelt (b. 1547), advocate or chief official to the States of Holland, who rose to preeminence as the ablest Dutch statesman during the conflict with Leicester. Oldenbarnevelt dedicated himself to the supremacy of the regent class and has been called by his learned biographer "the founder of the Republic of the United Netherlands."[96] This he was in the sense of having completed what others, most of all William of Orange, had struggled for. He performed this task in collaboration with Orange's youthful son, Prince Maurice, who filled some of his father's provincial offices and took on increasing military responsibilities, while Oldenbarnevelt directed political affairs.

The latter owed his ascendancy not to his office but to his exceptional abilities as administrator, strategist, and politician. Out of the almost indescribable complexity of the provinces' political institutions, with their many local bodies and intricate interplay of centralism and particularism, he fashioned a working government. It was the government of a decentralized republic, a federal union in which supreme authority lay in the States General, the congress of the provincial states, and in which the leadership of Holland, the dominant province, provided unity of policy and direction. It enshrined provincial autonomy and the practices securing it, yet enabled the new state to rise in a short span of years from weakness to a leading position in Europe. The republic was both an oligarchic and a constitutional polity. Power was shared by the provincial states and the States General, which were not popular bodies and owed no accountability to the people. It was their duty to carry on the government and maintain the country's privileges, rights, and freedoms.[97] The doctrine current at the time traced the republic's constitution to the alliance of provinces in the Union of Utrecht in 1579; it also held that formal sovereignty lay in the states. This last was the theme of a treatise written in 1587 by a Dutch jurist, which promptly acquired canonical status. It explained by medieval precedents that the states were and always had been sovereign; that their authority was the keystone safeguarding privileges and freedoms; and that there could be no differences between them and

---

[95] *Ibid.*, chs. 1–4, illuminates this process very interestingly; see also G. N. Clark, "The birth of the Dutch republic," for a helpful discussion.

[96] Den Tex, *Oldenbarnevelt*, v. 1, 166.

[97] *Ibid.*, v. 1, ch. 4, "Independence," provides a characterization of the political basis of his republic. Holland's preponderance, oligarchy, constitutionalism, and the rule of law were all equally prominent. See also the description of Dutch government in Parker, *The Dutch revolt*, 240–8.

the community because they derived their being solely by the commission of their constituents. This jural harmony of oligarchy, constitutionalism, and liberty became the theoretical rationale of the republic.[98]

The birth of independence coincided with the definite shift of the military balance in the republic's favor. After Leicester's departure, England was merely an ally whose representative acted as the English commander in the Netherlands. Prince Maurice became the general of all the fighting forces. By the end of the 1580s, the Spanish offensive had lost its momentum. The Armada required Parma to divert his resources to the south and the Channel coast in accord with Philip II's strategy, and the expedition's failure dealt a hard blow to Spain's morale and military effort. Then, in a further diversion, the king ordered Parma and his soldiers to France to support the Catholic League against the Protestant Henry IV. In 1590, Prince Maurice recaptured Breda, the beginning of a victorious campaign that in the next five years expelled the monarchy's troops from all of Holland and the northeastern provinces. It was in progress when Parma died in 1592. The States General was able to sustain the enormous costs of the war from the growing Dutch prosperity through trade, whereas the Spanish monarchy was increasingly strained for money and forced to divide its efforts between the Netherlands and France, as well as in its war with England. Spain's military involvement in the French civil war in the 1590s was a not inconsiderable factor in the Dutch advance. By 1600, Prince Maurice was already strong enough even to venture an invasion of Flanders in the hope of rousing the Spanish-ruled provinces, but he met with no success. The military situation gradually settled down to a stalemate preceding the cessation of hostilities. The conflict outlasted Philip II's generation. The pious king and world monarch in the Escorial died in 1598, bequeathing the war against the Dutch rebels and heretics to his successor.

VII

In 1609, Spain and the Dutch entered into the Twelve Year truce. It was not a peace because the parties could not agree on outstanding issues. The monarchy, which was not willing even yet to acknowledge rebel freedom or Protestant legitimacy, was led to this step by sheer exhaustion, having already terminated its wars with France and England some years before (1598 and 1604). For the Dutch, the truce meant de facto acceptance of their independence. One of the names that is frequently given to the long

---

[98] See Francis Vranck (or Francken), *A short exposition* (1587), of which an extract is printed in Kossmann and Mellink, *Texts concerning the revolt of the Netherlands*, 274–81. For characterizations of this work, *ibid.*, 49–50; Clark, *The birth of the Dutch republic*, and den Tex, *Oldenbarnevelt*, v. 1, 123, who calls it the "Magna Carta of the mercantile republic."

struggle in the Netherlands is the Eighty Years war. This takes in its entire span, including the Twelve Year truce, its expiration and the revival of hostilities in 1621, and the final settlement of 1648 in the Peace of Münster, when Spain finally accorded the republic of the United Netherlands full de jure recognition.[99] In reality, though, the Eighty Years war was a revolution and civil war that eventually turned into a war between imperial Spain and a Dutch sovereign state. The truce of 1609 sealed the victory of both the revolution and the new state born of its violence.

The revolution and truce left the Netherlands permanently split. Parma's conquests created the foundation of Belgium, the provinces of the Spanish Netherlands. Prince Maurice's victories consolidated the territory of the republic. The boundaries between the two were due to the arbitrament of war, not to ingrained, old, historical differences. The linguistic frontier between Dutch- and French-speaking provinces did not coincide with the political boundary; it ran well to the south of the latter right across the middle of the Spanish Netherlands.[100] Nevertheless, the southern provinces and the republic diverged more and more from each other. The one belonged to a civilization of Catholicism, monarchy, and a court; the other to a civilization of Protestantism, republicanism, and commerce. From this separation and the achievement of independence came a Dutch nation-state; from it also came eventually, although much later, a Belgian nation-state.

The revolution released the independent provinces for their phenomenal economic growth, the admiration and envy of Europe, in which Holland took the commanding part. The economic predominance that the Netherlands had possessed passed from its old centers in the south to others in the north. Amsterdam replaced Antwerp, badly damaged by war and its sea access along the river Scheldt permanently blockaded by rebel power, as a financial capital. A mass of refugees fled from Parma's conquests to Holland and the other free provinces, bringing their labor, skills, and capital. From the outbreak of the revolt to 1609, roughly a hundred thousand people left the Spanish-ruled provinces, many emigrating to the republic and thus contributing to the Dutch economic miracle.[101] The leap of expansion occurred in the 1590s and moved steadily upwards. The Dutch built their prosperity on a huge fishing industry, on their dominance of textile manufacture and export, and on cheap sea

[99] See G. Parker's essay, "Why did the Dutch revolt last eighty years?" *Transactions of the Royal Historical Society*, 5th ser., 26 (1976), for a discussion of the conditions that resulted in the longevity of the conflict.

[100] See Geyl, *History of the Low Countries: Episodes and problems*, ch. 1, for a concise discussion and map with the linguistic boundary of the divided provinces, also printed in the author's *The revolt of the Netherlands*, 180. Parker, *The Dutch revolt*, 229, contains a map recording the course of Dutch conquests.

[101] Parker, *The Dutch revolt*, 250, 254; but see also Chapter 6, n.33 of the present work.

transport and merchant fleets that outdistanced all competitors. They controlled the vital carrying trade between the Baltic and Southern Europe, bringing from Baltic ports grain, iron, and other heavy commodities, returning with herring, salt, and cloth. They pioneered trade routes across the Atlantic, around Africa, and in Asian seas, thus beginning the acquisition of a world commerce and empire in the East and West that directly challenged Spain and its dependent kingdom, Portugal.

Looking back from the 1590s, the basic cause of the revolt was stated by a sage observer, Francis Bacon. Philip II, he wrote, was resolved to reduce the Netherlands to "an absolute monarchy" and "a martial government like unto that which he had established in Naples and Milan, upon which suppression of their liberties ensued the defection of those provinces."[102] This, broadly, was the substance of the conflict, embracing also the issue of Protestantism insofar as the latter was related to political freedom. In its triumphant resistance, the Netherlands revolution became the first in the history of modern Europe to retain power and found a durable regime. Other early modern revolutions seized power but could not keep it. A few aspired to achieve change as great but failed. Only the Netherlands revolt succeeded in doing both.

This was not, of course, the result of conscious plan or intention. The Dutch rebels, although borne up by religious faith, had no design to mold history or change the world. Their political ideas were theoretically unadventurous, magnetized by the ideal of the normative past and indebted to the familiar corpus of principles vindicating the right to resist and remove rulers who become tyrants. They did not cherish novelties or rush headlong to embrace change. Nevertheless, step by step, out of the vicissitudes and experiences of revolt, they arrived at a republican order, a unique combination of old and new, in continuity with but also transcending their earlier history.

The Netherlands revolution resulted in a change of government and a change of regime. Did it also bring about a change of society? Certainly, in a measure, yes. It is tempting, if not entirely right, to speak of the Dutch republic as a bourgeois society and civilization. With monarchy also disappeared the social power of a royal court, dynasticism, and a traditional hereditary nobility of magnate families linked to the ruling house. The family of the prince of Orange alone remained to incarnate a dynastic element that at times during the seventeenth century came into acute conflict with the republic but also rendered it valuable service. A nobility, more numerous in some provinces than others, did continue to exist, but it was of little importance in Holland, the greatest of commercial

---

[102] F. Bacon, *Certain observations upon a libel*, in *Works*, v. 8, 193, 185; see Bacon's *Discourse in praise of the Queen*, in *ibid.*, v. 8, 137, where he repeats this point and compares the Netherlands revolt with the revolt of Aragon.

powers. Moreover, the republic made no provision for ennoblement. The members of the town councils and magisterial patrician strata became the new governing class, a class known collectively as the regents. Nowhere was this more true than in Holland, whose regents as a genuine ruling elite dominated its politics as they did the policy of the republic.

The Dutch republic was a mercantile commonwealth dedicated to business, commerce, finance, and empire and whose unprecedented economic expansion conferred wealth on its enterprising bourgeoisie and capitalists. The regent order had its roots in the bourgeoisie and trade. Yet, as a governing class it became more and more detached from active participation in economic life. Here we find again an example of the immense strength of the aristocratic principle, which irresistibly reproduced itself in the foremost commercial society of Europe. The regents gradually underwent "aristocratization," developing into gentlemen, a quasi-nobility socially and politically distinct from and superior in status to the bourgeoisie and citizens. They occupied themselves with government and in time adopted the attitudes and ways of life appropriate to an aristocratic order.[103]

Notwithstanding this evolution of the Dutch regent elite, the traits of a bourgeois civilization were nevertheless clearly uppermost in the republic. The difference between the northern independent and the southern Spanish-ruled provinces is well symbolized in the contrast between their great painters, the former's Rembrandt and Vermeer, the latter's Rubens and Van Dyck: Protestant subjectivism and domestic sobriety, on the one hand; and sumptuous Catholicism and courtly glorification, on the other. To their contemporaries, the United Provinces were most famed for their mighty trade, their mastery of the sea, their banks and low interest rates, and their industrious population, thriving cities, and agricultural improvements. With these achievements went their reputation for political freedom, for hospitality to refugees, and for a wide religious liberty maintained under the aegis of latitudinarian regent rulers. No state, wrote the Englishman, Sir William Temple, author of one of the most penetrating contemporary accounts of the republic, "was ever born with stronger throws, or nursed up with harder fare, or inured to greater labours or

---

[103] On the social changes connected with the formation of the Dutch republic, the decline of the nobility's position, and the emergence and evolution of the regent governing class, see the discussions by D. Roorda, "The ruling classes in Holland in the seventeenth century," *Britain and the Netherlands 2* (1962), and I. Schöffer, "La Stratification sociale de la république des Provinces Unies au XVIIᵉ siècle," in *Problèmes de stratification sociale: Actes du colloque internationale*, ed. R. Mousnier, Paris, 1968. J. Smit ("The Netherlands revolution," in *Preconditions of revolution in early modern Europe*, ed. R. Forster and J. Greene, Baltimore, 1970, 50, 53; stresses the social consequences of the conflict as a victory of the "bourgeois estates" and an "innovative, progressive, societal revolution."

dangers in the whole course of its youth."[104] To these, the ordeals of rebellion and consolidation of revolutionary power, he rightly ascribed the strength of the republic's prime.

[104] Sir William Temple, "Observations upon the United Provinces of the Netherlands" (1st ed. 1672), *Works*, 4 v., London, 1757, v. I, iii.

I2

*Revolutionary civil war:
the English revolution*

I

"If in time, as in place, there were degrees of high and low, I verily believe that the highest of time would be that which passed between the years of 1640 and 1660."[1] Thus wrote the philosopher Thomas Hobbes in considered judgment of the revolution in England against the Stuart monarchy. The English revolution, although resembling and typologically linked to the other revolutionary civil wars of the age, exceeded them all in numerous respects: the magnitude of its political change; its destruction of a state church and its battles over religious liberty; the breadth and significance of its ideological debates; its stimulus to social and democratic aspiration; its constitution making and republicanism; and its strong arousal of an insurgent radicalism from below. Moreover, the new regime created by the revolution also occupied a place of consequence on the international scene. The revolutionary state, after winning supremacy in England, promptly expanded beyond its limits to impose its conquest upon Scotland and Ireland. It waged war upon the Dutch, pursued colonial ambitions, and was sought by France and Spain as an ally. Nor was it ever vanquished by its enemies. When the revolution finally expired in 1660, with the return of the Stuart monarchy, it expired of bankruptcy, from its own inner failures to achieve a viable settlement.

In November 1640, just as the revolution was getting under way, Hobbes fled England to reside in France because he foresaw, he said, "a disorder comming on." Writing afterward from France, he noted how, before it turned to violence against itself, his country "was boiling hot with questions concerning the rights of dominion and the obedience due from subjects, the true forerunners of an approaching war." He lamented, too, the

---

[1] T. Hobbes, *Behemoth* (1679), in *English works*, v. 6, London, 1840, 165.

inroads that had been made by false political principles. "How many kings," he asked,

hath this one error, that a tyrant king might lawfully be put to death, been the slaughter of? How many throats hath this false position cut, that a prince for some causes may by some certain men be deposed? And what bloodshed hath not this erroneous doctrine caused, that kings are not superiors to, but administrators for the multitude?[2]

These populist beliefs stigmatized by Hobbes for their pernicious consequences are more or less familiar to us. We have met them already as part of the ideological armory of Huguenot and Dutch rebels, who had been among the first to give them extensive currency. The revolts in France and the Netherlands had run their course a half-century before England's began. But the three were akin in their combat against kings and absolutism, and the revolutionary tradition the two former helped to engender was powerfully reinforced and amplified by their successor.

The revolution began with the opening of the Long Parliament at Westminster on November 3, 1640. From its meeting sprang the immediate assault on the institutions of royal power in church and state. From its actions ensued the sequence of events that amputated royal authority, brought on armed struggle against Charles I in less than two years, and led after his defeat to the abolition of kingship and the House of Lords, the creation of a republic, and a series of political and constitutional experiments.

The genesis of the revolution involved some general features paralleling the earlier conflicts in France and the Netherlands. In England also, revolt was preceded by a shattering crisis of authority that undermined obedience and subverted the king's ability to rule. By 1640, a polarization had taken place between absolutism and its opponents that exhibited all the hallmarks of a revolutionary situation. Religion performed a similar seditious function, as Puritanism, Calvinism's English offspring, added its redoubtable strength to the alignment against the crown. As elsewhere, a large proportion of the governing class, the aristocratic order of nobility and gentry, had become alienated from the king's rule by his methods and policy. It was men belonging to this class who gave voice to the kingdom's griefs and headed the opposition that culminated in revolt.

Alongside these parallels, though, there were several features that made for consequential differences in the revolution of 1640–60 and its background.

By the early seventeenth century, England was a cohesive national state, better unified and integrated than any in Western Europe. The predeces-

[2] P. Zagorin, "Thomas Hobbes's departure from England in 1640: An unpublished letter," *Historical journal 20*, 1 (1978), 160; T. Hobbes, *De cive*, in *English works*, v. 2, London, 1841, xx.

sors of the Stuart dynasty had eliminated all internal rivals and established a comprehensive, unchallenged supremacy. The crown did not need to reckon with a still only partially subdued high nobility or to contend with autonomous provinces and their privileges. Central administration reached into all parts of the kingdom; local government was well harnessed to the royal state and its directives.

These characteristics were reflected in the character of the dominant class. Those of the aristocratic order, such as the elites who provided the greatest number of members in Parliament after Parliament and who also voluntarily served the crown in the higher offices of county administration, were becoming politically sophisticated. Indeed, they had evolved by the later years of Queen Elizabeth's reign into what might be called a national political class. They were now apt to be better educated than ever before. Increasingly, such men attended Oxford or Cambridge, made the continental tour, and spent some time in London at the Inns of Court, the center of the lawyers' professional and social life.[3] They were acquainted with public affairs and had come to share a genuine national horizon. Although imbued with ideals of obedience and service to the prince, they also felt a more impersonal loyalty to the state or commonwealth as exemplified in Parliament, the representative body of the realm. Only if such facts are borne in mind is it possible to understand how, with the rapid disintegration of the monarchical constitution after 1640, the opponents of Charles I were ready and able to assume the control of government.

In citing these considerations we should not forget, of course, that provincialism also remained a pervasive element in English society, as many regional and local studies of early modern England have shown. The shared interests and internal politics of county and urban communities interacted with and sometimes affected national politics. They exerted an effect upon the English revolution, too.[4] But it is important not to exaggerate or misconceive the influence of provincialism by the mid-seventeenth century. This is surely done when a leading student of the subject, in his zeal to correct an exclusively nationally focused history, goes so far as to say that "despite its ancient centralized government, the England of 1640 resembled a union of partially independent county-states or communities, each with its distinctive ethos and loyalty."[5] Such a description clearly overstates the case and in essence fits French provinces or Spanish regionalism

---

[3] See L. Stone, "The educational revolution in England, 1560–1640," *Past and present 28* (1964); W. R. Prest, *The Inns of Court under Elizabeth I and the early Stuarts 1590–1640*, London, 1972, chs. 1–2.

[4] R. Richardson, *The debate on the English revolution*, London, 1977, ch. 7, reviews some of the regional and local studies in connection with the revolution of 1640–1660, and is helpful also for its survey of other branches of the historical literature devoted to the subject.

[5] A. Everitt, *The community of Kent and the great rebellion 1640–1660*, Leicester, 1966, 13.

far better than English counties. Writers of this same school of thought similarly err when they try to explain the revolution of 1640 as though it were primarily an explosion of localist resistance to the central government.[6]

In England, provincialism coexisted in definite subordination with the national polity. It lacked the disruptive tendencies provincialism elsewhere persistently manifested. It was not fortified by legal immunities and could not graft itself upon local institutions like the French *parlements* or provincial estates. No county enjoyed autonomy or aspired to independence of the central government. There had been no provincial rebellion in England since the small insurrection in the north in 1569.[7] Even the relations and concerns binding leading country gentlemen to their communities expressed something beyond a merely old-fashioned, obstructive localism. They signified, rather, within the dominant context of the national polity, a conception of the proper balance between the central government and communities, so that the latter should not be unduly burdened or oppressed. This attitude was not inconsonant with a wider outlook upon the kingdom's interests; nor was it inconsistent with an opposition among county notables to Charles I's acts that transcended localism in being also based in part on general constitutional and political grounds.[8]

The role of Parliament was another distinctive feature in the background to the revolution of 1640. I have already referred in an earlier chapter to the position of the English Parliament and to some of the ways it differed from other representative assemblies.[9] Of course, it met only intermittently when and for as long as the king willed. In the earlier seventeenth century, it met in 1601, 1604–10 (five sessions), 1614, 1621, 1624, 1625, 1626, 1628–9, and twice in 1640. The longest intervals between successive Parliaments were thus seven and eleven years; the second of

[6] For examples of this view, see J. S. Morrill, *The revolt of the provinces*, London, 1976, and the papers by I. Roots and A. Everitt in E. W. Ives (ed.), *The English revolution 1600–1660*, London, 1968.

[7] See Chapter 9 in this book.

[8] J. S. Morrill, in an interesting discussion of the revolution from a provincialist standpoint, argues that the gentry opposed Charles I's policy not on constitutional and political grounds but largely because of its effects on local communities (*The revolt of the provinces*, 28, 30). This is very doubtful. What made opposition so dangerous before 1640, and carried it beyond provincialist limitations, was precisely that it could justify itself with constitutional arguments. The latter were essential in inspiring and legitimating the refractoriness of both the governing class and local communities to the king's demands. The same objection invalidates the contention that members of the governing class "almost always put concern for their own counties above any concept of the national interest" (C. Russell, *Parliament and English politics 1621–1629*, Oxford, 1979, 8). For an account of the linkage between county provincialism and national grievances in the case of Kent, see P. Clark, "Thomas Scott and the growth of urban opposition to the early Stuart regime," *Historical journal 21*, 1 (1978), and *English provincial society from the Reformation to the Revolution: Religion, politics and society in Kent 1500–1640*, Hassocks, 1977, chs. 11–12.

[9] See Chapter 4 in this book.

these, however, was most unusual in that it was a direct result of the quarrel between the crown and the House of Commons in the previous meeting in 1629. Even though it was not a permanent part of the government, however, the monarch had to turn to Parliament for direct taxes, to enact statutes, as well as for various consultative needs from time to time. And, despite its intermittency and dependence on royal summons, Parliament showed an awareness of its unique position in the polity that became, if anything, more pronounced in the early Stuart reigns; it possessed no less its own corporate memory, traditions, precedents, privileges, procedures, and official records, which gave its periodic meetings a persisting institutional life and continuity.

A number of recent writers have criticized previous studies of Elizabethan and early Stuart Parliaments for concentrating unduly on opposition, conflict, and confrontation with the crown at the expense of cooperation and consensus; they have stressed that Parliament's function was not primarily political; and they have attributed to historians both of Parliament and of the English revolution a false teleological conception that treats parliamentary developments as an irresistible advance toward supremacy culminating inevitably in political breakdown and civil war.[10]

These views claiming to put parliamentary history in the right perspective are themselves badly askew; were they applied consistently, as of course they cannot be, the parliamentary history of the earlier seventeenth century and the beginning of the revolution against Charles I, whose center was Parliament, would be incomprehensible.

Much as harmony and cooperation may have been the desired ideal, they were giving way in the Parliaments of James I and Charles I to serious quarrels and disagreements with the crown. This was why the Parliaments of the period passed so comparatively little legislation and, in the case of certain Parliaments, none at all. It was opposition, not accommodation, discord, not consensus, that predominated in most of the early Stuart Parliaments. The fact is so plain that revisionist scholars are compelled to acknowledge it themselves as soon as they turn from contentious generalities to the chronicle of parliamentary transactions.[11]

[10] For several statements of this revisionist position, see C. Russell, "Parliamentary history in perspective 1604–1629," *History 61*, 20 (1976), and *Parliament and English politics 1621–1629*, ch. 1; K. Sharpe, "Parliamentary history 1603–1629: In or out of perspective?" in *Faction and Parliament*, ed. K. Sharpe, Oxford, 1978; J. P. Kenyon, *Stuart England*, London, 1978, 32–6. An earlier expression of these views was G. R. Elton's essay, "A high road to civil war?" in *From the Renaissance to the Counter-Reformation: Essays in honor of Garrett Mattingly*, ed. C. H. Carter, New York, 1965. Among criticisms of the current revisionism, see the articles by J. H. Hexter, "Power struggle, parliament and liberty in early Stuart England," and D. Hirst, "Unanimity in the Commons, aristocratic intrigues, and the origins of the English civil war," both in *Journal of modern history 50*, 1 (1978).

[11] Many of the facts and particular discussions contained in C. Russell's *Parliament and English politics 1621–1629* are clearly at variance with its interpretive generalizations playing

Opposition in Parliament was not only vocal, it was organized and tended to grow stronger, as contemporaries noticed. Were this not so, it would be impossible to explain why the crown ran into such difficulties managing Parliament, why it tried so hard to influence parliamentary elections in its favor, why both James I and Charles I imprisoned leading members for their conduct, and why they were forced to resort to precipitous dissolutions.

Nor is there any assumption of teleology in observing, as contemporaries also did, that Parliament and the House of Commons in particular sought to expand their political influence and authority with new claims, procedural devices, and demands and that the Commons in the name of its privileges frequently infringed upon the crown's prerogatives and powers. (The revisionist claim that the House of Commons was a weak and ineffectual body, incapable of independent initiative and pulled by the strings of noble patrons in the House of Lords, is too unfounded to warrant any serious consideration.)

Moreover, the view that Parliament met not primarily for political purposes but to do the kingdom's business is decidedly one-sided, considering the numerous episodes when it *was* concerned with politics. Indeed, there was no way for such an institution, whatever else it was, not to be political. The declaration of grievances, bargaining over financial demands, and controversies with the crown often involved politics. It was from political reasons that the House of Commons devoted four days in 1610 to an unprecedented debate on impositions in which members denied the king's authority to increase customs duties without the consent of Parliament. Political differences appeared no less clearly in discussions of foreign policy in 1621 and in the historic debates on the limits of royal power in the Parliament of 1628 preceding the Petition of Right. Political animosity actuated some of the parliamentary attacks on royal officials and ministers. So much was politics at stake in the period that one of the biggest fears troubling members in the Parliaments of the later 1620s was that this great institution might not survive on account of royal dissatisfaction with its behavior.[12]

down political differences and opposition and underestimating the role of Parliament. This work, a perceptive survey of the Parliaments of the 1620s, is nevertheless not free of special pleading and of misrepresentations of the views it criticizes. Similarly, J. P. Kenyon's complaint about undue emphasis on conflict and confrontation cannot be easily reconciled with his following observation about the "breakdown of general cooperation which worried James I and irritated Charles I" (*Stuart England*, 33), nor with other subsequent discussions in the text. In the volume of essays edited by K. Sharpe, *Faction and Parliament*, the editor's own attempt to get parliamentary history into perspective by getting politics and opposition out is immediately followed by another essay on James I and "the growth of mutual distrust" between the king and the Commons.

[12] Some aspects of opposition and parliamentary politics are surveyed in P. Zagorin, *The court and the country*, London, 1969, ch. 4. The fears for Parliament's survival are strongly emphasized by Russell, *Parliament and English politics 1621–1629*, 54–5 and *passim*.

Parliament served as a prime forum for the governing class and as a significant object of attention for public opinion and the political nation. Along with the temporal nobility in the House of Lords, the House of Commons (which in 1640 had more than 500 members from 259 constituencies) was an aristocratic assembly composed mostly of landed gentlemen diversified by a small proportion (perhaps 20–25 percent) of lawyers, officials, and merchants. The gentry predominated in the representation not only of the counties but also of the boroughs and towns.

A venerable doctrine held that every Englishman was present in Parliament either personally or by proxy. But this formal theory of representation was being reinforced in the earlier seventeenth century by an increasing preoccupation in the House of Commons with its special representative relation to both constituencies and the country as a whole. On the one hand, members expressed a strong constituency consciousness, speaking of their duty to those who had sent them, implying even some idea of accountability. On the other hand, they dwelt equally on their duty to the kingdom, its liberty and welfare. Sometimes these obligations even seemed to take precedence over those to the crown.[13]

By the 1620s, a wider public concern with Parliament and its activities was increasingly manifest. The frequency of parliamentary meetings during the decade encouraged this trend. Notwithstanding a restrictive franchise and a skewed electoral system resulting in the underrepresentation of the commercial and manufacturing sectors of the population, the size of the electorate was also expanding. While additional boroughs gained the right to send members to Parliament, the ancient property qualification for the county franchise was being eroded by inflation, thus enabling more people to vote. The House of Commons itself consistently supported a wider franchise in particular constituencies on the ground of "common right." The electorate accordingly had not only increased by 1640 but also probably extended somewhat lower down the economic scale.[14]

The heightened attention to Parliament was equally reflected in the growing circulation of copies of speeches and of news letters reporting parliamentary affairs. Concurrently, contests in constituencies for seats between rival candidates, although still exceptional, multiplied rapidly. This in turn induced candidates to vie more for popular support and also led bigger numbers to vote. Greater participation in elections probably

[13] Zagorin, *The court and the country*, ch. 4; D. Hirst, *The representative of the people? Voters and voting under the early Stuarts*, Cambridge, 1975, introduction.

[14] Hirst, *The representative of the people?* treats this subject in detail. He estimates the total electorate in 1641 at about 300,000, out of a population of over 4 million, or between 27 percent and 40 percent of the adult male population. Unfortunately, he does not give equivalent figures for an earlier date in order to estimate the increase. Although all these numbers are tentative and subject to error, there can be no doubt of the growth of the electorate.

helped to promote political awareness and knowledge at the same time that it caused people to look even more to Parliament for action upon grievances. Election contests sometimes involved political issues rather than merely personal rivalries. Voters would then make the election an occasion for voicing their resentments by their rejection of a "courtier" candidate, that is, one who seemed too closely related to the Court.

Political differences and discontents in the beginning of Charles I's reign, when three successive Parliaments were called in 1625, 1626, and 1628, resulted in a keener interest in their meetings than ever before. The elections to the Parliament of 1628 brought a high in electioneering activity and the prominence of political issues, voter turnout, and demonstrations of hostility to the king's government. The elections in the spring and fall of 1640 to the Short and the Long Parliaments, held in a time of unprecedented crisis and of the greatest political excitement ever, surpassed even those of 1628 in all these respects. They also saw a record number of contests: At least sixty constituencies were contested in the spring and eighty in the fall, whereas the peak in the 1620s had been about forty.[15]

The development of political opposition in both Parliament and the nation is thus one of the inescapable realities of the period. Certainly, Parliament was never a revolutionary body prior to 1640. Even in its sharpest clashes with the crown, it never thought of or aspired to supremacy. Nevertheless, it showed itself far more refractory to royal control than its predecessors, and it repeatedly exceeded the limits within which the king wanted to confine it. Parliament's aggressive conduct provoked the crown's anger and concern, as it boldly challenged and attacked royal policies. Striving to extend its privileges, Parliament insisted on its right to debate and offer counsel on any matter affecting the nation's interests. Subjects turned to it more decidedly than ever before to express their grievances and to champion liberty and law. Without Parliament's crucial institutional role and political centrality, the movement against the Stuart monarchy would have been an entirely different thing than what it was.

II

The English revolution has been more intensively studied and discussed than any other prior to France's in 1789 and has received a variety of interpretations. To understand its inception, therefore, it will be well to state summarily what it was not.

Conformable to what I have said in earlier chapters about revolutionary civil wars and the deficiencies in the conception of the bourgeois revolu-

---

[15] *Ibid.*, pt. 2, discusses elections and their political impact; for figures on election contests, *ibid.*, 111–12 and app. 4.

tion, the revolution of 1640–60 was neither a class struggle, nor a bid for supreme power by a bourgeoisie, nor a conflict dictated by antithetical economic interests. Naturally enough, England in the earlier seventeenth century harbored many social and economic frictions; we have seen some of them manifested in the several agrarian outbreaks of the period.[16] But these antagonisms were both circumscribed and relatively unimportant. Such as they were, they were either overshadowed or absorbed within the general political polarization that had come about by 1640.

Nor was the revolution the inevitable culmination of a lengthy anteced-ent process of broad social change, as different scholars have wished to believe. Although the century before 1640, as I have previously pointed out, probably saw an exceptional degree of social mobility, this fact can-not explain the revolt against Charles I. Thus, the latter was not due to the "decline of the gentry" (which never happened), or to the "rise of the gentry" (which did happen but was only indirectly, if at all, related to the revolution's genesis). Neither was it a consequence of the "crisis of the aristocracy" (which also never happened and is merely an overdramatized description of a lengthy phase of adaptation by the titular nobility to an altered economic and political environment). Arguments, as we have seen, to connect the revolution with earlier long-term social trends and *conjonc-ture* have been singularly weak in demonstrating any genuine linkage be-tween the two.[17] However we construe these trends, it is fairly apparent that English society in the sixteenth and earlier seventeenth centuries re-mained fundamentally stable amid the changes it experienced: It certainly suffered no significant structural modifications or displacements, nor any disruptive economic innovations, to sow the seeds for the assault against the Stuart monarchy.

The revolution of 1640 grew out of the resistance to absolutism in a breakdown of government and regime. Its origin, as also its prevalent character at its inception, lay in the division between the Court and the Country, a conflict that signified the decline of the aristocratic governing class's support of the crown and the emergence within it of a fateful dis-affection.

The political system the Tudors created in the sixteenth century was based on the symbiotic relationship between the monarchy and aristo-cratic order through a reciprocity of patronage and service. Nobility and gentry were united in loyal submission to the prince, to whose govern-

[16] See Chapter 7 in this book.

[17] See Chapter 5 in this book. For a discussion of social interpretations of the English revolution, see the papers collected in L. Stone (ed.), *Social change and revolution in England 1540–1640*, London, 1965. Stone's *The causes of the English revolution 1529–1642*, London, 1972, contains an eclectic account of the social trends that allegedly underlay the revolution and greatly exaggerates their scale and impact, esp. 110–12, 134.

ment their cooperation was essential.[18] In James I's time, this system was exhibiting considerable strain; during Charles I's it broke down. *Court* and *Country* were terms that first became current in the 1620s, notably in Parliament, a pair of opposites exposing the germinating schism in the body politic.

Court referred loosely and vaguely to the crown and central government, its officials, dependents, and adherents, and to those associated with it by private and personal interest. *Country* designated the antithesis, men supposed free from or uncorrupted by court connection, who stood equally for their local community, the county or "country," and for the highest good of the "country" or kingdom as a whole. Devotion to community and nation alike was here combined in the one laden word, *Country*. In the House of Commons, members who opposed the court or crown were said to be "of" and "for" the "Country," and opposition noblemen in the House of Lords were sometimes called "country lords."[19]

The Court and the Country thus served to indicate divergent political positions or tendencies. They were not party labels, for nothing like parties existed, but they did suggest a spectrum of differences that increasingly diverged. The Court and a "courtier" in the controversies of the 1620s often implied partisanship, faction, and corrupt interest. The Country, in contrast, meant public spirit, patriotism, and dedication to the commonwealth. Opponents of the Court were seen in particular as champions of the liberty and privileges of Parliament and subjects. The Country, according to a contemporary writer, consisted of members of Parliament who believed that

being chosen for the Country, they are to be all for the Country, for the Liberty of the Subject, for the freedome of Speech, & to gain as much and as many Priviledges for the Subject from the King as is possible . . . then they are excellent Patriots, good Commonwealthsmen, they have well & faithfully discharg'd the trust reposed in them by their City or Country.[20]

It was members of this kind who came down hard on the theme of representation. When supporters of the Country opposition in the House of Commons declared, "Wee serve here for thousands and tenn thousands," "Let us remember that England sent us," "It concerns us to preserve the Countrey in freedom," and "We are entrusted for our country. If we lose our privileges, we betray it," they were envisaging the freedom of Parliament, communities, and commonwealth as a single, indissoluble whole.[21]

The distinction between the Court and the Country also tended to gather contrasting moral, religious, and even cultural overtones around itself. We

[18] See Chapter 4 in this book. [19] See Zagorin, *The court and the country*, 32–9. [20] Cited in *ibid.*, 37. [21] Cited in *ibid.*, 86–7.

have seen earlier that there was a vigorous tradition of anti-Court and anticourtier criticism, which was the negative and disillusioned side of the celebration of courtiership under absolute kings.[22] This found expression, too, in the burgeoning differences of the Court and the Country. The Court in this sense stood for corruption, the Country for virtue; the Court for urban sophistication and dangerous pleasures, the Country for rural simplicity and innocent enjoyments; the Court for addiction to novelty, the Country for fidelity to tried ways; the Court for crypto-Catholicism, the Country for stouthearted Protestantism.[23]

The growing currency of these names in the 1620s, premising tension and strife between Court and Country, was the symptom of a momentous political transition. It denoted the threatened dissolution of the organic political order binding the governing class to the crown. For men to conceive of the Country in opposition to the Court meant the opening of a rift in the political nation. It meant that the crown was no longer assumed to be the supreme embodiment of an integral authority. It revealed disunion, with the monarchy itself becoming a partisan in the quarrel in public life.

The Country first took shape as an opposition to the crown in Parliament. Neither it nor the Court were at all clearly defined blocs but rather fluid, diffuse, shifting groupings or alliances indicative of a certain political orientation or position. The Country, however, exhibited some resemblance to a party insofar as it contained an organized nucleus of activists who joined together to pursue their aims. They held private consultations and meetings to concert strategy, agreed on speeches and motions, and articulated general grievances. This was in the House of Commons, but they were also associated with some peers in the House of Lords who shared their views. Through their activity, oppositionist spokesmen achieved an influence in the Commons that undermined the parliamentary ascendancy and management of the king's ministers. Some of these Country adherents had further connections with each other outside Parliament. They were affiliated by family or friendship, engaged in business ventures together, and tended to share a similar Puritanism in religion. After Charles I in his displeasure dissolved Parliament in 1629 and refrained from calling another for eleven long years, this core of oppositionist politicians continued to exist. Those who belonged to it sat in 1640 in the Long Parliament, where their parliamentary expertise and previous expe-

[22] See Chapter 4 in this book. C. Uhlig, *Hofkritik im England des Mittelalters und der Renaissance*, Berlin, 1973, contains a good survey of the English anticourt literature; see also Zagorin, *The court and the country*, 43–7.

[23] See Zagorin, *The court and the country*, ch. 3; the discussion in Stone, *The causes of the English revolution*, 105–7; and P. Thomas, "Two cultures? Court and Country under Charles I," in *The origins of the English civil war*, ed. C. Russell, London, 1973.

rience of cooperation enabled them to assume its direction and management.[24]

Beyond Parliament, the dissension between the Court and the Country gradually affected the greater part of the political nation and kingdom. In some places, the Country was sustained by networks of gentry and urban oppositionists and by groups of Puritan sympathizers; moreover, besides organized manifestations of opposition, the king's rule frequently goaded subjects into spontaneous acts of defiance. If the government retained the support of London's financial tycoons, who were royal creditors and beneficiaries of its economic concessions, the bourgeois and commercial sectors as a whole became more and more hostile. As the anger of elites and communities against royal pressures intensified, the Court–Country difference developed into a fundamental split incorporating diverse tensions and grievances. By the close of the 1630s, the Court appeared to be ever more isolated, whereas the Country embraced nearly all of the governing class backed by massive general discontent.

Alienation from the Court stemmed from a whole series of royal actions that reinforced each other in their cumulative effects. For ten years until he was assassinated in 1628, the duke of Buckingham, supreme favorite of James I and Charles I, held a monopoly over power and patronage that aroused bitter intracourt jealousies and hatred at large. With singular ineptitude, the monarchy also contrived to get into wars with both Spain and France at the same time. English military efforts incurred nothing but failure abroad, and they bred a multiplicity of burdens and grievances at home. Parliament showed its distrust by refusing Charles I at his accession the usual grant of the customs revenue, which he continued to collect anyway, to the accompaniment of repeated charges of illegality. The House of Commons sought by means of impeachment to bring down the detested favorite Buckingham and turned a deaf ear to royal demands for money for the war. In 1627, the king in his financial straits and with a war on his hands commanded a forced loan from his subjects under threat of punishment. Although most complied, some refused, and about seventy gentlemen who declined to give were jailed without a legal cause shown.

These quarrels were further inflamed by religious controversies. Charles I identified himself with a new school of clergy, the Arminians, who were the agents of an Anglo-Catholic reaction in the national church. Whatever the various differences existing between Puritans and non-Puritans, the English church had been at one for over sixty years in its acceptance of the doctrine of predestination. The Arminians repudiated this doctrine, the keystone of Protestant orthodoxy, affirming instead that men had free will to cooperate with God in attaining salvation. They also pro-

[24] Zagorin, *The court and the country*, ch. 4.

moted ritualistic innovations redolent of Roman Catholicism, emphasized the sacrament over preaching, and claimed a spiritual jurisdiction for the bishops over the laity by divine ordinance. Although they were not much more than a small minority, the king gave the Arminians such preferment that they gradually came to dominate the church and episcopate. In turn, they preached in behalf of every royal command, exalting absolutism and proclaiming submission to the king's will as a religious duty. Considering Puritanism, moreover, as equivalent to rebellion, they set themselves by every means to silence it.[25]

The rise of the Arminians fomented a new division in the state church with dangerous political consequences. Puritanism was an old, deeply entrenched element in English religion which, despite periodic repression, could never be eradicated. Puritan ministers and their lay sympathizers still hoped for further reformation and persisted in various demonstrations of nonconformity. The Arminian ascendancy infuriated Puritans at the same time that it aroused the dislike and suspicion of earnest middle-of-the-road Protestants. It united both in opposition. The Arminians were fiercely denounced in Parliament for their innovations and provoked the wrath of the laity by their clericalist pretensions. A considerable body of opinion regarded Arminianism as nothing less than apostasy. Its ritualism, sacerdotalism, and rejection of predestination were commonly viewed as a betrayal of Protestantism and the entering wedge of popery. By favoring Arminianism's clerical adherents, the king only brought further hostility upon his government.

All these compounded frictions came to a head in a first big political crisis in 1628–9, foreshadowing the later crisis in 1640. The Parliament of 1628 met amid widespread protest and complaint, determined not to grant Charles I any money without redress of urgent grievances. Its insistence finally compelled the king to consent to the Petition of Right, a solemn reaffirmation of the right of subjects under Magna Carta and other old laws to be free of such injustices as forced loans and arbitrary imprisonment by royal command. Nevertheless, after the petition's passage, fresh quarrels arose over Arminianism and the denial of the king's right to the customs. These controversies caused a further confrontation in the session of 1629, which climaxed in an unprecedented scene of disorder in the House of Commons followed by Parliament's immediate dissolution. Charles imprisoned the most defiant members and vowed never to summon another Parliament.[26]

In a declaration published in 1629 after the dissolution, the king pro-

---

[25] *Ibid.*, 188–92; N. Tyacke, "Puritanism, Arminianism and counter-revolution," in Russell, *The origins of the English civil war.*
[26] The most recent account of the Parliament of 1628–9 is Russell's *Parliament and English politics 1621–1629*, chs. 6–7.

vided an involuntary testimonial to oppositionist strength in Parliament. He berated the House of Commons for its actions in recent years to extend its authority and privileges beyond all proper bounds by unprecedented invasions of royal prerogatives. He blamed these aggressions upon the sway exercised in the House by bold and ill-affected members. Never again, he said, would he permit such innovations, whose aim was to break through "all respects and ligaments of government" in order to usurp the power of the crown.[27]

Traces of this first crisis lingered briefly in scattered outbursts of disobedience and a cessation of exports by London merchants to protest the royal collection of customs dues without parliamentary authorization. The government soon surmounted these difficulties, however, and a period of relative quiet ensued. The wars with Spain and France were ended, thereby removing a main cause of expense. To all appearances, royal power remained invulnerable, and it exerted itself in the next years more forcibly than ever in many directions. Certain ministers of state, William Laud, the Arminian archbishop of Canterbury, and Thomas Wentworth earl of Strafford, president of the council in the north and governor of Ireland, with their slogan "Thorough," became in a high degree the detested symbols of a severe and unpopular rule.

Under the surface, nevertheless, discontents festered. The crown's numerous devices to extort money by exploiting its prerogative, its invasive weight upon county society, and its persecution of Puritan nonconformity vexed and angered subjects. Many groups and economic interests, gentry landlords, tenants, trading associations, and consumers, felt the adverse effects of the king's measures. Gradually all were welded into a common animosity against his government. By no coincidence, this decade saw the start of the great Puritan migration to New England under the auspices of the Massachusetts Bay Company, an enterprise founded by friends and adherents of the Country opposition. As did the Calvinist exiles who left the Netherlands, about twenty thousand Englishmen abandoned their native land between 1629 and 1640 for a new life and religious reformation in the American wilderness.

Then, toward the end of the 1630s, opposition raised its head again with renewed vigor, the prelude to a far bigger crisis to come than the earlier one of 1628–9. Its revival was due in particular to the introduction of ship money, a tax that the king first imposed on the maritime counties and then extended in 1635 into an annual exaction levied on the whole kingdom. The government justified this tax as necessary to maintain a fleet for defense at sea. Broad public sentiment nevertheless opposed it as downright unlawful because demanded without approval of Parliament.

[27] Printed in S. R. Gardiner (ed.), *The Constitutional documents of the Puritan revolution*, 3rd rev. ed., Oxford, 1936, 83–99.

Apart from constitutional objections, ship money also had an exceptionally heavy incidence. It was, in fact, a covert direct tax, which obliged many more people to pay than did previous imposts. A grievance to small tenants and lesser folk, a burden on communities, and an affront to legally minded gentlemen, it inevitably ran into increasing obstruction and resistance.

Ship money completed the alienation of the Country from the Court. Beyond any other measure, it was taken as conclusive evidence of the king's intention to consolidate absolutism. As head of the body politic, the crown in any case possessed a very ample supremacy and broad prerogatives. Included in the latter, as we have seen earlier, was a domain of discretionary absolute power that placed the king above the law when he dealt with what were called matters of state and policy. This was the received judicial opinion most recently reaffirmed in 1637 in connection with ship money. In a momentous court trial arising from the refusal of a leading Country oppositionist to pay, the majority judgment upheld the tax, several judges justifying it as an exercise of the king's "absolute power" for the safety of the realm, a power, they said, not limited by rules of law or the property rights of subjects. This was merely the reiteration of an old doctrine concerning the nature of the royal office but one that was now restated in the most highly controversial circumstances.[28]

If the monarchy were able to acquire an acknowledged right to lay a direct general charge on its subjects, its financial independence might be permanently secured. What need in that case would it ever again have for Parliament? In 1626, a Court spokesman warned the House of Commons that its opposition would cause the king to adopt "new counsels" spelling the extinction of Parliament. He reminded the members that in all Christian kingdoms parliaments had once existed; but at last, incensed by their turbulent spirit, the monarchs overthrew them all, so that England's alone survived. He therefore begged the Commons not to put the king out of love with Parliament by trenching on royal prerogatives. Charles I himself declared that the existence of Parliament depended entirely on his will and that as he found its fruits good or evil it was to continue to be or not.[29] It was this fear of Parliament's extinction that haunted members and Country oppositionists in the 1620s and that seemed to have come to pass after 1629. By one means and another, the monarchy in the 1630s was freeing itself of residual constraints upon its absolutism. Ship money was a giant step toward this end, investing the royal state as it did with a significant taxing power independent of Parliament's consent.

[28] M. Judson, *The crisis of the constitution*, New Brunswick, 1949, ch. 4, gives an account of the doctrine of the king's absolute power as expounded by lawyers and judges; see also Zagorin, *The court and the country*, 84–5; and Chapter 4 in this book.

[29] Zagorin, *The court and the country*, 87.

Possibly the king might have succeeded in the course his government pursued had it not been for the outbreak in 1638 of revolution in Scotland, which decisively affected the situation in England. Charles had created serious grievances in Scotland, too, and they were brought to the boiling point when he tried to impose a new liturgy more resembling England's upon the Scottish church. This egregious English interference with Scotland's religion precipitated a provincial rebellion whose symbol became the Scottish National Covenant.[30]

In 1639, the king raised an army to suppress the Covenanters' resistance, but it was a disaffected body with little inclination to fight. Desperately requiring English support at this critical juncture, he decided, notwithstanding his earlier resolutions, to hold a Parliament, which met in April 1640. He then discovered how far he had lost the loyalty of his English subjects. Parliament showed itself more favorable to the Scottish rebels than to royal needs. When the House of Commons declined to provide money and even threatened under opposition leadership to condemn the war against the Scots, Parliament was precipitously dissolved after sitting only three weeks.

The king then went forward with his military efforts, only to see his army retreat in disarray before stronger Scottish troops, who invaded England in August 1640 and occupied the northern counties. In this emergency, a call went up throughout the realm for the summons of Parliament. Helpless, Charles had to submit, and the writs were issued for a new Parliament to meet in November.

The Scottish rebellion thus released a parallel and unexampled crisis in England. The crown suffered a catastrophic loss of authority. Its vulnerability exposed, it could do nothing without the aid of its English subjects, who were generally hostile to its rule. Ship money collections dropped off drastically, as whole communities refused to pay. By 1640, the nation had gone on a virtual tax strike. County administration was ceasing to respond to commands from the center because the gentlemen who directed its machinery had lost confidence in the king. The force of public sentiment was concentrated against the Court and looked for deliverance to Parliament and to leaders of opposition. A crisis of obedience, authority, and confidence paralyzed the king's ability to govern and resulted in the collapse of sovereignty. There was no appearance of forcible resistance, which was unnecessary because the Scots, by taking arms in the name of their liberty and the reformed religion, had performed as surrogates for English opposition. In England, all that happened was that most of the aristocratic order turned away from the Court, including significant opportunistic defections within the Court itself.

[30] See Chapter 9 in this book.

Behind in similar attitude stood county communities and subjects with their convergent grievances. The monarchy had no means in these circumstances to coerce and to punish. It was almost wholly dependent for the execution of its mandates on the loyalty and cooperation of the aristocratic governing class. The latter's estrangement reduced it to impotence. Meanwhile, the royal army sat immobilized, and the Scottish rebel forces continued to occupy the north. Pending the completion of a peace treaty, Charles had to agree to maintain the Scots at a huge monthly cost. As the money for this end and also to pay the English troops could only come from Parliament, royal dependence on the latter was made even greater.

These developments created the essence of a revolutionary situation: a government unable to rule; a people no longer willing to be ruled in the former way. In the fall of 1640 political men and public opinion looked expectantly to the meeting of Parliament, from which much was hoped. The elections that preceded were more heavily affected by national issues than any in the past. The electoral influence of the crown had never been weaker. Held amid the collapse of royal power, the elections confirmed the Country's dominance and the Court's disintegration. Many opposition adherents were returned to the House of Commons, including members prominent in previous Parliaments. Charles I was left politically isolated, the initiative in the hands of the Court's adversaries.[31]

III

With the opening of the Long Parliament in November 1640, England crossed the threshold of revolution. Its meeting dates the beginning of the revolution in England as definitely as the meeting of the Estates General in May 1789 does the revolution in France.[32]

Both in its actuality and original ideal the revolution was dominated in the main by Parliament, the institution that constituted the chief basis of rebels' claim to legitimacy against the sacred authority of the king. Because of the union of forces arrayed against Charles I's methods of rule, it was relatively easy for Parliament and the Country to carry through a sweeping program of political reforms in the early months. This achieve-

[31] For these developments of 1629–40, Zagorin, *The court and the country*, 103–57, 114–18.

[32] There are many narrative accounts of part or all of the revolutionary decades of 1640–60. The fullest and still indispensable is S. R. Gardiner, *History of England from the accession of James I to the outbreak of the civil war 1603–1642*, 10 v., London, 1883–4, v. 10, *History of the great civil war, 1642–49*, 4 v., London, 1893, and *History of the commonwealth and protectorate, 1649–1656*, London, 1903. Gardiner's work was continued by C. H. Firth, *The last years of the protectorate 1656–1658*, 2 v., London, 1909. For the period up to 1647, a good modern narrative is C. V. Wedgwood, *The King's peace 1637–1641*, London, 1955, bk. 3, and *The King's war 1641–1647*, London, 1958. A shorter satisfactory narrative is I. Roots, *The great rebellion 1642–1660*, London, 1966.

ment of 1641 occupied the first stage of the revolution. Its second stage saw the disintegration of the Country alliance and a turnabout in the governing class, which gave Charles I a party and led in the summer of 1642 to civil war between Royalist and Parliamentarian. The continuance of the civil war brought on a splintering of the Parliamentarian side. The subsequent development of the revolution witnessed a multiplicity of internal divisions resulting in the emergence of the parliamentary army and its leader, Oliver Cromwell, to a position of power rivaling and at last superior to Parliament. Along with these events of the later 1640s and 1650s occurred the most singular phenomenon of the revolutionary era, an extraordinary outburst of democratic and radical agitation, a thrust among the middle and lower orders for citizenship rights, and a ferment of political discussion and argument, to which in its scope none of the other revolutions of the age affords a parallel.

One or two further general features of the revolutionary period may also be noted here.

First, in distinct contrast to the kindred earlier rebellions in France and the Netherlands, the revolt against Charles I was little threatened by external great-power animosities or involvement. Principally because of the long war between France and Spain, which lasted from 1635 until the Peace of the Pyrenees in 1659, England in the 1640s and 1650s remained effectively safe from intervention by foreign powers in its internal struggle. The French monarchy was further disabled by the outbreak of the revolution of the Fronde, the Spanish monarchy by the revolts in some of its subject possessions in the 1640s. True, the Scots intervened in England, first in 1644 as Parliament's ally and then later on behalf of the Stuart monarchy; but this was not so much a foreign involvement as the result of the association of the two countries in the union of crowns. Essentially, the English revolution was the least affected of all the civil wars of the age by external dangers.

Second, despite all its upheaval, the revolutionary period produced comparatively little in the way of significant agrarian disturbance or violence. Although small, scattered anti-enclosure riots took place in the 1640s in a score or so counties, there were no peasant insurrections. In certain areas, the rural population of small tenants who suffered under the depredations of the civil war reacted by demonstrations of neutralism and attempts to exclude military operations from their neighborhood. Generally, though, the English revolution was more notable for the relative absence than presence of any serious agrarian protest among its various effects.[33]

[33] B. Manning, *The English people and the English revolution 1648–1649*, London, 1976, 183–96, gives a recital of agrarian disorders that considerably exaggerates their importance. Certainly no peasant revolts accompanied the larger revolutionary movement.

Outside of Parliament, its main arena of action at first, the reality of revolution revealed itself in an immediate transformation of the political scene. An explosion of political consciousness after 1640 inspired newly activated multitudes to add their voices to the clamor for reforms. Parliament was surrounded by a forceful, observant public opinion that compelled it for the first time to act amid continual popular pressure. Something entirely new was the volume of petitioning. From London and many communities all over the kingdom came petitions of demands and grievances addressed to the two Houses, which stood at the center of an unprecedented upsurge among the English people that enabled the Country to impose its will.

The regime's collapse also liberated the press from any effective censorship, so that the Long Parliament opened the floodgates to a rising tide of publications dealing with public affairs. Even though Parliament itself was alarmed at the consequences of an uncontrolled press, it could do little to restrain the torrent. After 1640, the pamphlet became a vital part of revolutionary politics, a weapon of propaganda, agitation, and ideological debate. The sum of publications issued during the revolutionary period probably exceeded the entire output of the English press since the beginning of printing in England in 1475. At least 700-odd publications saw the light in 1641, at least 2,100-odd in 1642, a sign of the swift intensification of politicoreligious discussion. The same momentum gave rise also to the first English newspapers to report domestic events. These started as weeklies in the fall of 1641 and proved to be the precursors of an efflorescence of newspapers that came out in the following years in extraordinary variety and numbers and that served an important function as party organs.[34]

The revolution revealed itself, too, in the rapid emergence of sects and the reinvigorated Puritan thrust to achieve religious reform. For decades, the monarchy and bishops had maintained a stasis in the national church, frustrating the Puritan desire to see the completion of the long-sought reformation. But ecclesiastical authority broke down with the collapse of royal power, thus opening the prospect of significant religious change. The assembling of Parliament brought violent denunciations of the Arminians and bishops and initiated far-reaching controversies over the shape of the anticipated reformation. All the pent-up spiritual forces of the time sought release in the revolutionary years, thrusting England into an era of extraordinary religious development. Many Puritans wanted to abolish episcopal church government and replace it with a national presbyterian system; others favored retaining a reformed episcopacy stripped of its spiritual jurisdiction and secular functions, such as membership in the House of Lords; still others, congregationalists or Independents, were not

---

[34] See Zagorin, *The court and the country*, 203–6; and J. Frank, *The beginning of the English newspaper*, Cambridge, 1961, for the pamphlet and the press.

necessarily against a national church as long as individual congregations were left free from external constraint. But, although most Puritans looked to a reformed state church as their heart's desire, a proliferation of new religious groups began that rejected any inclusive national ecclesiastical institution. The growth of sectarianism and separatism, along with lay preaching and other forms of opposition to orthodoxy and coercive spiritual jurisdiction, was something the Puritans had not reckoned on. The sects created a religious diversity scandalous to Puritans yet impossible to prevent or eliminate. Moreover, both sectarians and congregationalists demanded religious toleration and liberty of conscience, thus injecting a highly divisive issue into the agenda of revolutionary politics. The quarrels among religious bodies became one of the most fertile causes of disunion as the revolution proceeded.[35]

Finally, we should note the inflation of hopes and the crusading fervor that seized many religious people as the revolution began. Enthusiasm and the expectation of wonders to come begot a revolutionary mentality eager to forward God's great work of renewal. To the pious, the Long Parliament seemed the beginning of a mighty transformation. Puritan preachers encouraged this apocalyptic mood, exhorting Parliament and their congregations to tear down Babylon and to plant reformation everywhere.[36] The passions, hopes, and militancy unleashed by revolution frequently erupted in disorder and incidents of violence. Well before the civil war started, the potential for physical confrontation was clearly evident. London especially, the heart of revolutionary England, witnessed scenes prefiguring the destruction of political order. Riotous crowds demonstrating at Westminster, mobs that threatened to assault bishops, unpopular noblemen, and the royal palace of Whitehall, repeated rumors of plots, and panic fears that the king was conspiring to use force against the Parliament all made for an atmosphere of tension that portended the engulfing violence to come.

In these unprecedented circumstances the first phase of the revolution was accomplished. Parliament's management lay in a loose confederation of Country oppositionists who acted as an informal leadership and through their ascendancy were able to guide its course. The group included John Pym, an experienced Parliament man and outstanding practical politician and orator who enjoyed great prestige in the House of Commons, John Hampden, another influential figure, and a number of fellow members who had taken part in the struggle against Charles I's government. They

---

[35] Zagorin, *The court and the country*, 227–35; a general treatment is given in W. Haller, *Liberty and reformation in the Puritan revolution*, New York, 1955.
[36] For this apocalyptic temper and its expression in the sermons preached to Parliament by Puritan ministers, see J. F. Wilson, *Pulpit in Parliament*, Princeton, 1969; and Zagorin, *The court and the country*, 345–6.

had friends and allies in the House of Lords and the support of Londoners who could mobilize the citizenry of the capital in behalf of the popular cause.[37]

Parliament's objectives at the outset were twofold, redress and reform, so as to set permanent limits on the king's authority. Thus, it immediately launched an attack upon the instruments of misgovernment and the institutions of royal power. Ministers of state, councillors, judges, and other offending royal servants were impeached. Archbishop Laud of Canterbury was imprisoned and in due course tried and executed. The earl of Strafford, the most feared of Charles I's advisers, was charged with treason for subverting the law and attempting to change England's government to a tyranny. He was executed in May 1641, after condemnation by an act of attainder, which the violence of the London mob forced the king to accept.

Along with its punitive measures upon malefactors, Parliament enacted a series of legislative changes, completed in the summer of 1641, that added up to a political and constitutional revolution. Because he was still so isolated, the king had no choice but to give them his assent. The Triennial Act mandated the meeting of Parliament at least every three years. The Court of Star Chamber, a great tribunal of the royal prerogative, together with certain other organs of prerogative government outside the system of common law, were abolished as illegal. The jurisdiction of the king's council was regulated in the interests of due process. The Court of High Commission, in which the bishops were prominent and which enforced the repression of Puritan dissent, was likewise abolished. Ship money, the collection of the customs without Parliament's consent, and other irregular exactions based on the royal prerogative were all declared illegal and annulled.

These statutory changes, which were seen as largely restorative, and the removal of illegalities performed a drastic surgery on royal authority. They took away most of the exceptional powers and prerogative institutions the Tudor monarchy had bequeathed to the Stuarts. They secured the future of Parliament and also deprived the crown of nearly all its significant sources of extraparliamentary revenue. They imposed new restrictions on the king's government to protect subjects' liberty and property against arbitrary power.[38]

Nevertheless, this battery of political reforms, the consolidation of the Country's victory, failed to restore stability or bring the revolution to an end. On the contrary, within a year the king was in a position to begin a civil war against Parliament in defense of his regality. What made this development possible? The explanation is twofold.

[37] Zagorin, *The court and the country*, 200–3. [38] *Ibid.*, 207–10, 217–26.

First, the king and the parliamentary managers remained separated by such a chasm of suspicion and mistrust that they could not collaborate to work the new constitutional arrangements. Angered and humiliated by his loss of authority and the pressures used against him, Charles did not think of accommodation; his main idea was, if possible, to strike a decisive blow against his adversaries. On their side, Pym and his friends were aware of the king's intentions and duplicity. They had evidence of royal plotting with some army officers to attempt force against Parliament and continually feared the danger of a coup. Thus, a ravaging lack of confidence maintained the breach in the body politic.

Second, because of their fears, Parliament and its managers embarked on a search for guarantees and security against the king. This need in turn compelled them to grasp at additional powers that went well beyond the bounds of their earlier reforming legislation. However, as Parliament pressed aggressive new demands upon the king, cracks and tremors appeared in the Country alliance. In both Houses, moderate members began to feel that the parliamentary leadership was venturing too far. They wanted stability based on the political changes already made and worried lest the insurrectionary spirit at large get beyond control. The spectacle of growing religious anarchy, mob disorders, and unruliness among the London populace only heightened their foreboding. It was this trend of opinion that presently destroyed the Country and begot from its split a Royalist party.

Already in May 1641, for fear lest the king suddenly dissolve Parliament, the managers put through an act providing that the existing Parliament could not be dissolved without its own consent. This measure did not redress a previous grievance but under cover of an emergency committed an extreme encroachment on the crown's traditional rights. Other usurpations followed that must be seen as the first tentative steps in the establishment of a rival sovereignty to the monarchy. The Houses issued military commands; they sent their own commissioners to Scotland; upon adjourning for a few weeks in September 1641, they created an unprecedented joint committee to function during their recess clothed with such broad authority that it resembled the germ of an executive government. Even more significant, they began to pass "ordinances" that bypassed the king's assent, the earliest hint of their acquisition of an independent legislative power.[39]

In August 1641, a peace treaty was finally concluded with the Scottish rebels, after which their troops withdrew and the English army was also disbanded. The king had yielded to all the Covenanter demands, leaving his Scottish realm virtually independent of the crown.[40] He then jour-

---

[39] *Ibid.*, 244–50.   [40] See Chapter 9 in this book.

neyed to Scotland, where he hoped by his concessions to build a party against his English opponents. While his Scottish intrigues played on Parliament's fears, there came the shocking news in November of the outbreak of revolt in Ireland, accompanied by reports of terrible atrocities against the Protestant settlers. The Irish Catholics had risen in the name of Ireland's freedom, exploiting the breakdown of central authority to imitate the example of Scotland and England. They declared themselves on the king's side against the English Parliament and Puritan faction that had deprived him of authority. The parliamentary leaders were convinced Charles had secretly encouraged the revolt. Even worse, they feared that, if he controlled the army that would be needed to suppress it, he would possess a sword to destroy his enemies and all that Parliament had won.[41]

The Irish rebellion aggravated political tensions and hastened the advent of civil war in England. To cope with new dangers, Pym and his party were determined to fasten additional fetters on the crown and take away Charles's legal right to command the military forces of the kingdom. Therefore, they put forward the unprecedented demand that the king submit his appointment of ministers and councillors to Parliament's approval. This far-reaching proposition was incorporated in the Grand Remonstrance, an inflammatory condemnation of Charles I's entire rule, which aroused a fierce debate and only passed the House of Commons by a slight majority at the end of November. In both the Commons and the House of Lords, members were now deserting the course set by Pym, and a new royalism was on the point of emerging.[42]

At the end of December, the king, having returned from Scotland, finally launched his oft-contemplated coup against his opponents, counting on a shift of opinion in his favor and the help of some demobilized army officers. First he tried to secure the Tower and then to arrest Pym and five other members of Parliament for high treason, but he was prevented by the violent reaction of the London populace. At the same time, the supporters of Parliament in London, who had built an organization of activists in the wards, captured the city government with their insurrectionary movement. They proceeded to establish an extraordinary committee of safety, which aligned the London municipality officially with the parliamentary leaders. Royalist partisans among the citizens were intimidated and rendered powerless by these developments. His attempt at counterrevolution a failure, the king felt himself surrounded by the hostility of the Londoners who had rallied to his enemies. Rather than look on at his humiliation, he left London on January 10, 1642, just as a half-century before his fellow monarch, Henry III of France, had been forced

[41] On the outbreak of the Irish rebellion, see Chapter 9 in this book.
[42] Zagorin, *The court and the country*, 254–69.

by the Day of the Barricades to leave Paris in May 1588. In Charles's case, too, an urban revolt had cost him his capital.[43]

After the king's departure from London, events moved inexorably toward civil war. Even though Charles's attempted coup dismayed many who were turning to his side, it did not stop the drift in his direction. His adversaries, backed by the mobs demonstrating at Westminster, relentlessly pursued their goals, despite the deepening differences in the House of Commons and acute frictions with the House of Lords, whose majority condemned their policy. Revolutionary pressures had steadily impaired the independence of the upper House and undermined its ability to hold out against the lower House's will.

Pym and his fellow managers insisted that the king surrender his military authority to Parliament. To satisfy Puritan opinion, they also pushed through a bill expelling bishops from the House of Lords, a major constitutional alteration in the composition of that body. The peers had to consent, despite their dislike of such a change, and the king did so too as a last concession. At the same time he made clear that he would never under any circumstances relinquish his rights over the militia. If any single issue was responsible for precipitating the civil war, it was this one of the disputed command of the armed forces, the *ultima ratio* of sovereignty.

In March, the two Houses boldly passed a militia ordinance, whereby they unilaterally invested themselves with full power over the kingdom's militia. They were now far along a path of constitutional-political innovation. The king, who was actively preparing for hostilities, declared the militia ordinance illegal. The ensuing intermittent negotiations between him and Parliament got nowhere, so great was the mutual mistrust. An irremediable quarrel between rival sovereignties was driving the former monarchical order to dissolution. In June, Parliament sent the king its Nineteen Propositions as its final demands for an accommodation. Because the propositions would have subjected his entire government in peace and war to parliamentary supervision, he of course rejected them. Compromise was evidently impossible. Parliament then voted to raise an army in its defense, and the king summoned all his loyal subjects to his standard at Nottingham. In August, with brushfires of strife already flaring up in many parts of the kingdom, the resort to arms began.[44]

---

[43] *Ibid.*, 269–94. V. Pearl, *London and the outbreak of Puritan revolution*, Oxford, 1961, provides a detailed treatment of London developments.

[44] For a closer view of the sequence of events leading to the civil war, see Zagorin, *The court and the country*, ch. 9.

IV

When the Long Parliament first assembled no one had anticipated a civil war, but in 1642 it came on with an irresistible momentum. Its onset involved a massive realignment in Parliament, the governing class, and the political nation. The Country coalition that had dominated the opening stage of the revolution fell apart as Pym's parliamentary leadership steadily drove the Houses to invade and appropriate the crown's lawful powers. In place of the former Court–Country antinomy and the latter's triumph, a new alignment supervened, giving rise to the Royalist and Parliamentarian parties that fought the civil war. The bulwark and leadership of this new royalism consisted of those in Parliament and the governing class who had previously supported the Country but had now gone over to the king. As one of its principal figures, the great contemporary historian of the revolution, Clarendon, wrote,

> . . . The King's party in both Houses was made up of persons who were strangers . . . to the Court, of the best fortunes and the best reputations in their several countries, where they were known as having always appeared very zealous in the maintenance of their just rights and opposed as much as in them lay all illegal and grievous impositions.[45]

For such men, the king had now become the champion of legal, constitutional, and religious order against Parliament's illicit and dangerous aggressions. For the Parliamentarians, on the other hand, unless the king were closely circumscribed and supervised by Parliament, liberty, law, and everything the revolution had gained or still hoped to gain would be in peril. Thus, the two Houses in a solemn manifesto on the eve of the civil war declared to "those who have sent us hither and intrusted us" with their estates, liberty, lives, and religion,

> . . . If the King may force this Parliament, they may bid farewell to all Parliaments . . . and if Parliaments be lost, they are lost; their Laws are lost, as well those lately made, as in former times, all which will be cut in sunder with the same sword now drawn for the destruction of this Parliament.[46]

The outbreak of the civil war elicited varied reactions. Among the aristocracy, resignation to its inevitability and unhappiness at having to choose between conflicting legitimacies were more common than either strong political commitment or enthusiasm. Many in both parties longed for a compromise that would bring an early peace – a vanishing prospect fated never to materialize, despite recurrent negotiations between the king

---

[45] Clarendon, *The history of the rebellion and civil wars*, ed. W. D. Macray, 6 v., Oxford, 1888, v. 2, 442.

[46] Cited in Zagorin, *The court and the country*, 322.

and Parliament. Neutralist manifestations surfaced in some counties, only to be borne down in the spreading violence. Puritans, on the other hand, were likely to regard the struggle as a sanctified war against evil.

In social composition, the two sides were largely indistinguishable, the governing class being itself divided. Within the House of Commons, the majority of members became Parliamentarians of one shade or another. Within the House of Lords, most noblemen joined the king, leaving their chamber in possession of the minority of Parliamentarian peers. The gentry appeared in sizable numbers in both parties, although more of them sided with the king. Bourgeois elites and the commercial, artisan, and urban strata generally were also fissioned in allegiance. Although more of them favored Parliament, and although London was of vital importance as a Parliamentarian stronghold, important towns like Newcastle and Bristol and many urban magistrates and citizens were decidedly Royalist. Among the agricultural population, small tenants and husbandmen often merely followed their landlords or were indifferent to the conflict, and some of the better-off yeomen and tenants adhered to Parliament. Regionally, the textile manufacturing districts and the counties of the south and east, where Puritanism was also strongly rooted, were predominantly Parliamentarian; the less economically developed counties of the west, southwest, and north, predominantly Royalist. This was far from being a clear-cut division, though; the king also had his supporters among the manufacturing interests, and some of the rich, populous counties were split and hotly contested by the two sides. The civil war in any case created conflicting alignments in every county and community. No preponderant socioeconomic differentiation accordingly separated the parties, each of which was also led by aristocratic elites.[47]

The advent of arms engendered hot ideological argument, which only intensified as the civil war continued. All through the sixteenth and earlier seventeenth centuries, English religious and political thought had maintained with considerable consistency the duty of subjects to submit to divinely appointed rulers. The Anglican church had continuously taught that rebellion was the worst of sins and the quintessence of all evils. Since Queen Elizabeth's accession, even despite sympathy and support for the embattled Protestantism in France and the Netherlands, not a single English Protestant writer had advanced any theoretical justification for resistance. The Country opposition of the 1620s and 1630s, wedded to legality, never broached the question of forcible resistance when attempting to withstand the pressures of Charles I's government. Only the Scottish Covenanters had justified their taking up of arms in defense of religion. In

---

[47] *Ibid.*, 336–40, contains a fuller account of alignments. See also the discussion in C. Wilson, *England's apprenticeship 1603–1763*, London, 1965, ch. 6. Manning, *The English people*, chs. 6–8, is a recent attempt to find a class struggle as the basis of the civil war.

England, however, the quarrel between the king and Parliament led to a decisive departure and breakthrough from political tradition, stimulating a mass of writings on behalf of popular sovereignty, the supremacy of Parliament, and the right of resistance.

The king and Parliament waged their own duel of manifestoes to win public opinion to their side. Due to Parliament's encroachments, the king, in a striking reversal of his earlier situation, was able to assume the posture of defender of the law and historic constitution. He condemned the two Houses' invasion of his rights and their exercise of the ordinance power to take over the militia as illegal and their subversion of the kingdom's constitution. For the Houses to make law without the royal consent, he declared, was to introduce "an Arbitrary way of Government."

The Houses responded by doing their best to minimize the novelty of their position. Before the Long Parliament, as also in the constitutional statutes of 1641, the opposition to the king had itself appeared as upholder of the law against absolute and arbitrary power. Steeped in reverence for the law, the Country's supporters were apt to be politically and intellectually conservative and devotees of the ideology of the normative past. It was in the name of the law that they had defended the rights and liberties of subjects. Now, however, the Houses found themselves compelled to maintain these rights and liberties by armed resistance against their sovereign.

In these circumstances, their main claim to legitimacy lay in the fact that even without the king they could describe themselves as Parliament. Still sitting in their usual place at Westminster, the Lords and Commons remained the representative body of the kingdom. Accordingly, they justified their resort to arms by exalting Parliament as bearing the supreme trust for the preservation of the commonwealth and its immemorial legal order. Because of this trust, they proclaimed Parliament's right to control the king when he failed in his duty. Although the Houses did not flatly assert that Parliament could make law alone, their defense of the ordinance power and of the seizure of the militia came to the same thing because they contended that Parliament possessed authority to declare what the law is and that its judgment was binding upon everyone. Furthermore, they repeatedly made a distinction between the king's office and his person. The royal office, they maintained, was expressed and exercised preeminently through Parliament, notwithstanding the personal wishes of its incumbent. This fiction absorbed the king's political capacity entirely in Parliament, thereby leaving him no regal will of his own. It also enabled the Houses to declare that Parliament was fighting Charles Stuart, not the king, a doctrine designed to avoid the stigma of rebellion. Despite its equivocations, however, Parliament could not really disguise the fact that it was propounding a revolutionary claim to supremacy and sovereignty independent of the crown.[48]

Besides the statements in official declarations, a crowd of writers clashed over the issues posed by the civil war. Royalists attacked the Parliamentarian case, invoking Scripture and law to deny a right of resistance against the king. In 1642, Hobbes, a Royalist exile in Paris, brought out his first published work on politics, *De cive*, later translated by himself into English, a philosophical analysis of sovereignty, law, right, and obligation that left no room for justifiable rebellion by subjects. Theorists of both sides were well aware of analogies with the earlier revolutionary civil war in France. Royalists cited it as a dread example of the evils of revolt, Parliamentarians made use of the *Vindiciae contra tyrannos* and other well-known Huguenot treatises supporting the right of the people and community against kings. Revolutionary political thought demonstrated a sufficient acquaintance with the monarchomach literature of the sixteenth century, and the *Vindiciae* itself was published in an English translation in 1648.[49]

Parliamentarian defenders adopted populist principles similar to those the Huguenots had formerly proclaimed. They maintained the superiority of the kingdom or community to the ruler and affirmed that the foundation of power lay in the people, contract, and consent. Some writers justified resistance by referring to the duty of inferior magistrates to restrain and prevent tyrannous government. But Parliamentarian ideology as a whole was much less concerned with the people or with the theme of the inferior magistrates than with the authority and position of Parliament. It placed its heaviest stress on the supremacy of Parliament as the corporate incarnation of the community. This conception was elaborated in both theoretical and antiquarian terms by various authors and seemed to best fit the circumstances of a conflict whose legitimacy depended on the representative assembly of the realm. It received its clearest and most uncompromising statement from Henry Parker, one of the cleverest of Parliamentarian pamphleteers, who placed Parliament over the king on the ground that it is, in essence, the people, the kingdom, and indeed the state itself.[50]

[48] Zagorin, *The court and the country*, 307–12, reviews the arguments in the declarations by the king and the Houses; see also J. W. Allen, *English political thought, 1603–1660*, London, 1938, 386–412, on the battle of manifestoes.

[49] Besides the Paris edition of 1642, three more editions of the Latin text of *De cive* were published in Amsterdam in 1647. Hobbes's English translation is in his *English works*, v. 2. On the use of Huguenot writings in the 1640s, see J. H. Salmon, *The French religious wars in English political thought*, Oxford, 1959, ch. 5.

[50] Henry Parker, *Observations upon some of his majesties late answers and expresses, 1642*. For Parker and Parliamentarian writings, see Zagorin, *The court and the country*, 348; and Allen, *English political thought*, 424–81.

The civil war ushered in a lengthy period of revolutionary government by Parliament and its successor regimes till 1660. Parliament set up its own independent rule, which confronted the king's in war and replaced it after victory. England thus became the first unitary national state in Europe to fall under the sovereignty and administration of a parliamentary assembly.

Parliament's rule was always collegial in character. Among the members active in affairs at the center were experienced men of high ability as politicians, organizers, and administrators. Pym remained the foremost director of the parliamentary cause, but he died at the end of 1643, worn out by his efforts to guide the Houses in meeting the exigencies of the war. Hampden, scarcely second in influence to Pym, died earlier the same year in battle against the Royalists. The leadership of the conflict against the king was carried on by other prominent members among whom the seeds of religious and political discord were already sprouting. Along with those in the House of Commons, some distinguished noblemen loyal to Parliament undertook both civil and military responsibilities in the prosecution of the war. The earl of Essex, one of the inner circle of Country oppositionists, became the first general of Parliament's army. It was in the bloodshed of the civil war that Oliver Cromwell, a Puritan gentleman and member of the House of Commons, first achieved prominence for his exploits as a fighting commander. Cromwell revealed himself as an immensely forceful personality and the possessor of outstanding political and military gifts. He alone, of all the men of the English revolution, was destined to become a great national leader, the strongest embodiment of its religious and political will.[51]

Parliament had to improvise its government at the same time that it fought the war. It did so mainly by adapting existing institutions, practices, and structures. That it was able, despite great confusions and inefficiency, to wield authority successfully and to conduct the fighting to victory was a testimonial to its institutional strength and leadership.

Essentially, Parliament's state power meant government by committee. Over all stood a committee of safety, composed of members of both Houses, which acted as a central war directorate and head of the executive. In 1644, when the Scottish Covenanters entered the civil war as Parliament's ally, their representatives were added to this committee, which then became known as the Committee of Both Kingdoms. During the entire period of parliamentary rule some such organ, named by and re-

---

[51] There are good studies and biographies of Cromwell by S. R. Gardiner, C. H. Firth, Christopher Hill, and others. For penetrating insight into his personality and beliefs, Thomas Carlyle's *Oliver Cromwell's letters and speeches* (1845), remains essential. W. C. Abbott (ed.), *The writings and speeches of Oliver Cromwell*, 4 v., Cambridge, 1937–47, is now the authoritative collection of Cromwell's words, accompanied by a valuable explanatory commentary.

sponsible to Parliament, exercised supreme executive authority. In addition, to deal with money and a mass of other business, Parliament appointed many standing and ad hoc committees, a method it had always used in its transactions.

Parliament financed the war by contributions, loans, fines and confiscations against Royalists, and an array of new taxes far exceeding the pre-1640 exactions of the crown. In the counties controlled by the Parliamentarians, the administration of taxes, local defense, and many other tasks were assigned to newly created county committees authorized and supervised by Parliament. These committees consisted mostly of county notables, men of the sort that traditionally occupied the higher offices of local government, and thus simply reflected the existing county power structure as much as possible.

Parliament's rule soon provoked the same frictions between the central government and localities as the king's had done. Wartime conditions disrupted the normal course of justice and the regular machinery of county administration. The extraordinary powers exercised by committees in Parliament and locally in the counties bred arbitrary methods, corruption, and violations of law. Even communities that supported the war nonetheless complained of the distribution of its burdens and showed more concern for their own interests than for national priorities. This was the expression of a familiar provincialism that inevitably confronted the revolutionary regime and ultimately contributed to the monarchy's restoration in 1660. But, as the war dragged on, its necessities overrode local considerations and provincialism. Parliament was forced to expand central control. Thus the English revolution, like nearly all the others that have conquered power (the Netherlands rebellion being a significant exception), only promoted greater governmental centralization, creating in the process a much stronger, more invasive state apparatus than the monarchy had ever possessed.[52]

It took Parliament four years to defeat the king. Like the Royalists, its forces were made up of both volunteers and a minority of conscripts – for by the summer of 1643 the Houses were compelled to resort to drafting men. The total number on either side probably never exceeded 60,000–70,000 troops. The fighting was marked not only by big pitched battles but by many local skirmishes and sieges of towns and garrisons. Problems of pay and desertion were continual. Although Parliament possessed superior material resources, not least because of the support of London, the earlier part of the war brought it more failures than successes and no sign

[52] On the organization of parliamentary government, taxes, county committees, and conflicts between localities and the center, see G. E. Aylmer, *The state's servants*, London, 1973, 9–12; D. H. Pennington, "The county community at war," in Ives, *The English revolution;* and Morrill, *The revolt of the provinces*, ch. 2.

of a decision. Weakness of military organization was among the difficulties that hampered the Parliamentarian cause. In addition to the army of the earl of Essex, general in chief, regional associations of counties raised their own armies under separate and rival generals. The result was a preoccupation with local interests and lack of unified command and strategy.[53] The year 1643 witnessed Royalist gains, so that Parliament was compelled to seek Scottish assistance. One of Pym's last important undertakings was to consummate the Solemn League and Covenant with Scotland in August 1643, a religious bond and political treaty whereby the Covenanters agreed to join the civil war as Parliament's ally. The Scots had their own interest in assuring Charles I's defeat; they were also very eager as the price of their aid to see the two countries united religiously on the basis of the institution in England of the same type of presbyterian church as Scotland's, a possibility the treaty itself envisaged.

The entry of the Scots helped to turn the balance against the king, but the Parliamentarian effort was beset by serious political as well as military problems, which were closely interlocked. Some in Parliament wanted an all-out prosecution of the war to a conclusive victory; others wished for a compromise peace at nearly any price; still others wanted Parliament to be strong enough to achieve a secure settlement with the king. These differences were attended by religious rifts, for by 1644 the Parliamentarian party was already quite at odds over the shape of reformation, whether there should be a state church on presbyterian lines with a compulsive uniformity or some freedom permitted for a diverse denominational life. Such disagreements not only affected Parliament but also infiltrated its army, creating animosities in the ranks between presbyterians on the one side and Independents and sectarians on the other.

In the fall of 1644, Cromwell, lieutenant-general in the parliamentary army, brought the military issue to a head. Cromwell belonged to the all-out war party in Parliament and supported religious Independency and toleration against presbyterianism. He charged his own commander, the earl of Manchester, and other generals with inaction and an unwillingness to fight the war to a victorious end for fear of the consequences of the king's total defeat. In a powerful speech in the House of Commons, he pleaded for "a more speedy, vigorous and effectual prosecution of the war" lest the kingdom grow weary of the name of Parliament. "If the army," he warned, "be not put into another method, and the war more vigorously prosecuted, the People can bear the war no longer, and will enforce you to a dishonourable peace."[54]

Parliament surmounted this crisis by a military reform that resulted in

[53] See C. H. Firth, *Cromwell's army*, 3rd ed., London, 1962, ch. 2, for an account of the royal and parliamentary armies at the beginning of the civil war.
[54] Printed in Abbott (ed.), *The writings and speeches of Oliver Cromwell*, v. 1, 314.

the creation early in 1645 of the New Model army, a consolidation of Essex's with two other regional forces strengthened by the recruitment of additional troops. This was the nearest thing to a national army that Parliament had achieved. A self-denying ordinance obliged members of both Houses serving in the army to give up their commands, which meant the retirement of Essex and other noblemen. An exception, however, was made for Cromwell, who was appointed lieutenant-general under Sir Thomas Fairfax, a veteran soldier, as commander-in-chief. The New Model was more regularly paid than its predecessors, better disciplined and led, and developed a keen fighting spirit under officers and chaplains inspired by religious fervor for the cause. In June 1645, it inflicted a great defeat upon the Royalists at Naseby, the first of a series of successes that drove the king's forces from the field. His army, suffering increasingly from disorganization and want of money, succumbed to a superior power. By the summer of 1646, the royal headquarters at Oxford had surrendered, and the civil war came to an end with Parliament victorious.[55]

V

The conclusion of the civil war placed the assorted problems of a settlement at the top of the revolutionary agenda. The religious and political divisions within Parliament and its supporters now shattered the Parliamentarian side into bitterly contending groups. The king, although defeated, still seemed indispensable to any permanent settlement, and he strove to exploit the disagreements among his erstwhile enemies. At length, Cromwell and his party of Independents, with the backing of the army, cut the Gordian knot. This they did at the end of 1648 by purging Parliament of offensive members, bringing Charles I to trial and execution, and instituting a republican commonwealth under the sole sovereignty of the House of Commons.

The establishment of the republic in 1649 closed the second and opened the third stage of the revolution. The events leading up to it reflected an inevitable process of differentiation and radicalization within the revolutionary camp. Quite against the intention of its initiators, the conflict against the king gave birth to novel perspectives and unforeseen aims. Thus, the latter half of the 1640s witnessed a determined fight for toleration against a repressive presbyterianism, along with the emergence of an organized popular movement against Parliament itself calling for various social reforms and democratic freedoms. An outpouring of pamphlets, petitions, newspapers, and broadsides fed the widening protest, which

[55] Firth, *Cromwell's army*, ch. 2, describes the creation of the New Model army; M. Kishlansky, "The case of the army truly stated: The creation of the New Model army," *Past and present 81* (1978), discusses the political background.

found a particular response among those who felt the burdens of the civil war the most. The New Model army was infected by these developments, too, and, becoming politicized, defied Parliament on behalf of its own and popular grievances. Instead of achieving a new status quo, the civil war thus seemed to have thrown England into the melting pot.

The toleration question was made inescapable by the chaotic multiplication of religious bodies and opinions outside the pale of the old Puritan and presbyterian orthodoxy. To its opponents, toleration was the parent of all heresies and a threat to social stability as well. Some of the sects rejected tithes, a professional ministry, and infant baptism; they held anticlerical and antinomian opinions and defended lay preaching. The congregationalists or Independents were more moderate but nevertheless denied the power of a national church over gathered congregations of believers. The presbyterians formed the Puritan main wing, those who wanted a compulsory national church with its disciplinary hierarchy of ministers, elders, classes, and synods along Calvinist lines. Presbyterianism had the support of the majority of Parliament, the Scots, most of the Puritan clergy, many Londoners, and the London city government. It was the religious correlate of a conservatism within the Parliamentarian side – a conservatism fearful of further change and the radical aspirations kindled in the civil war. In this sense, there was a political no less than a religious presbyterianism. The presbyterians would have suppressed the sects, silenced heretics, and enforced conformity on the nation. They were eager to obtain Charles I's endorsement of their church settlement in return for concessions. Their adversaries included the Independents in Parliament and the army, the Puritan ministers who favored congregational autonomy and opposed compulsion in religion, the several shades of political radicals, and the increasing number of sectarian separatists and their sympathizers of all sorts.

The contradictions of the revolution were demonstrated when Parliament finally voted in 1646 to establish presbyterian church government subject to its own ultimate authority. It had overthrown an intolerant Anglicanism only to substitute an intolerant presbyterianism. The decision entailed the end of episcopacy and was presently followed by the confiscation and sale of the lands belonging to bishops, deans, and cathedral chapters. The presbyterian dominion did not last long, however, being broken when the army and the Independents purged Parliament as the preface to a republican regime. The presbyterian church thereafter remained merely a half-formed, voluntary system, obliged to coexist with other denominations. Nevertheless, the controversies accompanying these religious changes were of the utmost import to the revolution's political and ideological history.

The central themes of toleration and liberty of conscience evoked the support of many minds. In 1644, the poet John Milton, whose pen in these years was largely devoted to politics, addressed a plea to Parliament against censorship. Upholding liberty of the press, he pictured the English as an awakening people eagerly searching for new light, who must be free to seek the truth in any quarter without hindrance. A little later, Milton stigmatized the presbyterians, whom he called the "new forcers of conscience," with the biting comment, "new presbyter is but old priest writ large."[56] To Milton, to Cromwell, and to many others, freedom of conscience for all the people of God was one of the essential freedoms for which Parliament fought the war. Clergy and lay authors, political theorists, sectarians, radicals, and pragmatic men of affairs all defended toleration from various angles. Rationalism, scepticism, and belief in the progressive revelation of religious truth; anticlericalism and laic rejection of any church's monopoly of spiritual authority or discipline; denunciation of persecution as un-Christian and immoral; pleas for the separation of church and state for the sake of both faith and civil peace; the economic benefits of religious freedom – all these arguments and more figured in the case for toleration.

True, tolerance or religious freedom were rarely advocated for all Christians. Few, for example, would have granted them to Catholics, alleged to be subservient to a foreign power, the pope. Jews, too, were commonly excluded, despite the philo-Semitism of some of the sectarians of the period. Generally speaking, however, the revolutionary era in its irresistible pluralism extended the bounds of confessional toleration more widely and developed its rationale more fully than at any time since the Reformation. These conditions enabled the other great prerevolutionary dissenting denominations besides Presbyterianism to root themselves firmly and achieve permanent existence. For Congregationalists, Baptists, and even such heterodox believers as Unitarians, the 1640s and 1650s were crucial years of development. Quakerism, too, was born in the 1650s; and, although then and afterward it suffered considerable persecution, it was able to propagate itself lastingly. Only the Dutch republic after its own revolt could compare with revolutionary England in the variety and relative latitude of its religious life.[57]

The toleration controversy helped to fertilize the ground from which the Leveller protest sprang in 1646–7 as a challenge to all the reigning powers. The first leftwing movement in English and, indeed, European

[56] J. Milton, *Areopagitica* (1644); "On the new forcers of conscience under the Long Parliament," printed in any edition of the poet's works among his sonnets.

[57] The ecclesiastical debates in Parliament, the opposition to presbyterianism, and the writings and ideas in defense of toleration are fully treated by W. K. Jordan, *The development of religious toleration in England*, 4 v., Cambridge, 1932–40, v. 3–4. London's relation to presbyterianism is described by V. Pearl, "London's counter-revolution," in *The interregnum*, ed. G. Aylmer, London, 1974.

politics, the Levellers embodied many of the radical ideals that threatened to drive the civil war well beyond its original aims. They were a genuine party, with their own propaganda, activists, leaders, loyal following, and program. Their objectives were the fullest liberty of conscience, social reform, and a democratic reconstruction of the polity. Earlier in the seventeenth century, the name *Leveller* had been borne by the rioters who attacked enclosures in 1607.[58] In the 1640s the Levellers were so called by their enemies, who charged them with wanting to level property. This was certainly untrue: If anything, they spoke for small property interests against big. They strove, unsuccessfully, for a further revolution of democracy within the revolution against the crown.

Despite some provincial offshoots, the Levellers remained predominantly an urban movement centered in London. Their supporters consisted mostly of small and middling people who opposed the presbyterian ascendancy and had also been hard hit by the effects of the civil war: effects that included heavy taxation, destruction of property, and economic depression throughout the 1640s. These adversities disillusioned many common folk into neutralism or Royalist sympathies as time passed. The Levellers, however, belonged to the committed Parliamentarians who demanded that the people be recompensed for their sacrifices in Parliament's cause. The most prominent of their leaders was John Lilburne, a religious sectarian and former officer in the parliamentary army who had been imprisoned without trial by the House of Lords for denying its authority over him. Courageous and incorruptible, Lilburne possessed an exceptional talent for dramatizing political issues and became the greatest popular tribune of his time as an agitator and pamphleteer. Through meetings, petitions, and a stream of tracts and manifestoes, he and his friends succeeded in creating a broad-based movement that advocated radical reform against Parliament itself.

The Leveller program welded together a multitude of complaints and grievances. It condemned monopolies, excise taxes, and other inequitable burdens on the people. It denounced the corruptions of members of Parliament and committees. It attacked religious persecution, censorship, and compulsory tithes. It called for free trade, the sweeping reform of the law and courts of justice, and the democratization of London's city government and guilds. It spoke of the decay of trade, the needs of the poor, and the abolition of imprisonment for debt.

Politically, the Levellers invoked the same principles against Parliament that the latter had used earlier against the king. With these principles as one of its points of departure, the Leveller program carried the idea of popular sovereignty to a new extreme. Thus, it insisted that Parliament

[58] See Chapter 7 in this book.

was no less accountable for its trust than was Charles I. Parliament was not an irresponsible authority but answerable to the people from whose consent it derived. This entailed that the king and the House of Lords, not being elected, had no standing or right to a negative voice in Parliament's deliberations. It also meant that supremacy resided in the House of Commons alone, with the further corollary that the House must be genuinely representative in its election and composition.

The Levellers expressed a severe indictment of Parliament, politically controlled by the presbyterians, for its oppressions and failure to ease the people's lot. They contended that the two Houses, sitting since 1640, no longer possessed legitimacy and had forfeited their authority. Accordingly, they repeatedly called on Parliament to dissolve itself and make way for a new representative.

It was in this connection that the Levellers advanced one of their most striking ideas. To reconstitute the polity, they proposed an Agreement of the People, a literal contract of government that would convey popular consent to the creation of a new political order. In 1647, they drew up such an agreement, the first of several versions, intended for individual subscription. In essence, it was a written constitution, the earliest designed for a national state to appear in Europe. Its purpose was to ordain as fundamental law the form, powers, and limits assigned by the people to the government they establish. With popular sovereignty as its ultimate basis, the agreement's central provisions included the supremacy of the people's representative without either king or House of Lords; universal manhood suffrage; and a reapportionment of seats and constituencies to assure the fairest representation in Parliament. It further prescribed equality before the law of all persons regardless of rank. Among the powers prohibited to Parliament was any compulsion in religion or form of worship.[59]

The Leveller program conceived of men fundamentally as participant citizens, rather than as subjects. This conception constituted its essential

---

[59] For the text of the 1647 Agreement of the People and later versions, see D. Wolfe, *Leveller manifestoes of the Puritan revolution*, New York, 1944, 223–8, which also contains other Leveller documents. There has been extensive debate by scholars on whether the Levellers were committed to universal manhood suffrage and how far they would have qualified it. The main argument against the view that the Levellers did believe in a universal franchise is in C. B. Macpherson, *The political theory of possessive individualism*, Oxford, 1962, ch. 3 and app., an interesting discussion that depends, however, on errors and misconceptions. To my mind, there can be little question that the essential thrust of the Leveller program was toward a universal franchise despite reservations in some of their statements that excluded servants and recipients of charity, as also, we must suppose, although this is not expressly declared, women. On various occasions, however, Leveller spokesmen also vigorously and unqualifiedly advocated universal manhood suffrage. For a balanced treatment of the problem, see K. Thomas, "The Levellers and the franchise," in Aylmer, *The interregnum*; and the remarks of I. Hampsher-Monk, "The political theory of the Levellers," *Political studies 24*, 4 (1976).

significance. Behind such a view lay a considerable transformation in revolutionary ideology.

Akin to other rebels of the early modern age, the Levellers began by seeking their justification in a mythical history and the normative past. To support their claims, they appealed at first to the ancient common law, Magna Carta, and especially to the idea of the Norman yoke – namely, that the Norman conquest had destroyed Anglo-Saxon liberty and fastened a six-century legacy of tyranny and injustice on the people.[60] This attitude naturally caused them to see the revolt against the king as the restoration and recovery of lost freedoms. But the Levellers soon came more and more to abandon the ground of the past and a restorationist perspective. Instead, they based their position increasingly on abstract reason, on what was due to man as a rational being formed in God's image, and on natural right. Even religious apologies for radicalism derived from God's law were subordinated to these overwhelmingly secular themes. The latter furnished them with their strongest justification for founding all government on consent as expressed through democratic institutions. Such principles were, of course, inherently universalistic in their meaning; they were also profoundly optimistic in their estimate of human capacity for self-rule. They served to sanction innovations, regardless of precedent, solely by virtue of what men might claim by natural right. "For whatever our Forefathers were," wrote a Leveller pamphleteer, "or whatever they did or suffered, or were enforced to yeeld unto; we are the men of the present age, and ought to be free." This signified a momentous transition in revolutionary thought: it displayed the shift from prevalent past-looking doctrines to universal ideals of reason and right as the support for revolutionary change.[61]

The period 1647–8 marked the high tide of radical politics and Leveller activity. In the spring of 1647, the New Model army was provoked to mutiny when Parliament decided to disband it without provision for its arrears of pay or indemnity for acts committed during the civil war. The army defied Parliament's orders, and twelve regiments elected agents, or "agitators," to represent them. In an unprecedented experiment in military democracy, the agitators combined with the regimental officers and top commanders, Fairfax and Cromwell, in a general council of the army to speak for the entire body. The troops then made a solemn engagement or covenant not to disband till both their own and the nation's grievances were remedied. In justification of the army's conduct, the general council declared:

[60] See C. Hill, "The Norman yoke," in *Puritanism and revolution*, London, 1958, esp. 75–82.

[61] For a fuller treatment of the Leveller writers, ideas, and program, P. Zagorin, *A history of political thought in the English revolution*, London, 1954, chs. 2–3; the citation is in *ibid.*, 22.

We were not a mere mercenary army, hired to serve any arbitrary power of a state, but called forth . . . by the several declarations of Parliament to the defense of our own and the people's just rights and liberties. And so we took up arms in judgment and conscience to those ends.[62]

These words announced the thunderous entrance of the army into the political arena in direct contravention of Parliament's authority. Officers and men were resolved to defeat presbyterian intolerance and prevent any treaty with Charles I that looked like a sellout. To these ends, the army did not hesitate to march on London to intimidate both Parliament and the municipal government. At the same time, its politicization and grievances rendered the army increasingly receptive to Leveller influence, which spread among the rank and file. The agitators and numbers of common soldiers became converts to the Leveller program.

The New Model's revolt was based on a coalition between Cromwell and the Independent officers and the more radical soldiers and Levellers, temporarily united against the threat of a presbyterian-dictated settlement with the king. In October 1647 the army general council, including some London Levellers, met at Putney to discuss the Agreement of the People as a possible platform for the kingdom.

These Putney debates have become deservedly famous as a classic confrontation of ideas in the immediate heat of revolutionary struggle. With uncompromising clarity, the Leveller spokesmen stated the case for a democratic polity, the vision of the future that inspired their efforts. They repudiated the existing regime of privilege, demanding to know whether the people and soldiers had fought the king only to remain slaves of the rich and powerful. Advocating a democratic republic, they argued strongly for a parliamentary franchise shorn of any property qualification as the birthright of Englishmen. The source of law is in the people, they asserted, who are born free and can only be subject to government by their own consent. "The poorest he that is in England," said one of them,

hath a life to live, as the greatest he; and therefore . . . it's clear, that every man that is to live under a government ought first by his own consent to put himself under that government; and I do think that the poorest man in England is not at all bound in a strict sense to that government that he hath not had a voice to put himself under.[63]

Cromwell and his officer followers, even though willing to see some reform of Parliament, rejected the Levellers' basic principles as dangerous

---

[62] Printed in A. S. P. Woodhouse, *Puritanism and liberty*, London, 1938, 404. The revolt of the New Model army is described in Firth, *Cromwell's army*, ch. 14; and, more fully, by M. Kishlansky, *The rise of the New Model army*, Cambridge, 1979, which modifies the view of the army's commitment to political and Leveller radicalism.

[63] See Woodhouse, *Puritanism and liberty*, which prints the Putney debates as they were taken down by the secretary of the army general council.

dreams conducive only to anarchy. To grant manhood suffrage, they argued, and to allow a voice to shirtless men who had no permanent "interest" in the kingdom would bring on the destruction of property. They opposed the appeal to natural rights, warning that such a claim opened prospects of unlimited change against all prescriptive rights and institutions.[64]

The Putney debates demonstrated the basic political differences between the Levellers and their soldier adherents, on the one side, and Cromwell and the more conservative Independents, on the other. It had also become apparent, meanwhile, that army democracy was undermining discipline and the authority of the commanders. After the Putney meeting, therefore, Cromwell procured the cessation of the army general council and the return of the agitators to their regiments. This put an end to rank-and-file participation as well as further Leveller influence in the direction of the army.

On the broader political scene, confusion reigned, and a settlement still appeared as distant as ever when Charles I finally took the step that led to his own destruction. After intriguing intermittently with all parties, the defeated monarch came to an accord with a section of the Scottish Covenanters to ratify presbyterianism in England on condition of his reinstatement in authority. The Scots had gone home following the civil war; they now prepared to return as the king's allies in order to see a royally endorsed presbyterian church triumphant in England. The English presbyterians were also deeply compromised by the Scottish intervention, and Charles was held guilty by his opponents of inciting a new civil war.

In the summer of 1648, amid serious Royalist insurrections, which broke out in several parts of the kingdom, a Scottish army invaded England. But the New Model smashed the Scots and also suppressed the risings everywhere. Then the army leadership and Independents took matters into their own hands in a decisive unilateral action. In December, they seized the king, occupied London with troops, and purged Parliament by the forcible expulsion of its presbyterian members. The truncated House of Commons voted three monumental resolutions, declaring that the people are, under God, the origin of all just power; that the Commons, as chosen by and representing the people, possesses supreme power; and that the enactments of the Commons alone, without concurrence of the king or House of Lords, have the force of law.[65] The House then established a high court of justice to try the king for tyranny, for betrayal of his trust, and for waging war on his people. Although the monarch denied the court's jurisdiction over him and refused to plead, his judges condemned him. On January 30, 1649, he was publicly beheaded before the royal palace of

64 *Ibid., passim.*
65 Printed in J. P. Kenyon, *The Stuart constitution*, Cambridge, 1966, 324.

Whitehall. With these stormy events, an English republic came into being.[66]

VI

Never had the principle of ruler accountability been given such a stark and visible exemplification as in the trial and execution of Charles I. Rebels, conspirators, and assassins had often deposed, imprisoned, and murdered kings. But English revolutionaries in 1649 were the first to try an anointed sovereign and strike off his head as a traitor to his people.

Regicide was followed by two acts of the House of Commons, or Rump Parliament, as it came to be called, formalizing the new situation. One abolished the office of king as unnecessary and dangerous to the liberty, safety, and public interest of the people; the other abolished the House of Lords on similar grounds (although it permitted loyal noblemen to sit in Parliament if duly elected). Somewhat later, in May 1649, a further act confirmed that England was now "a Commonwealth and Free State" under Parliament as "the supreme authority of this nation."[67]

The army's actions, regicide, and republic were vigorously defended by the commonwealth's apologists. Milton and a number of other publicists wrote on its behalf, making use of earlier monarchomach ideas and arguing from Scripture and historical examples, like the Dutch Act of Abjuration of 1581 against Philip II, that the people were free to remove kings and alter their government if they wished. Even Hobbes advocated submission to the commonwealth, despite the way it came to power. In 1651 in *Leviathan*, the fullest exposition of his political thought, he applied his analysis of sovereignty to point out that subjects ceased to be obliged to a sovereign who could no longer protect them. The clear corollary was that they may licitly transfer their obedience to the new sovereign who had emerged from the civil war and its aftermath. Hobbes himself gave personal effect to his teaching by returning home from exile in the same year.[68]

Nevertheless, the new republican regime was enmeshed in contradictions it was never able to resolve. The same was true of its successor, the

---

[66] D. Underdown (*Pride's purge*, Oxford, 1971) provides a detailed account and analysis of party alignments and events culminating in the purge of Parliament and its sequel. I have not felt it necessary in the text to discuss the complexities in defining presbyterians and Independents as political groupings or parties, a problem extensively considered by recent scholarship.

[67] Printed in Gardiner, *Constitutional documents of the Puritan revolution*, 384–8.

[68] J. Milton, *The tenure of kings and magistrates* (1649). T. Hobbes, *Leviathan* (1651), "A review and conclusion." For the political writings by Milton and others on the commonwealth, see Zagorin, *A history of political thought in the English revolution*, chs. 5–6, 114–15, and, for Hobbes, ch. 13.

protectorate of Cromwell, which was established in 1653 following the demise of the commonwealth at the hands of the army. All the interregnum governments suffered from identical and insoluble problems of legitimacy, which eventually resulted in the Stuart monarchy's return.

The commonwealth, although claiming to embody the sovereignty of the people, represented only a remnant of the former Parliamentarian party. The purge eliminated 270 members, leaving some 200 still qualified to sit in the House of Commons. This assembly, the Rump Parliament, governed England. It was a civil authority, yet it owed its position to the army, with which, nevertheless, there were many frictions. Its indebtedness to military force undermined its political legitimacy.[69]

The Rump was highly unpopular and reflected a much narrower sociopolitical base than the preceding parliamentary rule. The House of Commons had been sitting for such a long time that it had pretty well lost its mandate. By all appearances, the majority of subjects were shocked and alienated by Charles I's execution. Most of the aristocratic governing class that had previously stood with Parliament turned away from the commonwealth. Provincial animosities toward the regime were rampant. Inheriting debts and compelled to maintain a standing army, the Rump continued the heavy weight of taxation on the nation. Church lands had already been confiscated when it succeeded to power, but the abolition of the monarchy enabled it to sell off crown lands along with confiscated Royalist estates. In its financial operations and local administration generally, the Rump brought centralization to the highest pitch England had yet seen. The county committees were abolished and their functions transferred to supervisory parliamentary committees. Local offices were purged of unreliable elements. In county government, the Rump had to depend to a considerable extent on men of lesser status, small gentry and others, who did not belong to the traditional elite. In the towns, similarly, its primary support derived from people below the wealthiest bourgeois strata and from members of the sects and congregations.[70]

On the left, the Levellers opposed the commonwealth as altogether illegal. The party's hopes for a popular republic through the implementation of an agreement of the people had been dashed, and it considered the Rump no more than a self-appointed oligarchy. In 1649, several Leveller mutinies in the army were immediately crushed. Although the Leveller leaders continually attacked the government, the peak of their influence had passed, and they faced constant repression during the interregnum.

The installation of the commonwealth also arrested the revolution. The Rump, despite its origins in regicide, had no radical aims, and those sup-

---

[69] The composition, politics, and policies of the Rump are fully treated by B. Worden, *The Rump parliament*, Cambridge, 1974.

[70] For provincial reactions to the commonwealth, see Underdown, *Pride's purge*, ch. 10.

porters who looked to it for social reforms were gravely disappointed. Although sectarians, Independents, and some of the officers of the army urged the Rump to enact law reforms and other changes, it did virtually nothing on this score. It was an odd coalition whose leaders and members were mostly veteran politicians and gentlemen of established position, even including a few noblemen, who had no quarrel with the existing society. Some of them were genuinely committed to a kingless state; others decided to collaborate with the new order either in the belief that government must go on or for what they could get out of it. But the republican regime did not seek to realize any particular ideology or program and eschewed extreme policies.

The Rump's main objective was simply to retain power against its many enemies, and with the army's help it succeeded. First, in 1649–50, Cromwell undertook a hardhitting campaign in Ireland that ended the Irish rebellion and its alliance with royalism, thus eliminating the danger to the commonwealth from that quarter. Ireland was once again subjugated to English and Protestant supremacy. Then, in Scotland, a dominant faction of the now badly divided Covenanters rallied to Charles II, the executed monarch's heir, who accepted the National Covenant and Presbyterianism. To repel this threat, Cromwell invaded Scotland with his army and defeated the Scots at Dunbar in September 1650. A year afterward, he defeated them again at Worcester, when they in turn invaded England on Charles II's behalf. Their overthrow was followed by the English military occupation of Scotland and presently by Scotland's forcible incorporation with England.[71]

These conquests assured the survival of the commonwealth, which became a formidable power during its brief tenure. At home, all Royalist resistance was vanquished, and abroad the Rump was even able to wage a naval war in 1652 caused by political and commercial enmities on equal terms against the Dutch republic.

But the republican experiment foundered over conflicts with the army. The Rump could live neither with the army nor without it. Cromwell and his fellow officers were strongly critical of the Rump as a corrupt, self-perpetuating body that refused to relinquish its position. Insistently they pressed it to authorize new elections and then dissolve itself, as it had promised to do. Still the members clung to power, proceeding dilatorily with a bill for a new representative. It was necessary, of course, to provide safeguards against the election of Royalists and other adversaries of the commonwealth, but the Rumpers tried to assure that they should either retain their seats in a successor Parliament or control the latter's composition. Finally, the army leadership lost patience with their maneuvers,

---

[71] See Ch. 9 in this book for the fate of the Irish and Scottish provincial rebellions.

and in April 1653, at Cromwell's order, a body of troops expelled the Rump.

This act of military force left no government in England and blatantly advertised the supreme power of the army. After the long, costly struggle with the king, a settlement was still no nearer than before, and the gulf of instability yawned wide. By this time, though, Cromwell clearly bestrode the political scene as a leader of compelling charismatic authority. His invincible career as general, his destruction of the ancient monarchy, and his avowed dedication to the gospel all proclaimed that providence had designated him as its chosen instrument. It was thus as one specially appointed by God for some great work that many religious people and others still loyal to the revolution regarded Cromwell. The poet Andrew Marvell acclaimed him as "the war's and fortune's son," a kingly personality "fit for highest trust." Milton praised him as "our chief of men" who, "guided by faith and matchless fortitude," had reared his trophies in God's cause.[72] Millenarian enthusiasts also fixed upon Cromwell, whose conquests some sectarians held to portend the imminent fulfillment of the apocalyptic prophecies. Cromwell himself was convinced that he had been selected to execute judgment on God's enemies.

To fill the vacuum left by the Rump, the army council in 1653 summoned a handpicked Parliament chosen from the gathered congregations, sects, and loyal political men. This nominated assembly went on for only a few months and then resigned its position, hopelessly split between the advocates and opponents of law reform, the abolition of tithes, and other consequential changes.

Left again in naked control, in December 1653 the army officers installed Cromwell as head of state in a new regime, the protectorate, defined in an Instrument of Government. The latter was a formal written constitution ordained by the army and would doubtless have never even been conceived without the earlier Leveller conception of a fundamental charter for the state. The protectorate united England, Scotland, and Ireland in one government. Under the title of lord protector, Cromwell was designated chief magistrate; he was to share supreme authority with a new Parliament representing all three countries and elected on a changed but little democratized franchise that excluded Royalists.

The Cromwellian protectorate was the last significant effort to achieve a settlement out of the irreparable disruption of the revolution. It marked a sharp turn to the right after the republic, vesting executive authority as it did in a single person, even if limited by Parliament. The conservative trend of the protectorate was further emphasized when, in 1656, some of Cromwell's supporters proposed to make him king. He refused the prof-

[72] A. Marvell, "An Horatian ode upon Cromwell's return from Ireland"; J. Milton, "To the Lord Generall Cromwell May 1652."

fered crown, but his office became hereditary in his family, and a second chamber, analogous to the House of Lords, was added to Parliament. Many who were weary of insecurity and the military basis of revolutionary rule welcomed these developments as a gradual return to the former monarchical constitution. Cromwell was apparently persuaded himself that stability lay in that direction and might well have assumed the kingship had he lived much longer.

Domestically, the protectorate, buttressed by its standing army, was impregnable against enemies, and it occupied a no less commanding position internationally. Cromwell pursued a Protestant and imperial foreign policy of aggressive nationalism: peace with the Dutch; alliance with France; and war with Spain, which gained England the possession of Jamaica in the West Indies and Dunkirk in the Spanish Netherlands. English military and naval power as a revolutionary state far surpassed what it had been for well more than a half-century under the monarchy.[73]

Yet the protectorate was not a political success. Cromwell failed to get on with his Parliaments, which tried to cut down his powers and modify the government. Opposition appeared against the newly formed Cromwellian court. The army's conspicuous presence and expense, plus the continual threat of its political interference, made for great unpopularity. Defenders of parliamentary supremacy, republicans, and people who had vainly called for social reforms accused Cromwell of betraying the good old cause for which the civil war was fought. A few radicals even urged tyrannicide against him as the destroyer of liberty. The protectorate was unable to acquire legitimacy and depended mostly on the army and Cromwell's personal preeminence. With his death in September 1658, his office passed to his son, Richard. The army, however, felt no loyalty to a Cromwellian dynasty, and the protectorate soon collapsed, thus reopening the vacuum at the center. By then the restoration of monarchy was not far off.

Coincident with the first years of the interregnum and the installation of the protectorate, a small but highly vocal millenarian movement proclaimed its appearance on the political scene. Apart from the millenarian anabaptist dictatorship at Münster in 1534 and the activity of Thomas Müntzer and his disciples in the German peasant war, this was the sole eruption of millenarian militancy in an early modern revolution.[74]

Some scholars have pointed to (and, indeed, considerably exaggerated) a millenarian strain in traditional Puritanism itself. Before the revolution, certainly, there was a good deal of academic millenarian speculation in

---

[73] J. R. Seeley, *The growth of British policy*, 2 v., Cambridge, 1895, v. 2, pt. 3, chs. 1–3, contains a penetrating discussion of the foreign policy and wars of the commonwealth and the Cromwellian protectorate.
[74] See Chs. 6 and 7 in this book.

English Protestantism, and the 1640s began with high hopes of a thoroughgoing reformation that helped to foster a mood of apocalyptic excitement among the pious. Witnessing the fall of the Laudian church, Puritan ministers pictured England as the nation God had chosen over all others for the fulfillment of his providential plan. But such sentiments, the fruit of early revolutionary optimism, were by no means identical with the subsequent millenarian faith, which in its driving urgency and attraction to violence impatiently awaited the rule of the Saints.[75]

Probably the strongest impulsion to the emergence of the millenarian Fifth Monarchists was the execution of Charles I. Some sectarians interpreted this cataclysmic event as the beginning of the destruction of all kings and kingdoms and the fall of the tyrannical fourth monarchy prophesied in the Book of Daniel. Convinced that they were living in the last days, they announced the coming of a new heaven and a new earth in the fast-approaching millennium, which would usher in the Fifth Monarchy, the thousand-year reign of Christ and his Saints.

The commonwealth was a heavy disappointment to these believers because of its failure to introduce desired social reforms in preparation for the impending millennium. They placed great hopes, though, in Cromwell, whom they saw as the first of the elect and another Moses charged with delivering God's people. After Cromwell became lord protector, however, he incurred their bitter enmity. They regarded him thenceforth as a renegade to Christ who had ambitiously assumed a tyrannical power. Disillusionment only intensified their eschatological ardor: The enthusiasts of millenarian revolution only embrace disaster as a sure harbinger of the eagerly expected supernatural transformation. In pulpit and press, Fifth Monarchy preachers urged violence and insurrection against Cromwell's government. As the movement was more effective in agitation than concerted action, however, Cromwell had no difficulty in controlling and suppressing any danger it presented. In 1661, soon after the Restoration, a bloody rising in London by a small group of Fifth Monarchists in behalf of King Jesus was the last pathetic outbreak of millenarian militancy.[76]

Fifth Monarchism formed around the separatist clergy who invoked the Biblical apocalypse to propound a vision of social justice and destruction of antichrist and the ungodly. Its devotees were mostly urban, and its greatest following lay in London, where the Baptist and other congregations contained hotbeds of enthusiasts. Its numbers, never large (ten thousand is one estimate), included a large proportion of cloth workers and

[75] Both Wilson, *Pulpit in Parliament*, and W. Lamont, *Godly rule*, London, 1969, seem to me to read much more of a millenarian component into English Puritanism than is justified, as does also C. Webster, *The great instauration: Science, medicine and reform, 1626–1660*, London, 1975, ch. 1.

[76] B. Capp (*The Fifth Monarchy men*, London, 1972) provides a valuable account of the history and ideas of this millenarian movement.

other mechanical occupations, as well as some ministers, a few profession-als and gentlemen, and some of the soldiers and officers of the army.[77]

The movement is primarily of interest for its ideology, which inter-twined theocratic elitism with radical social protest. Like earlier mille-narian outbursts, Fifth Monarchism projected itself as "a revolution within the revolution." More important, it belonged to the revolution's declining period and was a reaction to fading, not rising expectations of a new polit-ical order. It appeared, moreover, in the aftermath of the Leveller move-ment's defeat. Secular radicalism having failed, it was now the turn of eschatological radicalism.

Fifth Monarchy preachers embraced some of the same demands and grievances the Levellers had stressed. They often employed the concep-tion of the Norman yoke to explain the long tyranny Englishmen had suffered. They condemned the heavy taxes on the people and denounced covetous rich men and corrupt lawyers. They would have abolished the legal profession and the courts altogether, as well as put an end to tithes and excises. They would have done away no less with lords of manors and "all oppressions and grievances in the tenure of lands." They called, too, for the export of the revolution. "Our armies and navies and churches," a millenarian wrote, should "in the name of Jesus proclaim liberty to the oppressed ones of other nations."[78]

In place of unrighteousness, Fifth Monarchy men envisaged a dominion of the Saints in readiness for Christ's kingdom on earth. They took the belief in inward grace to its extreme, holding that none but the elect (to whom they, of course, belonged) had a title to magistracy. "What right," demanded one of their manifestoes, "can meer natural and worldly men have to Rule and Government?" The Saints, they declared, are members of a heavenly state and commonwealth, and it is for them alone to exercise the authority given by God.

Fifth Monarchists would also have had the Bible as the only law. They demanded the acknowledgment of Christ's legislative power by establish-ing Scripture and the Mosaic code as the law of the land. Their fanatical literalism led them to propose death for moral offenses, atheism, and pro-fanation of the Sabbath; at the same time, they pointed out that the mu-nicipal law of Moses, unlike English law, did not make theft a capital crime but only required double restitution. God's law, they said, opens its mouth for the dumb and pleads for the poor and the needy; the beastly law of the world opens its mouth for those with a large purse and sends the poor empty away.

---

[77] *Ibid.*, ch. 4.

[78] Citations in this and the next two paragraphs are taken from Zagorin, *A history of political thought in the English revolution*, ch. 8, which discusses Fifth Monarchist political ideas; see also Capp, *The Fifth Monarchy men*, chs. 6–8.

The Fifth Monarchy movement was an outgrowth of the radical sectarianism that proliferated so luxuriantly during the revolution. It was an amalgam of humanitarian lament for the oppressed and apocalyptic vengeance fantasies against worldly power. It looked only to a miraculous theocratic utopia and had no care for rights or for men as citizens. Unlike Müntzer in the German peasant war (whose memory Fifth Monarchist writers defended), it actually tried to advance some elements of a program in its yearning for justice. But it shared an identical faith in the soon-to-be-consummated destruction of the sinful order of history, and, like Müntzer, it would have borne witness to millennial transformation by violence against the ungodly and unsparing dictatorship of the Saints.

VII

The interregnum years were fertile in reforming aspirations and projects of all kinds. The Rump Parliament tried to control immorality with acts that made serious secular offenses of adultery and fornication, profanation of the Sabbath, and swearing and cursing.[79] Longstanding complaints of the expense and injustices of legal proceedings and the courts gave rise to a host of proposals for law reform, one of the most popular issues of the day. Writers called for curbing fees and lawyers, abolition of that "black puddle," the Court of Chancery, for its abuses, conversion of all pleading from law French to English, introduction of elected juries, lay judges, and decentralized county courts, provision of a land registry to avoid frauds and litigation, and correction of the inequitable penalties in the criminal law and the treatment of debtors. Despite widespread agitation and discussion, however, these ideas bore scarcely any fruit.[80]

Numerous reformers occupied themselves with schemes of practical improvement for the benefit of the nation's spiritual and material welfare. Samuel Hartlib, a utopian-minded German who lived permanently in England, played a key part in many of these efforts. He was the central connecting figure of a wide circle of writers and thinkers concerned with the reform of education and the universities, trade and manufactures, the relief of poverty, science, and medicine. Highly active in the 1640s and 1650s, Hartlib placed great hopes in the revolution's possibilities and promoted numerous projects looking toward the betterment of man's estate.[81] Merchants, politicians, and pamphleteers likewise engaged in extensive discussion of economic policy and organization and propounded innova-

---

[79] C. H. Firth and R. S. Rait, *Acts and ordinances of the interregnum 1642–1660*, 3 v., London, 1911, v. 2, 383–9, 393–6.

[80] See D. Veall, *The popular movement for law reform 1640–1660*, Oxford, 1970.

[81] See Webster, *The great instauration*, for a comprehensive account of Hartlib's activity and these reforming projects.

tive recommendations for the advancement of agriculture, commerce, industry, and shipping.[82] If these designs had but little effect at the time, they testified nonetheless to the stimulating effects and many-sided interest in amelioration produced by an era of experiment.

In the domain of political thought, the interregnum continued the ferment of the preceding decade with the formulation of a significant theoretical republicanism, the expression of some extraordinary communist ideas, and the concluding version of Hobbes's work on politics.

The publication of *Leviathan* in London in 1651, with its four parts on man, the commonwealth, the Christian commonwealth, and the kingdom of darkness, marked the appearance of the greatest masterpiece of English political philosophy and represented Hobbes's most comprehensive statement of his principles on this subject. It contained a thoroughly secularized view of political life and obligation that afforded slight comfort either to Royalists, whose sentiments for Charles I Hobbes himself had shared, or to doctrinaire defenders of the republic. The author portrayed man as a restless, competitive being, actuated equally by fear of death and by an incessant desire for power after power. Hobbes made use of the concept of an original state of nature to demonstrate the terrible insecurity of men who, although free, are placed in a condition of war of all against all without a sovereign to protect them. He based the rationale of government and subjection on the human passion for self-preservation as a natural right. The latter impels men to accept the dictate of reason, which teaches them to renounce the absolute freedom of the state of nature for the sake of peace, security, and even the good life. The political order depends on contract: not a contract, though, between the sovereign and people but among the people themselves, who covenant with one another to convey their power to the sovereign, who commands them all and whose coercion can enforce obedience.

Hobbes invested the sovereign, whether one, few, or many, with formidable attributes, including the sole right to legislate, to tax, to interpret Scripture, and to define the rules of good and evil. He considered these attributes the logical corollary of the sovereign's function to preserve peace and held that sovereignty could be neither divided nor limited without its end being defeated. In denial of the great body of revolutionary monarchomach and resistance theory, a further corollary of his argument held that the sovereign and the people or community were not joint parties to a contract, and thus the former could never be charged with breaking its conditions. One of his most drastic departures from tradition was his conception of law, which he defined exclusively as a command emanating

[82] See M. James, *Social problems and policy during the Puritan revolution 1640–1660*, London, 1930, ch. 7 and *passim*; and W. K. Jordan, *Men of substance*, Chicago, 1942, 215–48, the latter concerned with the ideas of Henry Robinson on economic reform.

from the sovereign's will. This radical view completely divorced the notion of law from any substantive content of justice and gave it a purely formal character.

Reflecting on the calamities of civil war and "that dissolute condition of masterlesse men, without subjection to Lawes, and a coercive Power to tye their hands from rapine and revenge," Hobbes naturally strove to fortify absolute power. But if absolutism was one great part of his thought, another part allied him with the liberalism expressed by the revolutionary theorists of his time. Thus, he was thoroughly individualistic in his standpoint and regarded the commonwealth solely as a contrivance of the interest of individuals in peace and security. He also shared the hostility of many laymen and sectarians to the clergy's authority in politics and intellectual matters. He detested clerical obscurantism and preferred that the sovereign permit considerable freedom of religion. He instructed the sovereign to direct its rule to the safety and happiness of its subjects: Rebellion, he warned, is the inevitable consequence and punishment of bad and negligent government. Most important of all, he justified the political order no less than the Levellers had on the basis of natural right, which in his case signified the prepolitical human claim to life as well as, if possible, to "contentment" and "commodious living," the objects for which sovereignty is itself ordained. And, insofar as natural right was his root conception and point of departure, Hobbes left subjects, at least implicitly, a standard by which to judge and even to reject a sovereign power that no longer fulfilled the ends for which it existed.[83]

Of the several exponents of economic equality and utopian communism during these years, the most noteworthy by far was Gerrard Winstanley, a thinker whose originality and penetration modern scholarship has come to recognize. Winstanley was entirely a product of the English revolutionary experience and was inspired to speak by the intense hopes and bitter disappointments of the 1640s. He comes to notice first as a small cloth merchant in London financially ruined by the civil war. Immersed in the milieu of radical sectarianism, a questioner, a visionary, and a mystic, he began in 1648 to write tracts that expounded a religion of love, universal redemption, and Christ's restoration of the whole creation. Soon he developed these thoughts further to identify God with the spirit of reason dwelling immanently within the world. God and Jesus are not in a place of glory beyond the skies, he said, but are present in all things as the reason and righteousness destined to rule in every man and woman. These ideas, expressed in words of exceptional tenderness and beauty, amounted

---

[83] For a fuller discussion of Hobbes's thought along the lines in the text, see Zagorin, *A history of political thought in the English revolution*, ch. 13, which also includes the cited passages. An excellent general exposition of Hobbes's political ideas is contained in M. M. Goldsmith, *Hobbes's science of politics*, New York, 1966.

to a spiritualistic pantheism imbued with the faith that Christ would soon lift mankind's curse and fill the earth with righteousness.

Early in 1649 Winstanley published *The new law of righteousness*, announcing his revelation of communism as the ethical and spiritual meaning of Christ's teaching. The origin of evil lay in private property; reason and the righteousness of Christ lay in the equal possession of the earth, which would restore man to his pristine good. "So long as such are Rulers," Winstanley wrote, "as cals the Land theirs, upholding this particular propriety of Mine and Thine, the common-people shall never have their liberty, nor the Land ever [be] freed from troubles, oppressions, and complainings." Hence Christ, the light of reason, requires that all mankind have a freedom in the earth. Winstanley coupled this radical interpretation of reason with his insistence that men look for their felicity in this world. The clergy who preach for gain only deceive the people by speaking of righteousness in another life; but "I tel you . . . it must be seen by the material eye of the flesh: and those five senses that is in man, shall partake of this glory."

Shortly after the appearance of this tract, Winstanley and some of his followers occupied and began to work the parish common lands at Saint George's Hill in Surrey. They called themselves Diggers and True Levellers. In carrying on communal cultivation, they desired to testify to the coming redemption of the world, when the earth again exists as a common treasury freed from the evil of covetousness and private property. They disavowed the use of force against landlords but would set an example of true religion by their act of working and sharing together.

The Digger experiment lasted only a few brief months due to the animosity of the neighboring tenants, parson, and gentry, who drove the colony away. Several similar ventures that sprang up elsewhere under Digger inspiration were also short lived. But in manifestoes written to justify the Diggers, Winstanley continued his attack upon private property with a passionate critique of the contemporary order. For him, Christ was the "head Leveller," the spirit of love that stands for "communitie." He condemned the nation's ruling powers for promising freedom but maintaining bondage. The common people, he charged, are still under the Norman yoke in servitude to the clergy, gentry, and landlords. But the people did not spend their blood and money in the civil war only to maintain the Norman tyranny. Now that the kingly office is abolished, manor lords, the offspring of monarchy, must also be abolished. Although England is supposed to be a free commonwealth, he said, "If I have not freedom to live in peace, and enjoy food and rayment by my Labors freely, it is no Commonwealth at all."

Winstanley grounded these criticisms in a general view that saw property as the dominant force and cause of conflict in social life. All men's strivings and struggles, according to his understanding, revolved around the possession of the earth. It is the desire for the earth that motivates the actions of the gentry and the sermons of the clergy. The basis of all laws consists in the disposal of the earth. And, above all, the essence of freedom lies in the unrestricted right to use the earth. When the gentry summoned the people to fight against the king, they only intended their own freedom, while they left the people under the slavery of manor lords. All that wars have done in the past is to remove property from a weaker to a stronger hand without lifting the "curse of Bondage." The law upholds property, forcing the poor to work for landlords at low wages and imprisoning them if they refuse. If they beg, they are whipped: "And truly most Lawes are but to enslave the Poor to the Rich." Should the poor man protest his lot and recall the words of Scripture that the poor shall inherit the earth, "the tithing Priest stops his mouth with a slam," saying that this "is meant of the inward satisfaction of mind which the poor shall have, though they enjoy nothing at all."

In 1652, Winstanley gave final expression to his beliefs in *The law of freedom*, a plan of an ideal communist society, which he dedicated to Oliver Cromwell. This work, although apparently seriously intended as a design for reform, belongs to the classic utopian genre and ranks not far below Sir Thomas More's famous *Utopia* in its humanity, trenchancy, and intelligence.

The foundation of Winstanley's proposed commonwealth is the free enjoyment of the earth, which removes not only outward bondage but the inward bondages of the mind, such as envy, pride, fear, sorrow, and madness. Private property in the land and its products, wage labor, and money are all abolished. Families live separately with their personal possessions, but common storehouses distribute all goods and working materials according to need. A popularly elected parliament and local officials govern the nation and its communities and supervise the communal economy. Winstanley here abandoned his former opposition to coercion and instituted penal provisions, although assured that common ownership would eventually make them superfluous as men gained understanding of freedom. The refusal to work and the hiring of labor were punishable by a year's hard labor, the buying and selling of land or its fruits by death.

Ministers elected annually in each parish would conduct Sunday observances to consist of discussions of national affairs and discourses on "Physick, Chyrurgy, Astrology, Astronomy, Navigation, Husbandry," and other arts and sciences. The only true knowledge, Winstanley declared, is in the "secrets of Nature." To know these secrets is to know the works of God; "and to know the works of God within the Creation, is to know God himself." No other knowledge of God is possible for man. The clergy advise against trusting reason and promise a hell or happiness after death to divert attention from injustice in this world. Men, however, asserted Winstanley, must find their happiness on earth while they are living. Schools are to instruct all children in useful arts, languages, and every kind of knowledge found by experiment and observation, the only true knowledge. Many secrets of nature, he held, would be discovered when mankind enjoyed the freedom of the earth: For "Kingly Bondage is the cause of the spreading of ignorance," but "when Commonwealths Freedom is established . . . then will knowledge cover the Earth."

Such ideas suggest a mind that had traveled far beyond most of its contemporaries. What intellectual influences may have acted upon it are hidden from view. Possibly Winstanley was acquainted with More's *Utopia* as well as with some of Francis Bacon's works and with writings by occult Hermetic philosophers who touched certain themes resembling his own. During a short period of activity, however, he arrived at an original pantheistic religion embracing community as the highest of ethical principles. Whether this religion be termed a spiritualistic materialism or a materialistic spiritualism is all one because the two are ultimately the same. It was a unique faith, centered entirely upon this world, joining Christ, reason, redemption, and the freedom of command ownership in a single vision of a transformed society.[84]

The political ideology of republicanism was a late growth of the revolutionary era that developed only in the 1650s. The Levellers fought for a democratic republic but did not produce any distinctively republican theory. The creators of the commonwealth in 1649, although they subscribed to the maxims of popular sovereignty and a right of resistance, had no commitment to a doctrinaire republicanism. If they abolished kingship, they did so mostly due to practical exigencies rather than to any belief in a republic as the best form of government. Nonetheless, the interregnum in its continued unsettledness offered an encouraging atmosphere for republican ideas. Following the extinction of monarchy, men educated in the classical and humanistic tradition began to look to formal republican models as their preferred polity. The opponents of the Cromwellian protectorate included republicans or "commonwealthsmen," who rejected military despotism and rule by a single person. In the five years preceding the Restoration, republicanism reached its apogee, taken up by writers

[84] Nearly all of Winstanley's writings are printed with an illuminating introduction in *The works of Gerrard Winstanley*, ed. G. H. Sabine, Ithaca, 1941. For the quotations in the text and a fuller treatment of Winstanley's ideas, see Zagorin, *A history of political thought in the English revolution*, ch. 4, which also discusses several other communist writings of the period. C. Hill, *The world turned upside down*, London, 1972, ch. 7, contains an account of Winstanley placed in the essential context of the multitudinous sectarianism and antinomianism of the revolutionary era; Hill's *The religion of Gerrard Winstanley, Past and present supplement* 5 (1978) is a stimulating attempt to investigate the evolution and nature of Winstanley's religious beliefs.

and politicians as a fashionable doctrine and as the last remaining alternative in the quest for settlement. This final effort to rescue the revolutionary cause was no more successful than its predecessors, but it added substantially to the era's harvest of political ideas.

One writer largely dominated the republicanism of this brief moment of its efflorescence: James Harrington, whose principal work, *The commonwealth of Oceana* (1656), was the inspiration for a whole school of republican theorists. Harrington derived his conceptions from such different sources as the republicanism of classical antiquity, Machiavelli and Hobbes, who were prime influences on his thought, and the history of Venice, the famed republic, which legend said had survived unchanged for a thousand years. From these materials he created an original synthesis in *Oceana*, a thinly disguised utopian fiction showing how England could be shaped into a lasting republic or free commonwealth.

Harrington's primary insight was that the form of government and sovereignty depended on the distribution of landed property by an inevitable necessity. The balance of property is the foundation; government, the superstructure. In an absolute monarchy, all or most of the land is owned by one man; in a regulated monarchy, the land is owned by the crown and a small nobility; in a commonwealth, landownership is widely diffused among the people. Only when balance and superstructure are in accord can government be stable. Harrington believed that social change in England since the end of the fifteenth century had placed the balance of property in the people. The earlier feudal balance founded on the crown and nobility had thus given way to a popular balance. This transformation in turn inevitably resulted in the breakdown of the polity and the civil war. His theory of the balance made Harrington conclude that "the dissolution of this government caused the war, not the war the dissolution of this government." Accordingly, he held that recognition of this fact through the formation of a free commonwealth was England's sole route to peace, harmony, and order.

Harrington composed a detailed picture of a model republican state that combined popular sovereignty with aristocratic gentry leadership. Government, he believed, is an art "peculiar unto the Genius of a Gentleman." One of the republic's essential institutions was an agrarian law limiting the amount of land anyone could possess in order to preserve a permanent popular balance. Regular rotation in office and the use of the ballot for voting were also provided. Rule lay in an executive magistracy and a bicameral parliament consisting of a popularly elected assembly and a senate chosen on a property franchise. The senate alone had the right to debate, the assembly alone the right to legislate, thereby assuring the supremacy of both public interest and deliberative wisdom in the republic's government. As regards religion, Harrington permitted a national church under parliament's authority but took care to require liberty of conscience and denied any power to the clergy as a danger to civil peace.

In spite of its somewhat fantastic character as the portrait of a utopian commonwealth, Harrington's *Oceana*, as well as his other writings, was filled with perceptive ideas and observations. His analysis of forms of government, his comparison of republics, and his comments on a citizen army, public assemblies, colonies, and related topics formed a treasury of republican doctrine. He advocated a republic not only as a historical necessity but in the firm conviction, which he shared with Machiavelli, that it is the best foundation of civic virtue and the public good. In common with that of other revolutionary theorists of the time, his political faith was dominated by the conception of man as a free citizen. He was so convinced of the theory of the balance that he thought a republic with the proper institutions could be as long-lived as the world. He was no less convinced that kingship had become an impossibility in England because of the social changes that had taken place. He and fellow republicans were still clinging hopefully to this belief even as the Restoration stared them in the face.[85]

VIII

In April 1659, the protectorate collapsed when the army chiefs deposed Cromwell's son, Richard. A rapid succession of futile expedients to preserve the "good old cause" ensued, attended only by deepening confusion, uncertainty, and irreconcilable quarrels among army officers, old Parliament men, republicans, and sectarians. The revolution was breathing its last like a dying patient who continually changes his bed without allaying his distemper. Meanwhile, the great bulk of political opinion had swung strongly toward kingship. In February 1660, the decisive step in this direction was taken after General Monck, the English commander-in-chief in Scotland, brought his troops to London and, in response to an overwhelming demand, recalled the Long Parliament as it had been prior to the military purge twelve years before. Its members met, a ghost from the past, and, having provided for a successor Parliament, formally dissolved themselves at last. The newly elected Parliament then convened, including the House of Lords, and summoned Charles II, who returned from exile in May 1660 to a jubilant welcome. With this the Restoration was accomplished.[86]

[85] *The political works of James Harrington*, ed. J. G. Pocock, 1977, contains *Oceana* and other writings, preceded by a discussion of Harrington's ideas and influence. See also Zagorin, *A history of political thought in the English revolution*, chs. 10–12, for another account of Harrington and republican theorists.

[86] The final events leading to the Restoration are discussed by A. Woolrych, "Last quests for a settlement 1657–1660," in Aylmer, *The interregnum;* G. Davies, *The Restoration of Charles II 1658–1660*, San Marino, 1955, contains a detailed narrative.

The Restoration took place without any conditions. Hardly the work of Royalists, it was due primarily to former Parliamentarians who turned to the Stuart monarchy as the sole means of reestablishing a legitimate and stable polity. It was apparently desired by nearly the entire aristocratic order, as well as by London's government and most of the citizenry. In 1642, London had abandoned Charles I; in 1660, its weighty support helped to reinstate Charles II. The army acquiesced in the Restoration because it shared the general feeling and because the soldiers had been promised all their arrears of pay on demobilization; those officers who would have opposed the event were discredited and powerless.

Kingship and the Stuarts thus came back peacefully, by consensus, not by force of arms, and as the decision of Parliament. With them also came the restoration of Parliament itself, freed from further military intervention. Civil authority was again supreme, and a standing army henceforth regarded by Englishmen as dangerous to their liberty. It was also of moment that just as revolutionary and interregnum government did not inflict a "red" terror of brutal repression upon political enemies, so the Restoration was not accompanied by a "white" terror or great political proscription. The act of indemnity and oblivion that Parliament passed in 1660 wiped out the past by pardoning everyone who had taken arms against the king, save for fifty-odd men, most of whom had participated in Charles I's trial and death. Of these regicides, thirteen were condemned and executed.

The civil war may have killed a hundred thousand Englishmen, besides its innumerable casualties in wounds and sickness. It destroyed untold amounts of property. The revolution's magnitude, with its successive overturnings, makes it tempting to believe that it must have wrought some enduring changes politically and socially. The truth, however, is more complex and qualified. To be sure, the civil war and overthrow of the monarchy was an experience that could never be erased. Moreover, Parliament had taken over the government and administration of the state and could not simply return to its pre-1640 position. But the revolution, by its failure to achieve a durable regime, left many issues unresolved. At the Restoration, the entire corpus of legislation passed since 1642 without the royal assent was expunged as void. The control of the militia was reinstated in the crown. The act of 1642 expelling the bishops from the House of Lords was repealed, and they took their place in Parliament again. The great constitutional reform statutes of 1641 remained in effect; however, although they assured the regularity of parliamentary meetings and deeply restricted the royal prerogative, they by no means settled the future relations between the crown and Parliament.

Hence, it is understandable that the post-1660 era, far from being a period of consensus and harmony, was increasingly embroiled in bitter political and party strife. At least once in Charles II's reign, the difference between the crown and its opponents in Parliament and the country looked as if it might end in civil war. If the king could no longer dispense with Parliament, the course of events after the Restoration demonstrated nevertheless that royal absolutism or a fresh breakdown of the state remained real possibilities. With the succession of James II in 1685, it seemed that absolutism would win. It took a second revolution in 1688, coupled with the military intervention of William of Orange and James II's deposition, before this danger was finally removed by means of an evolving political settlement that made Parliament supreme.[87]

Socially as well, the revolution, for all its convulsion, wrought no lasting transformation. The same aristocratic order that dominated English society before 1640 emerged intact and ascendant after 1660. The two intervening decades brought troubles, dislocations, financial woes, and political fragmentation to the traditional governing class but not any loss of social power. It might be supposed that revolutionary rule led to permanent changes in the distribution of property and fostered the rise of many new men and families, yet even this was not the case. From the later 1640s, Parliament sold nearly £2.5 million of church lands to finance its expenses; the interregnum governments for the same reason sold confiscated lands of the crown valued at £3.5 million and Royalist estates values at over £1 million. At the Restoration, however, all these sales of confiscated property were invalidated, and the lands required by law to be returned to their original owners. The purchasers, a miscellaneous lot of private individuals and speculators, corporate bodies, and soldiers, made what terms they could and accepted the consequence. In contrast to confiscated lands, the lands that Royalists had sold voluntarily in order to pay fines levied on them by the state were not affected by the Restoration. Despite the losses they may have suffered by such sales, though, aristocratic families weathered their difficulties as a rule and were thus able to maintain their accustomed position after 1660. The revolution, therefore, did not bring about a displacement of the dominant class or produce any long-term effects on the fortunes of landed society or the distribution of landownership.[88]

Probably the most enduring consequence of the revolution was the change it made in beliefs and values. The destruction of the state church,

[87] See the comments of J. R. Jones, *The revolution of 1688 in England*, London, 1972, introduction.

[88] J. Thirsk, "The sales of royalist land during the interregnum," *Economic history review*, 2nd ser., *5*, 2 (1952), and "The Restoration land settlement," *Journal of modern history 26*, 4 (1954); H. J. Habakkuk, "Landowners and the civil war," *Economic history review*, 2nd ser., *18*, 1 (1965), and "The land settlement and the Restoration of Charles II," *Transactions of the Royal Historical Society*, 5th ser., *28* (1978); see also the summary by C. Wilson, *England's apprenticeship*, 108, 133–4.

the multiplication of denominations, and the many-sided debate over toleration deeply undermined the assumption that the nation must be a single religious society. The revolutionary experience severed religious membership from civil subjection, and it lent strength to the conviction that religious and political freedom must go together. If tolerance and liberty of conscience had yet to be fully established, morally and intellectually they had made a great advance, which powerfully weakened the principle of compulsion in religion. In this fundamental matter, the revolution crossed the frontier into liberalism and certainly showed that it had the future in its bones.

Similarly, the political arguments, programs, and ideas of the revolutionary era offered new prospects for government and for freedom. No revolution in early modern Europe was as fertile or extensive in its political speculation. In their defense of resistance and the community's right to control or remove kings, theorists took up previous conceptions derived from their own and continental traditions of ruler limitation, which they enriched and amplified. At the same time, the revolution brought forth a stronger, more fully developed populism than had ever yet appeared in Europe. The emphasis on natural right, the thrust of the Levellers toward equal citizenship and a democratic republic, the controversies over the suffrage and parliamentary reform, the insistence on the political accountability of Parliament and government to the governed, the demand to base the state on a written constitution that ensured representation and established the limits of authority, the radical meanings given the doctrine of popular sovereignty and consent, the restriction or denial of the magistrate's power in religion, the attacks on economic privilege and vested interests, the social radicalism of some reformers and the visionary utopianism of others, and the formulation of republican precepts by Harrington and his followers added up to an imposing body of ideas with an influential life before them. The English revolution came closer than the other revolutions of early modern Europe to the enunciation of general principles of political and religious liberty. More than any of the rest, it embodied aspirations that clearly prefigured the liberal society still far off in the future.

13

Revolutionary civil war: the Fronde

I

The urchins and hooligans of seventeenth-century Paris used to have a game, one prohibited by the authorities, of shooting at people with a *fronde*, or sling; by this same term, too, contemporaries designated the revolution of the Fronde and its actors, the Frondeurs.

A sling may seem a toy, yet it can do deadly harm. Correspondingly, most of the Fronde's historians have tended in different ways to consider it as a dangerous rebellion, yet one that was vitiated by a paradoxical levity. Particularly the part taken in it by fashionable men and women of the high nobility has caused it to be regarded as lacking the deep seriousness a proper revolution should display. The themes of enigma, confusion, and even senselessness also run through some accounts of it, owing to the discrepancy between its violence and apparent character as an attack upon absolutism and the vanity, cynicism, and playacting ascribed to its aristocratic participants.[1]

Thus, in a representative verdict Ernest Lavisse, author of a standard depiction of the subject, called the Fronde "a game, but an abominable game." Louis Madelin summed it up as "a failed revolution" in which the nation never took part. Victor Cousin, a distinguished *savant* who wrote

[1] For themes in the historiography of the Fronde, see E. Kossmann, *La Fronde*, Leiden, 1954, one of the best works on the subject, which stresses its enigmatic character. Among the most helpful general accounts besides Kossmann's for the understanding of the Fronde are P. Doolin, *The Fronde*, Cambridge, 1935; A. L. Moote, *The revolt of the judges*, Princeton, 1971; R. Mousnier, "The Fronde," in *Preconditions of revolution in early modern Europe*, ed. R. Forster and J. Greene, Baltimore, 1970; and R. Bonney, "The French civil war 1649–1653," *European studies review 8*, 1 (1978). R. Bonney, *Political change in France under Richelieu and Mazarin 1624–1661*, Oxford, 1978, contains many valuable details and comments. R. B. Merriman, *Six contemporaneous revolutions*, Oxford, 1938, 50–70, also includes a discussion of the Fronde. An old-fashioned political narrative is given by J. B. Perkins, *France under Mazarin with a review of the administration of Richelieu*, 2 v., New York, 1886, v. 1, ch. 9, v. 2, chs. 11–15. See also the works cited in n. 2.

much about the aristocratic society of the period, described the Fronde as a series of intrigues with no serious object, an event without grandeur, and a pastime for gentlemen, wits, and belles. "To the ladies especially," he remarked, "the Fronde belonged."[2] The duke of La Rochefoucauld, himself a leading Frondeur whose *Maximes*, partly distilled from its experience, belong to the enduring classics of moral reflection in French literature, referred to the Fronde as "a sad farce."[3]

Such judgments not only indicate the ambiguous status of the Fronde in the succession of European revolutions but direct our notice to a presumed futility in it that calls for explanation in relation to the sociopolitical order that produced it. But whether inscribed by futility or not, by no means can the Fronde be dismissed as a merely superficial event. Lasting from 1648 to 1653, it was a drawn-out, destructive conflict in which fundamental issues were at stake. Moreover, it brought a collapse of rule and a civil war that menaced the French royal state with the most serious resistance to its authority during the whole long span between the earlier wars of religion and the revolution of 1789.[4]

In contrast to the parallel English revolution, which came as the sequel to a prolonged period of civil peace, the Fronde was the culmination of repeated unrest and insurrections during the preceding decades. We have already seen the political disorder of France in the earlier seventeenth century and how frequently it was smitten with agrarian, urban, and provincial revolts. The Fronde embraced just about every kind of disaffection. It was a fuse for the simultaneous explosion of all the festering grievances, factious animosities, and political resentments incited by the monarchy's absolutist thrust. It released in a final paroxysm of resistance half-subdued elements and institutions the monarchy had long sought to make unconditionally subservient to its will. If, as we have previously noted, hatred of fiscality was the predominant theme of seventeenth-century French revolts, then the Fronde was the greatest antifiscal revolution in France's history. But it was considerably more than this as well. The reigns of Henry IV and Louis XIII had seen a series of aristocratic conspiracies, particularly against the dominance of Richelieu, and noble involvement in various revolts. The Fronde brought the nobility into play again in an ultimate decisive encounter at the summit of the polity that pitted princes of the blood and *grands* against the crown. Officials and magistrates had often supported or sympathized with localized antifiscal movements. The Fronde, a climax of defiance by officials, found its initi-

---

[2] E. Lavisse, (ed.), *Histoire de France depuis les origines jusqu'à la Révolution*, Paris, 1903–11, v. 7, pt. 1, 42; L. Madelin, *Une révolution manquée: La Fronde*, Paris, 1931; V. Cousin, *The youth of Madame de Longueville*, trans. F. Accord, New York, 1854, 72–4.

[3] Cited in A. Krailsheimer, *Studies in self-interest from Descartes to La Bruyère*, Oxford, 1962, 82.

[4] See the discussion of revolutionary civil war in Chapter 10 in this book.

ating center in the kingdom's most eminent body of them, the judges of the Parlement of Paris. It encouraged an assertion of claims on behalf of the *parlements*, the Estates General, and the nobility to control or restrain the monarchy's power. Naturally, it precipitated popular outbreaks, so that Paris more than once became the scene of crucial interventions by the mob. It ramified into some of the provinces also, absorbing local conflicts, exploiting anticentralist discontent, igniting diverse provincial Frondes. In short, the Fronde reflected a polarization that forced a breakdown of the royal state.

The revolution of the Fronde unfolded in two stages, the first dominated by the Parlement of Paris, judges, and officials, the second by the princes of the blood, *grands*, and nobility. Between the two, of course, were continuities and interconnections, for France in 1648 resembled a thin crust stretched over a powder mine, and the ensuing blow-up was the reaction of an entire society.

The revolution originated in Paris itself, from the action of the crown's sovereign courts, the first rebellion in the kingdom's capital since the days of the Catholic League and Henry III in 1588. The broader background to its origin has been sketched in earlier chapters.[5] *Conjoncture* in this instance contributed not a little, due to the severely depressed conditions of the time. Paris and its surrounding region, the smaller peasants of the countryside and *menu peuple* of the capital, suffered the woeful effects of heightened disease and mortality, scarcity, and dearth. The last years of the 1640s were among the worst of the century. In the Paris market, grain prices after 1645 rose four and five times over their previous level to a peak in 1650–1, their highest point since 1590. This was an aspect of the "crisis of the seventeenth century," of which we have previously spoken, and only intensified the opposition to exactions and the hated *hommes de finance* of the fiscal apparatus who fattened at subjects' expense. Sporadic tax riots in Paris prior to the outbreak of the Fronde bore witness to the anger of the *pauvres gens* against new imposts.[6]

The exceptional hardship of the time was aggravated by the cost of France's interminable war with Spain, dating from 1635, which was the principal reason for the monarchy's insensate fiscal exploitation. The war, a legacy from Louis XIII and Cardinal Richelieu, was part of the European Thirty Years war but continued when the latter was finally ended in October 1648 by the treaties of Westphalia. This Franco–Spanish conflict went on till 1659, a breeding ground of revolt in both monarchies. Many modern students like to think that a realistic explanation of a nation's pol-

---

[5] See the discussion of French conditions in Chapters 5 and 7 in this book.

[6] See O. Ranum, *Paris in the age of absolutism*, New York, 1968, 201–3, 207–9, 220, which reproduces the graph of grain prices compiled by Baulant and Meuvret. Ch. 10 of this work, dealing with the Fronde, lays considerable stress on conjunctural factors.

itics presupposes the priority of domestic over foreign imperatives in its policy, a view enshrined in the German maxim of "der Primat der Innenpolitik."[7] The French war against Spain, however, was a case in which the reverse was true. One of the paramount objectives of Richelieu's statecraft was the achievement of Bourbon France's preponderance in Europe over Spain and the house of Habsburg, and to this goal he made domestic policy subservient, even at the price of the crown's harmony with its subjects. The determination to subjugate every element in the realm, which led the Bourbon monarchy to ride roughshod over privileges, to suppress the political liberties of the Huguenots, and to teach a harsh lesson of obedience to the nobility, was actuated not only by its commitment to the state's supremacy but by its need to be free of internal obstacles in waging its struggle for European hegemony. La Rochefoucauld remarked on this fact, commenting in his *Mémoires* that Richelieu "wished to establish the king's authority and his own by the ruin of the Huguenots and the great houses of the realm, in order to attack the house of Austria and abase its power."[8] If the Frondeurs wanted peace with Spain, as they did, they did so because the connection between peace and relief from autocratic government seemed obvious.

The administrative measures and innovations resorted to by Richelieu and his patron, Louis XIII, according to a modern scholar, resembled a dictatorship or monocracy more than monarchy; the war necessitated absolutist, even dictatorial methods, and royal government could only be wartime government.[9] This oppressive rule was justified on behalf of the regime by well-developed doctrines of reason-of-state and absolutism. A number of political writers, echoing the views of Richelieu himself, held that the interests of the state superseded the ordinary principles of law and justice and the rights of groups and individuals. They maintained, to paraphrase Pascal, that the state has reasons of which subjects and private men can know nothing. Hence, in case of conflict, its safety must be preferred to lesser values. Although advocates of this opinion ingeniously strove to harmonize it with the dictates of religion and the public good, it provided an explicit rationale to place the royal state above moral or any other considerations if necessity so required.[10]

[7] The centrality of this principle, particularly for Germano-Prussian history in the nineteenth and twentieth centuries, was stressed by Eckart Kehr (d. 1933), a young nonconformist scholar of the Weimar period whose writings were resuscitated after World War II and have exercised a strong influence in German historiography in reaction to earlier traditions; see his essays, *Der Primat der Innenpolitik*, ed. H.-U. Wehler, 2nd rev. ed., Berlin, 1970.

[8] Cited in R. von Albertini, *Das politische Denken in Frankreich zur Zeit Richelieus*, Marburg, 1951, 108.

[9] Mousnier, "The Fronde," 132; "Quelques raisons de la Fronde," *La Plume, la faucille et le marteau*, Paris, 1970, 284.

[10] The role and character of reason-of-state doctrines in Richelieu's time is fully discussed in W. F. Church, *Richelieu and reason of state*, Princeton, 1972, which also contains an analysis

Such principles were reinforced by conceptions highly exalting the monarchy's unitary sovereignty and divine sanction. Absolutist theories in the hands of Jean Bodin and other writers had flourished in France ever since the later years of the sixteenth century as an answer to the populist theses and defense of rebellion propagated first by the Huguenots and then by the Catholic League; by the time of Louis XIII and Cardinal Richelieu, they held the field as the dominant, virtually unchallenged political ideology of the age. During the period leading up to the Fronde, they received their most authoritative statement in Cardin Le Bret's *Of the sovereignty of the king* (1632), a treatise by a jurist who had been a royal intendant and was the leading French political theorist of his generation.

Le Bret conceived the king as the very image of God's government of the world. He ascribed to the crown the complete monopoly of public authority, including the right to tax and to make and change laws at will. The king was not bound by the customs or ordinances of the land and possessed full freedom of action in matters of state and public affairs. Le Bret did not, of course, consider the crown exempt from all limits, of which he listed a number such as divine law and the property rights of subjects. Nevertheless, he emphasized that the king could not be restricted by the judicial powers of the *parlements*, or by the Estates General, or by the princes of the blood, all of whom are subject to royal control and have no share in public authority. He specifically rejected the claims of the *parlements* to ratify the king's acts, affirming that they were only royal delegates who had cognizance of the disputes of particular parties and no jurisdiction over matters of state. Moreover, he unreservedly justified royal fiscal exactions and pointed out that war had obliged France's kings to use their absolute authority to raise *tailles* and subsidies from their people without consent. This power, according to him, was an essential attribute of the sovereignty pertaining to the crown, against which no privilege can stand. Nor did he hesitate to authorize a breach of the norms of justice when the state's higher good was in question. He also interpreted the crime of *lèse-majesté* in such a draconian way as to prohibit any manifestation of political opposition or criticism as an offense against the prince.[11]

With good reason, Le Bret's work has been described as the "great apology of Richelieu's government."[12] It expressed in juridical and theoretical

of the cardinal's policy and contemporary political ideas. The only possible reservation one can have about this indispensable study is that it takes at times a too favorable view of Richelieu's actions and motives. For further discussion, see also von Albertini, *Das politische Denken*, 175–95.

[11] C. Le Bret (1558–1655), *De la Souveraineté du roy*, Paris, 1632. For discussions of this work and current absolutist theories, see Doolin, *The Fronde*, ch. 4; von Albertini, *Das politische Denken*, 39–42 and *passim*; and Church, *Richelieu and reason of state*, 266–76.

[12] Doolin, *The Fronde*, 84.

terms the thorough authoritarianism of the monarchy's relation to its subjects. Yet, in reality, this authoritarian order was only the obverse of the repeated seditions and obstructions with which the Bourbon monarchy contended. Because French institutions were such a confusion of rival jurisdictions and countervailing powers, and because group immunities, autonomist traditions, and noble insubordination were so strongly rooted, without an overriding royal will at the center, the polity would have tended toward deadlock. In this particular respect, France could be likened, as already remarked, to a *"société bloquée,"* a stalemated society. Kossmann, the most perceptive historian of the Fronde, has commented on these anomalies and the consequent "incompletion" of the state before the Fronde, terming it a "typically baroque" organism in its contradictory pulls and tensions.[13] This is true, and it explains the autocratic severity of Richelieu's state-building efforts.

Thus, it was on theoretical foundations such as Le Bret laid down, eliminating the possibility of the slightest populist checks to regal sovereignty, no less than at the behest of hard practical exigencies, that Richelieu as first minister labored to extend and consolidate the regime of absolutism. It was accordingly the governmental structure he left behind him that the Fronde attempted to demolish.

II

Richelieu's death in 1642 and Louis XIII's in 1643 raised the curtain on the immediate prelude to the Fronde. The new king, Louis XIV, being only five years old, the government became a regency of the queen mother, Anne of Austria, advised by her all-powerful confidant and first minister, Cardinal Mazarin, a diplomat of Italian extraction whom Richelieu had recommended as his successor. Mazarin's policy was identical with Richelieu's: its prime goal was the defeat of Habsburg Spain, whatever the cost. This purpose ruled out the likelihood of any relief from the rigors of the previous reign. The government, though, was inherently more vulnerable during a royal minority and found itself faced by mounting unrest. Political opposition presently magnified into an acute crisis of authority, which, as in other cases we have seen, led to a revolutionary situation and a head-on collision between the regime and its adversaries.

Grievances due to financial problems and royal administrative pressures gave the crisis its momentum. In the hope of beating Spain to its knees, the regency adopted every possible fiscal expedient until the government

---

[13] On the *"société bloquée,"* Chapter 10 and its n. 79 in this book; on France's "baroque state," Kossmann, *La Fronde*, ch. 1, esp. 22–3, 27, 29. The phrase "the incompletion of the state" ("l'inachèvement de l'Etat") was first used by Lavisse (*Histoire de France*, 50) in his narrative of the Fronde.

stood on the verge of bankruptcy. Up to 1646, French military victories in the Spanish Netherlands gave promise that Spain might be compelled to conclude a disadvantageous peace, but these were then followed by reverses in Catalonia and Italy that dimmed the prospect of success. The Spanish monarchy in any case was grimly determined to maintain the fight against its Bourbon rival. Thus, the only thing that might have vindicated Mazarin's sway remained beyond his grasp.

Meanwhile, the weight and continual introduction of fresh taxes caused vehement complaint. Bureaucratic officials, one of the monarchy's chief props, were bitterly antagonized by their treatment. They had to submit to cuts and nonpayment of salaries, forced loans and contributions, and multiplication of new offices, which were put up for sale to the detriment of the interests of existing occupants. Among the sorest points to all the higher *officiers* of the crown was the spread of the system of royal intendants under Richelieu. The intendants were dispatched into the provinces with extraordinary commissions empowering them to supersede the functions of venal officeholders and the regular forms of administration. They invaded the jurisdiction of provincial magistrates and finance officials, short-circuited judicial procedures, and in particular were assigned major responsibility for levying and collecting taxes. The direct agents of absolutism against bureaucratic inertia and recalcitrance, they were authorized to employ every sort of coercion to execute the crown's decrees.

Another theme of protest was the extortionate practices of the tax farmers, the *partisans* or *traitants*, with whom the crown contracted to collect part of its taxes. Massive deficits caused by the war necessitated the government to raise huge loans at high interest and to anticipate its income. To entice lenders and the syndicates that farmed its taxes, it had to screw more revenues from its subjects. The situation was an ever-worsening, vicious circle from which no escape was possible under existing circumstances.

Paris, too, was violently irritated by royal exactions. The regency levied fines on all shops and buildings erected in the *faubourgs* since 1548, and it placed higher duties on goods entering the city. The government also tried to manipulate the interest payable on the *rentes* or bonds issued on the municipality's security. These and similar devices, invented by Mazarin's superintendent of finances, were injurious to nearly every segment of the Paris population, the poor and lower orders, bourgeoisie, and officials. Parisians anyway considered the entire financial administration ridden with corruption and were extremely hostile to Mazarin's ascendancy. Moreover, it was commonly believed that the minister wanted to prolong the war solely for his own profit and to make himself indispensable. This idea seemed that much more plausible when it became apparent from the negotiations to end the Thirty Years war that France would conclude peace with its other opponents while hostilities with Spain proceeded as before.

The regency's exorbitancies encountered a critic in the Parlement of Paris, the greatest civil and criminal jurisdiction in the kingdom and highest of the crown's sovereign courts. The Parlement's exercise of the right of judicial review to remonstrate against royal edicts and refuse them registration, without which they could not become law, was an old thorn in the monarchy's side. Such review with its accompanying debates offered endless opportunity to obstruct, delay, and modify royal legislation. The king could compel registration by his direct command, a command most solemnly delivered in a special session of the Parlement known as a *lit de justice*. Louis XIII and Richelieu, however, made strenuous efforts to eliminate the political interference of the judges and had frequently subjected them to punishment for their conduct. In 1641, in one of his strongest steps to curb its pretensions, the king in a *lit de justice* prohibited the Parlement from intervening in matters of state and also strictly limited its powers of issuing remonstrances. From the royal viewpoint, the registration of edicts was only a formalism, and the judges had no business to scrutinize the actions of the king and his council; they were to confine themselves to deciding between parties and refrain from meddling in policy or reason-of-state.

Even with its nails thus pared by Louis XIII, though, the Parlement of Paris was not an institution ever to be taken lightly. For the regency, ruling in the name of a minor, its sanction was particularly important. It was such a venerable, complex body with such wide competence, both judicial and administrative, that no one could precisely define where its powers ended. As the first of the sovereign courts, it ranked in authority above the rest – the Cour des Aides, Grand Conseil, and Chambre des Comptes – as well as above the provincial *parlements*. Owing to the honorary membership in it of princes of the blood, noblemen who bore the title of peers of France, and prelates, it even attributed to itself a representative character, which caused it to consider itself equal or superior to the Estates General.

The Parlement of Paris consisted of ten chambers or divisions, of which the Grand' Chambre was most senior and important. A hierarchy of nearly two hundred judges, plus other lawyers and a host of lesser staff, formed the regular *parlementaire* world. The chambers had their own president judges, the eight of the Grand' Chambre headed by the first president standing highest in respect and influence. As the pillar of the legal order, the court was an organ of legitimacy very necessary to the monarchy, indeed, standing in close symbiotic relationship with the latter, hence the difficulty of keeping it in bounds. To ignore or override the Parlement's views was impolitic because doing so inevitably put into question the validity of the decree or policy to which it took exception. The judges, proprietary magistrates with their own professional esprit de corps, enjoyed great prestige. Their ability at the behest of the senior judges to act in concert by a plenary assembly of all the chambers, combined with their strategic position in stating grievances, certainly made them politically formidable. Like most lawyers, they tended to be very conservative. The institution they served was an integral part of the crown itself, one they regarded as the very throne and depository of kingship, and they were fully committed to the ruler's sovereign authority. For them, however, this allegiance was tempered by legality as manifest in the Parlement's obligation of judicial review. In addition to all these considerations, the members of the Parlement, like those of the other sovereign courts, had their own vested interests to protect as officeholders, which made them strongly critical of the governmental autocracy of recent years.[14]

To obtain acceptance of its financial legislation, the regency did not hesitate to use threats and intimidation against the Parlement. There was nothing new in that – Louis XIII had done the same – but such treatment was less prudent and seemed more questionable under a child monarch. When in 1644 the government threatened a *lit de justice* to obtain ratification of a forced loan, the Parlement responded that "it was an extraordinary and unparalleled act for a king who was still a minor to hold a *lit de justice* and have edicts verified by the exercise of his absolute power." On another occasion, the regent imprisoned and exiled several counsellors for defying an order, provoking a judicial strike in two of the chambers as a result.[15] Recurring disputes testified to the strained relations caused by the Parlement's desire to moderate the barrage of exactions and the queen regent's and Mazarin's contempt, circumvention, and disregard of judicial objection.

During 1648, a further series of clashes took place that catalyzed revolt. They started in January with a *lit de justice*, the second one of the reign, which the regent had ordered to enforce the registration of a group of fiscal edicts, including the creation of some new offices. The Parlement's advocate general, whose job was to present the royal demand, prefaced it by a memorable oration condemning the regime's fiscal oppression. He lamented the ruin of the country under the weight of imposts, the miseries of the provinces and towns, the bitter poverty of the peasants, and the attacks on the sovereign courts, all to support the luxury of the tax farm-

---

[14] See Chapter 4 in this book; and J. Shennan, *The Parlement of Paris*, London, 1968, which contains a history of the court as a legal and political institution; a chart in *ibid.*, app. 1, illustrates its organization. The latter is also described in an excellent analysis of its role and the government's dealing with it and other officials in Moote, *The revolt of the judges*, 20–3, and chs. 1–3. Bonney, *Political change under Richelieu and Mazarin*, 23–5, and ch. 11, summarizes Louis XIII's attempts to exclude the Parlement from interfering in affairs of state and provides an account of the sovereign courts and their disagreements with the government.

[15] Shennan, *The Parlement of Paris*, 257.

ers. No less boldly, he also criticized the exercise of absolute power in a *lit de justice* to stifle discussion of legislation, even implying its illegitimacy.[16]

Although the edicts were registered, the chambers proceeded all the same to meet a few days later in plenary assembly to examine their validity. The regent denounced the move as unprecedented, asserting that the court had no authority to consider legislation after it was registered. From this ensued a struggle over several months while the government tried to put a stop to the Parlement's objections and while the latter persisted in attempts to block or modify the offending measures.

The rift became wider still at the end of April over the renewal of the *paulette*, an issue of the utmost concern to officials. The *paulette* was the privilege, conceded by the crown for nine years at a time, that permitted officeholders to make their posts hereditary on payment of an annual premium (*droit annuel*).[17] The government now confirmed it to the Parlement gratis, while offering it to the members of the other sovereign courts and the provincial *parlements* only if they would forego their salaries for four years. Outraged at this proposition and further provoked when the regent threatened to withdraw the privilege altogether, all four Paris sovereign courts entered into discussions in defense of their interests. They then resolved to act jointly by uniting in a special assembly in the Chambre Saint Louis, the hall in the Palais de Justice that was the seat of the Parlement's Grand' Chambre.

The Parlement's Decree of Union of May 13, 1648, proclaiming the conjunction of the four Paris sovereign courts, may be regarded as the starting point of the revolution of the Fronde.[18] The decision with all its potential implications was certainly seriously open to question from a juridical standpoint. According to the government,

to make of four sovereign companies a fifth without order from the king and without legitimate authority is a thing without precedent and without reason, the introduction of a kind of republic in the monarchy, of a new power which could pose a dangerous threat to the established government order.[19]

The decree signaled the formation of an extraordinary coalition of judges and officials, high bureaucratic elites and representatives of the robe, in a

---

[16] This speech by the advocate general, Omer Talon, became notorious. A summary with citations is in *ibid.*, 260–1; and Kossmann, *La Fronde*, 42–4.

[17] See Chapter 4 in this book.

[18] Doolin (*The Fronde*, 6–7) quotes the text of the Decree of Union. Kossmann has puzzled over the date of the Fronde's commencement, owing to his belief in the absence of any revolutionary purpose in the Parlement's acts (*ibid.*, 49, 53, 68). I agree, however, with both Moote (*The revolt of the judges*, 126–7, 140) and Bonney (*Political change under Richelieu and Mazarin*, 53, 190), among other writers, that the Fronde's beginning was the Decree of Union by the Parlement of Paris.

[19] Cited in Shennan, *The Parlement of Paris*, 264.

direct assault upon the monarchy's absolutism. This development was the more striking considering the many rivalries and conflicts of jurisdiction among bureaucratic officeholders that were a permanent feature of the French polity. Long-smoldering resentments, though, plus their treatment by the queen regent and Mazarin, succeeded in welding them together temporarily on behalf of what was called at the time "la cause commune de la robe."[20] Of course, many *officiers* not members of the sovereign courts likewise threw their support to the Chambre Saint Louis. The treasurers of France, for example, the corporation of officials who administered the royal bureaus of finances throughout the kingdom, were equally aggrieved on account of the *paulette*, slashes in salary, and usurpation of their functions by the intendants and tax farmers. To look after their collective interests, they maintained a permanent delegation in Paris. Following the Decree of Union, their representatives, too, appealed for help to the Parlement of Paris and sent a violent circular letter to all of the bureaus of finances, calling on the treasurers to concert with other local officials and to forward statements proving the nefarious conduct of the intendants and tax farmers. The *élus* also, another corporation of finance officials who administered the *taille* in the *élections*, although they were bitter rivals of the *trésoriers*, were similarly aroused, and their representatives in Paris turned to the sovereign courts for redress of their grievances.[21]

The regent was determined at all costs to prevent the execution of the Decree of Union and alternately tried threats, punishments, including arrest of judges, and conciliatory gestures, all to no avail. In spite of repeated prohibitions and charges of illegality and sedition, the Parlement, egged on by its more militant members, insisted on discussing how the decree was to be implemented. In June, the king's council of state formally annulled the proposed union as a contempt of authority, declaring that the court had no power but what the crown committed to it. Even this action did not deter the Parlement, which by now in its acrimonious exchanges with the regent and ministers was being cheered by crowds of thousands of Parisians for its stand. The judges stuck to their guns, leveling accusations against governmental abuses and defending their right to call the Chambre Saint Louis into being.

Finally, in fear of the effects on the difficult financial and military situation if the controversy continued, the queen regent capitulated. On June 30, she consented to the execution of the Decree of Union. The Chambre Saint Louis, an extraordinary convention of thirty-two deputies

---

[20] Bonney, *Political change under Richelieu and Mazarin*, 53.
[21] For the treasurers, see J.-P. Charmeil, *Les Trésoriers de France à l'époque de la Fronde*, Paris, 1964, 267–9; both treasurers and *élus* are dealt with in the essay by R. Mousnier, "Recherches sur les syndicats d'officiers pendant la Fronde," in *La Plume, la faucille, et le marteau*, Paris, 1970.

representing the four Paris sovereign courts, accordingly met for the first time that same day.

The Chambre Saint Louis remained in session four weeks, in which time it adopted a series of twenty-seven articles providing for extensive fiscal and political reform. As the deputies had no right to legislate, they sent their recommendations one after another to the Parlement for deliberation and action. The Parlement decreed a number of them on its own authority, thereby clearly assuming a legislative function. Thus, it was by its own decree that the court ordained one of the first articles of the Chambre Saint Louis abolishing the royal intendants. Other articles were presented to it at its own request in the form of royal declarations, which it then proceeded to modify as necessary. All along, the judges had to wage a continual battle of political argument and legal maneuver with the government. The harassed regent and Mazarin, even though on the defensive, did their best to weaken or prevent enactment of the more extreme articles. Both sides were fully aware that what was at stake was the preservation or subversion of absolutism and the fiscal regime.

The Parlement's opposition and the concessions forced upon the government raised widespread hopes in Paris and the provinces of the reduction of taxes and other burdens. The conflict with the judges was conducted in full public view, and the provincial *parlements* were naturally apprised of the course of events. In July, to appease the popular clamor, the queen regent was forced to dismiss the superintendent of finances, one of the most hated symbols of corruption and misgovernment. The privilege of the *paulette* was also unconditionally confirmed to all the sovereign courts. As the political conflict lengthened through the summer of 1648, the crown's financial position became critical in the extreme, with resistance to tax collections increasing and the tax farmers, who were among the chief targets of the sovereign courts' offensive, refusing to advance money in such uncertain conditions. In the sequel, the state, no longer able to service the payments on its loans, actually had to declare bankruptcy.

Mazarin and Anne of Austria never had out of their minds the contemporary revolution in England, which had destroyed the power of Louis XIII's brother-in-law, Charles I. They were quite determined that the French monarchy would not tread a similar path. While their embroilment with the Parlement continued, on August 20 a French army under the prince of Condé won a big victory against Spain at Lens in the Spanish Netherlands. This success encouraged the regent to venture a repressive stroke to put an end to the Parlement's aggressions. On the 26th, she suddenly had two of the most outspoken judges seized and imprisoned, one of whom, the elderly Pierre Broussel, was particularly known and respected for integrity.

Far from having the effect intended, the step provoked Paris to insurrection. As the news of Broussel's arrest spread, shops closed, crowds gathered, and barricades of chains, beams, and barrels were promptly thrown up, more than twelve hundred of them, it was reported, blocking the streets and the bridges across the Seine and making the movement of troops impossible. The next two "days of the barricades," a reminiscence of the urban revolt of May 1588, saw a huge popular protest. Mobs filled the area around the Palais de Justice and the Palais-Royal, the regent's residence, calling, "No Mazarin," and "Long live the king, long live the Parlement, long live Broussel." The multitudes who took part in these scenes were, by report, a mixed lot of affluent bourgeois, merchants, shopkeepers, better-off and petty artisans, and other manual occupations, *menu peuple* of all sorts. It may even have been the bourgeois elements who started off the demonstrations that momentarily turned the capital into an insurgent camp. In spite of disorders, however, not much violence erupted, apart from stones and threats hurled at several of the ministers.[22]

The situation looked very dangerous, and on the 27th a delegation of *parlementaires* followed by big crowds went to the regent to seek the release of their fellow magistrates. They warned her of the consequences of intransigence: "It is a question of nothing less than the loss of the city of Paris, and, through its example, of all the others of the kingdom. This affair involves the preservation of the State and Royalty."[23] The members of the Parlement themselves were under intense pressure from the populace, which demanded that they act in defense of their colleagues and the court's independence.

However distasteful, there was nothing for the regent to do but submit and order the freeing of the two judges. Broussel appeared in triumph the next day, hailed by the citizens and welcomed by the Parlement. With this the tension subsided, and the city returned to calm.

The Parlement did not incite the insurrection of August 26–8, but it was borne forward and profited by it. An intelligent pamphleteer observed that during the days of the barricades the judges were the "absolute masters of Paris," with a hundred thousand men in arms at their orders.[24] The royal government after this eruption had to retreat unless and until it was prepared to apply military force. In mid-September, Anne of Austria

---

[22] The days of the barricades of August 1648, and the events leading up to them, including the establishment of the Chambre Saint Louis and its sequel, are described in Kossmann, *La Fronde*, Moote, *The revolt of the judges*, and other standard accounts. For a detailed discussion of the crowd, see J.-L. Bourgeon, "L'Ile de la Cité pendant la Fronde: Structure sociale," *Paris et l'Ile de France, Mémoires 13* (1962). R. Mousnier ("Quelques raisons de la Fronde") presents a close description and analysis of these "journées révolutionnaires parisiennes."

[23] Cited in O. Ranum, *Paris in the age of absolutism*, 214.

[24] *Lettre d'avis à Messieurs du Parlement de Paris* (1649), in C. Moreau (ed.), *Choix de Mazarinades*, 2 v., Paris, 1853, v. 1, 375.

with the king and Mazarin withdrew from Paris to Saint-Germain to be out of range of the city's hostility, refusing all requests to return. There the Parlement sent its committees to negotiate over the remaining articles of the Chambre Saint Louis. The regent and minister had finally decided to yield to the sovereign courts, biding their time until in a position to suppress the monarchy's rebellious subjects. A royal declaration, which was approved and registered by the Parlement on October 24, 1648, gave effect to the concessions won in the months-long struggle.

The declaration accepted the whole program of the Chambre Saint Louis and, according to Mazarin, "abolished the best part" of the monarchy.[25] Included among the reforms achieved by the Parlement and sovereign courts were suppression of the intendants and extraordinary commissions; substantial reductions in present and future of the *taille* and indirect taxes; measures to prevent and punish the abuses of the tax farmers; restoration of officials' salaries; prohibition of new fiscal edicts and offices unless freely discussed and ratified by the Parlement; abolition of recently created offices; and finally, as a safeguard against arbitrary arrest, the provision that no member of the sovereign courts or other person was to be imprisoned by royal order longer than a day without appropriate legal process.[26]

These reforms struck at the foundations of absolutism and autocratic rule. The Parlement of Paris, through its right of judicial review, affirmed its authority to control and restrict the will of the crown in the name of law. In effect, it erected itself into an independent constitutional arbiter between king and subjects. In so doing, it threw down a serious challenge to the principles of absolute monarchy and reason-of-state. True, the program of the Chambre Saint Louis dealt largely with fiscal matters and did not explicitly confront in general political terms the issue of absolute royal sovereignty. However, by their insistence on the elimination of intendants, complete freedom of debate and suffrage in approving royal edicts, and prevention of arbitrary arrest, the sovereign courts showed that their objective was to dismantle absolutism. It was also true that one of the principal beneficiaries of the intended changes was the class of venal officials. Nevertheless, the Chambre Saint Louis's articles were important for other interests as well. They sought to redress common fiscal grievances, to lighten the weight of the *taille* on the peasants and the burden of indirect imposts on taxpayers, and to curb the regime's oppressions against subjects.

The judges in their contestation with the government were never anything but conservative and legalistic. They acted from a combination of professional and political motives and in their own eyes were far from

[25] Doolin, *The Fronde*, 21.
[26] The above is a bald and somewhat simplified summary. For a more detailed, technical treatment, see *ibid.*, 20–1; and Moote, *The revolt of the judges*, 158–67.

being rebels. Their posture was restorationist, professing fidelity to tradition and prescription, condemning innovation. As elites of the robe, they could hardly have been radicals. They kept their opposition within moderate bounds and showed no desire for institutional transformation or even for a thorough overhaul of the royal financial system.

Yet, a conservative impulse behind revolutionary change is what we have often seen in the rebellions of early modern Europe.[27] The Parlement's commitment to law and the belief in the normative past furnished it with a convincing ground to reject the absolutist design of Bourbon state building. "The opposition altered the constitution," comments one of the Fronde's historians, "but . . . altered it to make it conform with the ancient constitution of the state."[28] In this political context, even a restorationist project was bound to acquire a novel import, and, if the Parlement's envisaged reforms had become permanent, instead of not outlasting the Fronde they would have eventuated in an altered status quo by the barriers they raised to royal sovereign power. At the same time, the Parlement's demands and actions inevitably served to legitimate resistance and to set other forces in motion by its example.

III

The accord of October 1648 was simply a brief truce preceding the outbreak of civil war. The regent did not mean to keep her agreement with the Parlement. Although she returned to Paris, after frequent quarrels she withdrew once more in January 1649 to Saint-Germain. From there she ordered the Parlement into exile for its unwarranted and disobedient behavior. On its refusal, royal troops commanded by the prince of Condé laid siege to Paris to reduce it to obedience. The judges organized the capital's defense, directing the raising of money and fighting men and

---

[27] Some of the Fronde's recent historians have differed on whether the judges were really "revolutionary" or not. Kossmann holds that they were no such thing because their objectives were superficial and never included a transformation of the political system or significant social change (*La Fronde*, 31–2, 55–6, 68–9). Moote calls the judges serious reformers, not revolutionaries, their legalism being their chief strength (*The revolt of the judges*, 168–71). Mousnier, in contrast, holds that the Parlement's attitude was genuinely "*révolutionnaire*," that it wanted limited monarchy and even opened the way to a republic and that it stood for a revolution opposed to the other "centralizing and in a measure egalitarian revolution of the absolute monarchy" ("Quelque raisons de la Fronde," 282). Doolin, on the other hand, asserts that the idea of revolution was in complete contradiction to "the professed theory of the movement" and that to the judges innovation was "criminal and the principle of their attacks upon the government" (*The Fronde*, xiii). These assorted views only serve as another illustration of the confusion and disagreement among modern scholars about the meaning of revolution and also, in several instances, of the difficulties resulting from trying to read back into the past the post-1789 idea of revolution as a conscious will to sociopolitical transformation.

[28] Doolin, *The Fronde*, xiii.

superintending a coalition of the city's public authorities. They were supported as in the days of the barricades by masses of the populace in revolt against material and political grievances and the execrated first minister.

In a duel of declarations, the government condemned the Parlement of Paris for usurpations "without example in past ages." It accused the magistrates, whose authority derives solely from the sovereign, of taking over "the government and administration of the state." Because of the court's transgressions, the regency announced the king's decision "to extinguish and suppress this Company and to withdraw the power which they hold of us."[29]

In response, the Parlement justified its actions by adducing precedents for the position it held itself entitled to occupy under the crown. It denounced Mazarin's sway as minister as an illicit intrusion upon the monarchy and affirmed that it was in arms for the "common preservation" and against the "tyranny" of Mazarin, not against the king. In an audacious move, it proceeded to try Mazarin (in absentia, of course) and sentenced him to expulsion from the royal councils and the kingdom.[30]

The breakdown of royal authority and advent of civil war were accompanied by a sudden expansion of public opinion reflected in the proliferation of the press. Revolutionary circumstances gave birth to an outspoken freedom of criticism, which inspired and sustained the Fronde. From the latter part of 1648, a swelling volume of news sheets, official statements, satires and burlesques, and serious works of controversy aired and debated the issues of the day. The former mechanisms of royal censorship were helpless to prevent the flow of publications and the productions of seditious authors. "One half of Paris prints or sells pamphlets," commented a journalist, "the other half writes them."[31] Not since the revolutionary movement of the Catholic League in 1588 had the press been so bold or prolific in probing political events.

Under Cardinal Richelieu, the government had taken special care to control and utilize the press in its interest. The *Gazette*, an official newspaper, was founded in 1631 as a propaganda organ edited by Théophraste Renaudot, one of Richelieu's journalists. During the siege of Paris, Renaudot was established among the regent's entourage at Saint-Germain, where he continued to produce the *Gazette* on the government's behalf. The Frondeur rival of this royalist newspaper was the weekly *Courrier françois*, which served as the Parlement's voice and was described as so successful

[29] *Ibid.*, 81. [30] *Ibid.*, 73–4; Moote, *The revolt of the judges*, 193.

[31] C. Moreau, *Bibliographie de Mazarinades*, 3 v., Paris, 1850–1, v. 1, xxx–xxxi. The introduction to this work in v. 1 contains a survey and discussion of the press and propaganda during the Fronde. On the same topic, see also R. Anger, *Die Flugschriftenpublizistik zur Zeit der Pariser Fronde 1648–1652*, Münster, 1957; and M. Grand-Mesnil, *Mazarin, la Fronde, et la presse 1647–1649*, Paris, 1967.

that "bread did not sell better."[32] Renaudot also composed some anonymous broadsheets, which were smuggled into Paris for distribution. One of February 1649, entitled *Read and act*, a defense of the regency government scattered in the streets, was addressed to the "poor people of Paris"; another, *To whoever loves the truth*, to the "poor Bourgeois of Paris." Both sought to exploit social resentments by charging that the seditious adversaries of the government acted exclusively from motives of self-enrichment and personal interest.[33]

But the great majority of writings of the time were antigovernment and pro-Frondeur. Because the prime target of the pamphleteers was Mazarin, the name *Mazarinades* has been applied to the whole mass of literature produced during the Fronde. The liberty of discussion and intensification of political argument the conflict produced may be estimated from the output of the press. Between January 1649 and October 1652, the major period of the Fronde, more than four thousand Mazarinades appeared, and the total number emanating from the revolt was probably about five thousand, if not higher.[34]

These writings, according to their bibliographer, "dealt unhesitatingly with the highest, the most difficult, the most inflammatory questions . . . the constitution of the state, the rights of the king and of the people, the privileges of the princes, the aristocracy."[35] The incitement to this ferment was given by the resistance of the Parlement of Paris. It was the Parlement, declared a Frondeur memoirist, that began the "revolution" and thereby admitted the people "into the sanctuary. It lifted the veil which should always cover everything that can be said or believed about the right of peoples and of kings, which never accord so well as when left in silence. The hall of [the Parlement] profaned these mysteries."[36]

The political propaganda of the Fronde of the Parlement concentrated its fire on Cardinal Mazarin and the defense of the Parlement's high position in the state. In a typical outburst, one author ranged over the minister's base origins, his evil conduct, his disregard of justice both human and divine, and his stirring up of subjects to rebellion by his thievery and persecution and denounced him as the "disturber of the public peace, the

---

[32] Cited in Moreau, *Bibliographie de Mazarinades*, v. 1, x–xi. For Renaudot's work as a royal propagandist in the Fronde and earlier, see H. Solomon, *Public welfare, science, and propaganda in seventeenth-century France: The innovations of Théophraste Renaudot*, Princeton, 1972, 206–11 and *passim*.

[33] Solomon, *Public welfare, science, and propaganda*, 207. The two pamphlets, *Lis et fais* and *A qui ayme la vérité*, are reprinted in Moreau, *Choix de Mazarinades*, v. 1, 179–90.

[34] Moreau's *Bibliographie de Mazarinades* contains over four thousand titles, and subsequent supplements by other editors such as Socard (1886) and Labadie (1904) list additional entries. For estimates of the total number, see Anger, *Die Flugschriftenpublizistik*, 29–30.

[35] Moreau, *Bibliographie de Mazarinades*, v. 1, xiv.

[36] Cardinal de Retz, *Mémoires*, ed. A. Champollion-Figeac, 4 v., Paris, 1873, v. 1, 131.

enemy, destroyer, loss, and ruin of all France."[37] Writers affirmed that the revolt was against the tyrannical domination of Mazarin, not the king. They celebrated the antiquity of the Parlement of Paris, comparing it with the Roman Senate, and described it as having the authority to judge between kings and people.[38] Another champion of the Parlement emphatically denied that either it or the city of Paris were guilty of rebellion because both remained faithful to the laws. Looking at several contemporary revolts, he pointed out that the Parisians had done nothing resembling the actions of the Catalans, the people of Naples, or the furious English against their rulers.[39] Against all such views, a royalist publicist declared that the basic question at issue was "whether the king or the Parlement will be obeyed in France."[40]

The most noteworthy statement on the Parlement's side was *A letter of advice to messieurs of the Parlement*, an anonymous pamphlet of 1649 that attracted wide attention by its cogency and force. The author wrote to persuade the judges to hold out against any weak accommodation with the government. Among the causes of France's recent evils, he listed, along with venality of office and the tax farmers, the Parlement's own failure to live up to its exalted position in the state. He reminded it that it was the father and protector of the people against oppression, France's sun and tutelary genius, and that without its consent the king could do nothing of consequence. Yet for thirty years France had been enslaved by Richelieu and other ministers who have tried "to make pass as legitimate a politics of tyranny." "We are so accustomed to slavery," remarked the author about Bourbon rule, "that we are no longer able to believe our fathers were ever free."

He justified resistance on the authority of the Parlement. The king, in his view, although sovereign, was not a despot and must govern in conformity with the law; and the people under subjection still retain their "natural liberty" and the private property in their goods. Thus, if the monarch commits oppression and abuses the power granted him by God, he ceases to be a king, and the people are exempt from obedience. By the "people" in this connection the author noted that he didn't mean particular persons, but "Estates" and "the *parlements*," which have the right to approve edicts and taxation and to decide if they are just. He appealed to

---

[37] *Lettre d'un religieux*, 1649, in Moreau, *Choix de Mazarinades*, v. 1, 93 and *passim*.

[38] *Lettre de chevalier Georges de Paris* (1649) in Moreau, *Choix de Mazarinades*, v. 1, 150, 168.

[39] *Decision de la question du temps* (1649) in Moreau, *Choix des Mazarinades*, v. 1, 250–52.

[40] *Le Roi veut que le Parlement sorte de Paris* (1649) in Moreau, *Choix des Mazarinades*, v. 1, 191.

the Parlement to stand fast to its duty because it serves as the people's "deliberative voice" and as their "deputies."[41]

Besides such subversive spokesmen, some of the highest nobility were also involved in the Fronde of the Parlement. The *grands* allied themselves with the judges' resistance and eventually took over the revolt. During the siege of Paris, the two greatest noblemen of France remained loyal to the regency despite their resentment of Mazarin: Gaston duke of Orléans, Louis XIV's uncle, a vacillating, indecisive figure; and Louis prince of Condé, a Bourbon and royal cousin, descendant of the Huguenot leader of the sixteenth century, and one of the most famous soldiers of the age, who commanded the army blockading rebel Paris. In due course, the latter was to become the principal Frondeur chief. The aristocratic group of the Parlement's supporters included the duchess of Longueville, Condé's sister, Paul de Gondi, coadjutor archbishop of Paris, the prince of Conti, Condé's brother, the duke of La Rochefoucauld, and various other dukes, princes, and noble personages. These members of illustrious houses held provincial governorships as well as other influential positions that made them dangerously powerful.[42]

Among them were vivid, exceptional personalities. Madame de Longueville, a captivating princess whose husband was governor of Normandy, was one of the most glamorous women of her time and a fearless spirit in the revolt. Gondi was a brilliant writer, conspirator, and politician with a strong base in Paris who, under his later title of Cardinal de Retz, left the most famous of the memoirs of the Fronde. La Rochefoucauld, a lover of Madame de Longueville, possessed a mind of the finest intelligence and penetration, as evinced in his subsequent *Maximes*.[43]

These and other prominent noble rebels, men and women, husbands and wives, rivals, mistresses, and lovers, were affiliated through their shifting personal liaisons as well as by their common political opposition to Mazarin and the regency government. Indeed, in their case the personal and political were so closely interwoven as to be inseparable. They wanted to reverse the policy of the monarchy and to overthrow Mazarin's ascendancy. They also wanted to secure offices, pensions, and favors for themselves. In their eyes, the Fronde provided an occasion for the display of gallantry, valor, and their talent for intrigue in making and unmaking factional combinations.

---

[41] *Lettre d'avis à Messieurs du Parlement* (1649), *passim*, in Moreau, *Choix des Mazarinades*, v. 1, 358–407.

[42] For the provincial governorships of the noble Frondeurs, see Bonney, *Political change in France under Richelieu and Mazarin*, 294–5.

[43] At the time of the Fronde, La Rochefoucauld was known by his earlier title of prince of Marcillac.

The interplay of motives among the Frondeur *grands* may be perceived in the *Mémoires* of Cardinal de Retz, a younger son of a great family who became an ecclesiastic for dynastic reasons without a religious vocation until undergoing a spiritual conversion in his later years. His *Mémoires* were apparently written in the decade before his death at sixty-five in 1679.[44] In tracing the origins of the Fronde, he pointed out that the kings of France had not always been absolute monarchs such as they became afterward. He delivered a harsh judgment on Richelieu, an unscrupulous politician who "formed in the most legitimate of monarchies the most scandalous and the most dangerous tyranny which has perhaps ever enslaved a state." It was Richelieu, according to Retz, who habituated Frenchmen to a servitude unknown to their fathers and began to punish the magistrates of the Parlement for speaking the truths their oaths obliged them to uphold with their lives.[45]

Retz was thus not devoid of political convictions. He clearly believed in the idea of some kind of constitutional limit upon royal sovereignty which, as the nineteenth-century critic Sainte-Beuve pointed out in his essay upon Retz, was "the first serious thought from which the Fronde proceeded."[46] Yet his lucid self-consciousness was dominated at every moment by untrammeled egoism and a thirst for glory. He treated the revolt as a theatrical performance in which he aspired to play a leading and heroic role. So he consistently pictured himself in his *Mémoires*.[47] If he believed in certain principles, nevertheless the mainspring of his actions, as of those of other aristocratic Frondeurs, was what Kossmann has aptly called "an ideal of self-interested cynicism and refined Machiavellianism."[48] Retz's Machiavellian attitude appeared most strikingly in the scattered reflections he devoted to the "science of faction," as he termed the conduct of revolutions.[49] He took a perfectly amoral view of such movements, analyzing how they are to be managed and how one becomes the "chief of a party." He stressed the irrational factors that excite the frenzy of the people and expressed nothing but contempt for the Paris mob, with which he was a popular and influential figure.[50] He brought the same quality of detached

[44] See J. H. M. Salmon's excellent biography, *Cardinal de Retz: The anatomy of a conspirator*, London, 1970, which also discusses Retz's writings.

[45] *Mémoires*, v. 1, 119–21; see also *ibid.*, v. 1, 128, for remarks on the destruction of ancient laws and the "establishment of an authority purely and absolutely despotic."

[46] C. Sainte-Beuve, *Causeries du lundi*, 3rd ed., 15v., Paris, 1857–72, v.5, 49. (This is the *Causerie* of October 20, 1851.)

[47] See Krailsheimer, *Studies in self-interest*, ch. 4, an incisive and sensitive treatment of Retz.

[48] Kossmann, *La Fronde*, 151–2.

[49] *Mémoires*, v. 3, 380. Retz also sometimes used the term *révolution* (e.g., *ibid.*, v. 1, 130), meaning by it a convulsion of the state. His interest in revolutions also led him to refer frequently to the civil war of the later sixteenth century, the Huguenot party, and the Catholic League, for comparisons and contrasts.

[50] See Salmon, *Cardinal de Retz*, ch. 14, for a survey of Retz's ideas.

analysis to his portrayal of all the partisans involved in the Fronde. Although he was a completely individual personality, with his selfish ambition and calculation of interests, his passion for glory, and his antiabsolutist political opinions, Retz exemplified some of the typical features animating the aristocracy in the revolutionary civil war.

During the ten-week siege of Paris, the royal army tried to starve the city into submission by cutting off its supplies, a strategy that was only partially successful. The Parlement's troops led by its noble adherents undertook minor sorties against the blockaders. Both sides limited their operations, neither wanting to drive the civil war to extremes. England had demonstrated how revolution could get out of hand, and, at the news of Charles I's execution on January 30, 1649, the Parlement outdid itself in its declarations of abhorrence and condemnation of this act.[51] The judges, moderates as most were anyway, headed a shaky front, which probably could not have survived a long struggle. The mob recruited from the inferior populace provided the most dynamic support for Paris's revolt, but its unrest had begun to alarm the bourgeois and propertied strata.[52] The municipal administration in the Hotel de Ville had actually refused to associate itself with the capital's resistance, and dissensions had emerged between the sovereign courts themselves. Similarly, the regency government's problems were compounded by the growing disorder in the provinces, and it was particularly fearful of Spain's alliance with the Fronde at the invitation of aristocratic rebels.

Hence the Parlement and queen regent both found it expedient to begin negotiations to conclude their hostilities. The Treaty of Rueil between them, approved in April 1649 despite riots in Paris against a peace, generally preserved the status quo. The reforms of 1648 were confirmed, an amnesty was granted to everyone in arms against the crown, and Mazarin remained in power as first minister. This was a limited victory for the Parlement and its goals but left a situation that was highly fluid and unstable.[53]

IV

The peace of Rueil was only an illusory respite. Although it terminated the Fronde of the Parlement, it could not halt the wider movement of revolt and political breakdown. The Frondeur *grands* were not provided for in the settlement and continued to be highly disaffected toward the regency regime. Disobedience and resistance had deeply enfeebled the

[51] See P. Knachel, *England and the Fronde*, Ithaca, 1967, 87–91.
[52] See Bourgeon, "L'Île de la Cité pendant la Fronde."
[53] The negotiations and the treaty of Rueil are discussed in detail by Moote, *The revolt of the judges*, 208–19.

monarchy's authority. The provinces were out of control and drifting into anarchy. Amid all the troubles encompassing it, the royal regime still had to carry on at its frontiers the war with Spain.

The second stage of the Fronde was sustained chiefly by factions of the high nobility with Condé, a prince of the blood and renowned general who had won famous victories for France, as its key figure.

Condé, to be known in later life as "le grand Condé," was not yet thirty years old in 1649. An intrepid soldier, he had none of the gifts of a statesman or political leader but felt entitled by his birth to a great influence in the direction of affairs, especially during a regency. Although Mazarin's sway was anathema to him, he refrained from supporting the revolt of the Parlement. At that time he had said, "My name is Louis de Bourbon, and I don't want to shake the crown."[54] After the treaty of Rueil, however, he demanded enormous rewards for his services to the government during the siege of Paris. He aspired to political primacy and domination of royal patronage. Due to weakness, Anne of Austria and Mazarin appeased him with great concessions, and as a result some of the noble participants in the earlier Fronde became very jealous of his position. In this manner, Mazarin, a master of political flexibility, tried to foment dissensions among his many enemies. But he and the regent found Condé's ambitions implacable. So in January 1650 they took the extreme step of suddenly imprisoning him along with his brother and brother-in-law, the prince of Conti and the duke of Longueville.

This coup precipitated a new crisis and the resumption of the civil war. Condé's family, friends, and allies appealed to the Parlement of Paris for the release of the three princes, incited revolt in the provinces, and solicited Spanish intervention on their behalf. The *grands* of the first Fronde united with Condé's partisans against Mazarin. The latter's position became so untenable that in February 1651 he ordered the princes freed and left France. Following his release, Condé hoped to dominate affairs, but this was unacceptable to Anne of Austria, to whom Mazarin remained indispensable. She strengthened the royal position in September by having Louis XIV, now fourteen years old, declare his majority, thus ending the regency and enabling him to act in his own name. At the end of 1651, Mazarin, recalled by the king and the queen mother, returned from his brief exile, after Condé had already plunged into full-scale rebellion with the noble Frondeurs.

The Fronde of the princes and nobility was undirected by any clear political will or aim. It possessed no unifying center, ideas, or program. Fractured and dispersed, it was a mélange of the many discontents that had sparked the Fronde from its inception, evincing no consistent theme

[54] Retz, *Mémoires*, v. 1, 296.

save for the unpredictable play of aristocratic alignments and ambitions. This second period of the Fronde failed to realize any coherent purpose. The revolution simply became a vehicle of disintegration, tearing apart the fabric of political order but putting nothing in its place, giving full rein to the many centrifugal forces goaded into resistance by Bourbon absolutism.

This was the final struggle of the *grands* to dominate the government's policy and preserve some independence from the royal state. Condé as a dynast occupied a powerful position. Some of the officers and regiments he commanded against Spain were more loyal to him than to the crown and joined his revolt. He possessed a numerous clientele of noblemen and others in his hereditary possessions and controlled extensive patronage in the provinces he governed in the crown's name. The governorship of Burgundy had been in his family since 1631. In 1651, he exchanged it for that of Guienne, where he and his family enjoyed considerable popularity and the Fronde lasted the longest. He was allied to other magnates who also wielded large resources of provincial patronage.[55] Even the duke of Orléans, Louis XIV's uncle, affiliated himself with the noble Fronde in 1652 because of enmity to Mazarin, and his daughter the duchess of Montpensier, the greatest heiress in France, became one of its heroines.

The rebel *grands* did not hesitate to seek Spanish support for their cause. They had previously done so in 1649 and 1650, when they made agreements with Philip IV of Spain for aid in money and men. From the Spanish Netherlands, an army in union with their revolt invaded France in the summer of 1650, penetrating into Champagne and threatening Paris, only to be defeated eventually by royal troops. In November 1651, Condé concluded a further treaty with Spain that provided for subsidies and the aim of immediate peace negotiations to end the Franco–Spanish war. Just as Richelieu and Mazarin had intervened during the 1640s to assist the revolts in the Spanish monarchy, so the latter did the same against France during the Fronde. *Realpolitik* gave the Spanish government every reason to respond to the Frondeurs' appeal; the rebels opposed Mazarin's war policy, and the prolongation of civil conflict seriously weakened the French monarchy's military efforts.[56]

By its assault on the central government, the Fronde instigated revolt and turmoil in the provinces. The example of the Paris sovereign courts lit the spark of some local Frondes and at the same time initiated the pro-

---

[55] On the subject of Condé's position, resources, and connections, there are helpful comments by Lavisse, *Histoire de France*, 51–2; and Bonney, *Political change in France under Richelieu and Mazarin*, 286, 292, 296. See also P. Lefebvre, "Aspects de la 'fidelité' en France au XVIIe siècle: Le Cas des agents des princes de Condé," *Revue historique 250*, 507 (1973).

[56] See Bonney, "The French civil war, 1649–1653," 78–82, for a discussion of Condé's and the Fronde's relation to Spain and Spanish intervention.

cess of disintegration of the monarchical state's authority, which reached an extreme during the Fronde of the nobility.

The government's recall of the royal intendants from most of the provinces after 1648, as required by the reforms of the Chambre Saint Louis, was followed by antifiscal outbreaks in many parts of France.[57] Among the mass of subjects and in what may be termed the popular Fronde, antifiscalism was the most common feature. The belief was prevalent that it was no longer necessary to pay taxes. All the *pays d'élections*, where the intendants had been vitally involved in financial administration, were afflicted by antifiscal disturbances. Rumors of the reduction and cancellation of imposts led to taxpayers' strikes. Peasants in many places refused to pay the *taille* and resisted collections with violence. The regular tax officials often lacked the means to coerce the recalcitrant because royal troops were stretched thin in fighting both a foreign and a civil war. The Fronde represented the culmination in the lengthy succession of French rebellions of which resistance to royal fiscality was the dominant motive.[58]

The revolution in the provinces was in no way a single struggle and consisted merely of some separate fragments of revolt amid the general decay of order. In the first period of the Fronde, the Parlement of Paris communicated with and sought the support of the provincial *parlements* but never entered into union with them. The longstanding rivalries between the sovereign courts and corporations of officials (often exploited by the monarchy in the past to its advantage) made a conjunction or mutual assistance between them impossible. The provincial *parlements* (there were nine of them) shared the typical grievances of venal officials, and some were also angered over the government's introduction of the Semester, which imposed an additional term upon the court and meant the creation of many new offices.[59] Nevertheless, the other *parlements* did not want to become satellites of the Paris court; similarly, the Parlement of Paris, which considered itself superior in dignity and authority to the rest, wanted to have a free hand in dealing with the government. Thus, notwithstanding the analogous complaints that spurred the opposition of the kingdom's *parlementaires*, their failure to cooperate soon undermined "la cause commune de la robe" and enabled the monarchy to negotiate with

[57] By the reform of the Chambre Saint Louis, the intendants were abolished in all but six provinces, which contained theaters of war in the Franco–Spanish conflict. Here the intendants were restricted to military administration and deprived of any jurisdiction over finances; see Moote, *The revolt of the judges*, 161; Bonney, *Political change in France under Richelieu and Mazarin*, 55–6, 60.

[58] *Ibid.*, 225–8, contains a survey of antifiscal revolts in the Fronde; and see Y.-M. Bercé (*Histoire des Croquants: Etude des soulèvements populaires au XVIIe siècle dans la sud-ouest de la France*, 2 v., Geneva, 1974, v. 1, 489) for the comment that rejection of imposts was the essential characteristic of the "popular Fronde."

[59] The provincial *parlements* at the time of the Fronde were those of Aix, Bordeaux, Dijon, Grenoble, Metz, Pau, Rennes, Rouen, and Toulouse.

them piecemeal. Just as the Parlement of Paris made its terms with the government in the Treaty of Rueil, so the provincial *parlements* used the crisis to gain their own particular concessions from the regime.[60]

Although after 1648 the provinces sank more or less into anarchy, local Frondes only developed in certain provinces as a result of particular circumstances. They occurred only where a provincial *parlement* headed the resistance to a royalist governor, or where the authority of a Frondeur governor was effective in bringing his province into revolt.[61] Such, for example, despite the innumerable complications in each, were the Frondes in Provence, Guienne, and Normandy.

In Provence, the Fronde and ensuing civil war was basically a confrontation between the Parlement of Aix and the intransigent Mazarinist governor, the count of Alais. The Parlement with popular support fought to oust him and gain redress of its own and provincial grievances. This conflict absorbed local feuds, caused outbreaks in Aix and other towns (Aix went through its own Day of the Barricades) and was continued in the fractionated Fronde of the nobility. In Guienne, the Parlement of Bordeaux led the revolt of the province against the hated Mazarinist governor, the duke of Epernon, which resulted in civil war. Then, split in various ways, Guienne became a base for the prince of Condé's partisans and noble rebellion, Condé himself succeeding Epernon as governor in 1651 as a concession extorted from the crown. Bordeaux, involved in internecine strife, remained the last bastion of the Fronde's battle against central authority. In Normandy, the Fronde was begun by the Parlement of Rouen, whose magistrates nursed grievances going back to the punishment inflicted on them nine years before for their inaction in the provincial rebellion of the Nu-pieds.[62] The duke of Longueville, the Frondeur governor, helped to carry on the conflict in Normandy until, like the Parlement of Rouen, he made his own terms with the monarchy and Mazarin.[63]

The civil war unleashed in the provinces by the events of 1648 was unstructured and uncoordinated. It consisted of multiple manifestations of collective violence without any bond or overall organization. Localized peasant insurrections, urban disorders, factional divisions of many kinds

[60] The relations during the rebellion between the Parlement of Paris and the provincial *parlements* are discussed by Moote, *The revolt of the judges*, *passim*; and see Bonney, *Political change in France under Richelieu and Mazarin*, 64–7.

[61] For this view, which I have adopted, see Kossmann, *La Fronde*, 118.

[62] See Chapter 9 in this book.

[63] Kossmann, *La Fronde*, *passim*, contains surveys of the Frondes in Provence, Guienne, Normandy, and several other provinces. Aix and Provence are discussed in detail by S. Kettering, *Judicial politics and urban revolt in seventeenth-century France: The Parlement of Aix, 1629–1659*, Princeton, 1978, ch. 8, and R. Pillorget, *Les Mouvements insurrectionnels de Provence entre 1596 et 1715*, Paris, 1975, 567–705. Normandy is treated in the narrative of P. Logié, *La Fronde en Normandie*, 3 v., Amiens, 1951–2.

in towns and provinces, popular resistance to royal and rebel soldiery alike, mingled in the general upheaval. The conflict between parties of Frondeurs and Mazarinists was less a reflection of general political issues than of local quarrels and particularist interests. Provincial Frondes did not merge to realize common aims; they remained unconnected movements of revolt, related only through their similar anticentralist character. No other revolutionary civil war of the early modern period was more fragmented, more lacking in central control, or more steeped in localism and provincialism.

The torrent of Mazarinades continued in full spate during the Fronde of the nobility. The *grands* employed their own pamphleteers. Retz published some clever libels of his own and also used other writers to promote his opinions and interests. Condé retained writers in his service such as Claude Dubosc Montandré, one of the ablest journalists of the time. Aristocratic Frondeurs utilized the press alike to pursue their personal vendettas and to express their political opposition.[64]

There was no break or sharp distinction in political ideas between the first and second stages of the Fronde. As always, Mazarin's tyranny remained one of the chief objects of denunciation. The institution of monarchy itself was never called into question. Indeed, Mazarin's position as first minister could be the more vehemently attacked because it was alleged to have no legitimate standing and to detract from the ruler's own authority.

The critique of absolutism and assertion of limits on royal power continued to be the Fronde's predominant and central theme. Besides the claims advanced in behalf of the Parlement of Paris, Frondeur writers also emphasized that the princes of the blood must be consulted in the government of the kingdom. This was a general point, although it acquired additional pertinence during the regency and before Louis XIV came of age. Condé protested against the regent's appointment of councillors without his consent, for by law "the Princes of the Blood are born Counsellors of the State." The Parlement of Paris, of which the princes of the blood were honorary members by birth, similarly affirmed their right to participate in the government.[65] A declaration of the princes in 1650 demanded that "to restore the State to its original form" a "legitimate Council of the Princes of the Blood" should be established, also to include officers of the crown and persons "descended of great Houses and ancient families."[66]

---

[64] For mention of some of Retz's tracts and of various authors employed by him and others, see, e.g., Retz's *Mémoires*, v. 3, 92–5, and the editor's notes; and also Moreau, *Bibliographie de Mazarinades*, v. 1, introduction, *passim*. Salmon (*Cardinal de Retz*, 192–5) reviews several of Retz's pamphlets. On Dubosc Montandré, see Kossmann, *La Fronde*, 108–10.

[65] See the passages cited in Doolin, *The Fronde*, 70–1.

[66] *L'Union ou association des princes, sur l'iniuste détention des princes de Condé, Conty, et duc de Longueville* (1650) in Moreau, *Choix de Mazarinades*, v. 2, 64.

Some writers propounded populist and constitutionalist doctrines in defense of the Fronde. Dubosc Montandré affirmed in various pamphlets that the king's will should not be accepted as valid or for the good of the state unless it accorded with the will of the princes of the blood, the *parlements*, and the people. For such ideas he was charged with speaking the language of the rebels in England.[67] Another pamphleteer perhaps drew on earlier monarchomach precepts in rejecting royal "absolute power" as incompatible with France's laws and customs. He declared that the people's resistance to oppression, far from being a case of disobedience or rebellion, was "legitimate war," justifiable by law and religion. Distinguishing royal tyranny from legitimate kingship, he claimed that the latter "depends on the will and choice of the people." Like other writers, he stressed the responsibility of both the *parlements* and the princes of the blood in restricting sovereign power.[68]

Claude Joly, a Paris priest associated with Retz and the aristocratic Frondeurs, presented the fullest discussion of limited monarchy in 1652 in a large work on public law. Joly held that monarchy stemmed from the election of the people and that kings are subject to the laws of their kingdom. Examining France's polity and legal writers, he concluded that the king was not alone in possessing authority to govern but shared it with the *parlements*, princes of the blood, and Estates General. To the *parlements* and Estates General he allotted an independent power to consent to legislation and taxes. Joly's conception would have transformed the absolute monarchy of Bourbon state builders into a constitutionally limited supremacy.[69]

As Joly's treatise indicated, the troubles of the Fronde stimulated a momentary spurt of political interest in the Estates General, which had not been convened for over forty years. In 1649, the regent summoned the Estates General, only to put off its meeting indefinitely because of its possible dangers. In 1651, an assembly of nobility in Paris that supported the Frondeur princes called anew for the Estates General. In its request, the nobility cited the country's rampant violence and revolt, vaunted its own preeminent role in the state, and declared that a general meeting of three orders was the infallible ancestral remedy to preserve the kingdom from destruction.[70] The regent pretended to consent but again contrived to postpone the convening indefinitely lest it further noble pretensions.

[67] See the passages cited in Kossmann, *La Fronde*, 109–10.
[68] *Le Raisonnable plaintif sur la dernière déclaration du roy* (1652), in Moreau, *Choix de Mazarinades*, v. 2, 452–65, *passim*. Doolin (*The Fronde*, 115–21) prints some extracts from this anonymous tract in behalf of limited monarchy.
[69] C. Joly, *Recueil de maximes véritables et importantes pour l'institution du roy* (1652). See the discussion of this work by Doolin, *The Fronde*, 121–34.
[70] *Requeste de la noblesse pour l'assemblée des éstats généraux* (1651), in Moreau, *Choix de Mazarinades*, v. 2, 230–40.

The Parlement of Paris was also opposed to the Estates General, which it disliked as a possible rival to itself. One of the judges expressed the prevailing opinion when he said that the Estates General can only act by means of petitions and on its knees, whereas the Parlement ranks above it and stands as a mediator between the people and the king.[71] Thus, despite some discussion of its importance, demands to revive the Estates General bore no fruit. By the time of the Fronde, however, the Estates General was an obsolete and little-regarded institution. Even had its meeting materialized, it probably would have failed to serve as a focal point for effective action in the revolt.[72]

V

During the Fronde of the nobility, the Parlement of Paris remained unaligned, pursuing a wobbly path of neutrality or mediation amid its own differences and a fantastic confusion of factions and interests. Courted by the government, rival *grands*, and aristocratic Frondeurs, it allied itself with none. It condemned the government's imprisonment of Condé and his two relatives but also condemned the subsequent rebellion of the princes. It maintained its strong opposition to Mazarin, protesting vehemently when he returned at the end of 1651 from exile, but at the same time was anxious about the deepening anarchy of the kingdom. Although its revolt was past, the Parlement was witnessing all the effects of the decomposition of the state its resistance had initiated.

The civil war in 1651–2 was fought between the royal armies and those of Condé and his magnate allies in engagements scattered over the provinces. The monarchy's troops included German mercenaries, Condé's some Spanish contingents and six thousand mercenaries of the duke of Lorraine. In the fall of 1651, the queen mother and king abandoned Paris to show themselves to their subjects and support their armies with their presence. Mazarin rejoined them a few months later on his return to France. The main aim of the queen and the minister was to reenter the capital in triumph. Despite a few successes, the position of the Frondeur princes gradually deteriorated. They were driven from their main strongholds in the south and west, save for the insurgent city of Bordeaux. In the central provinces the fighting went against them, and Normandy was neutralized.

---

[71] Cited in Kossmann, *La Fronde*, 99.

[72] For the failed attempt to revive the Estates General during the Fronde, see *ibid.*, 99, 190–3; and Moote, *The revolt of the judges*, 295–6. Doolin (*The Fronde*, 145–6) notices some of the writings favorable to the Estates General, remarking that they are "comparatively rare." Assemblies of nobility, like that in Paris in 1651 which called for a convention of the Estates General, were another aspect of the Fronde's disorder and symptom of royal weakness. The subject is discussed by J.-D. Lassaigne, *Les Assemblées de la noblesse de France aux XVIIe et XVIIIe siécles*, Paris, 1966, pts. 1–2.

By the spring of 1652, the civil war was narrowing to the region around Paris. In April, Condé left his army of about six thousand men and proceeded suddenly to Paris with the hope of gaining it for his cause. The Fronde had begun in Paris; there in the summer of 1652 it was also to undergo its climactic moment and decisive reverse.

The city was infected by growing tensions caused by the proximity of the contending armies. Provisioning was difficult and popular unruliness once again manifest in its anti-Mazarinist fervor, as in the days of the barricades and the siege of 1649. On his arrival, Condé first tried to persuade the Parlement to support his revolt but failed. Then he began to incite the populace and play on fears of social upheaval in order to intimidate the judges. Incendiary placards and pamphlets called on the people to rise against the "Mazarins," the partisans of the minister. A few writings of even more radical bent appeared attacking the king, the Parlement, and the princes alike as enemies of the people. During May and June there were repeated incidents of disorder. A violent demonstration at the end of June threatened the Parlement, demanding "death to the Mazarins" and "union with the princes." The situation became even more critical a few days later, when Condé's troops entered Paris after fighting a battle right outside the city gates.

Violence reached a peak on July 4 at the Hotel de Ville, where a huge crowd including soldiers waited impatiently while, inside, deputies of the sovereign courts and other public bodies discussed how to preserve order. Shooting began, and an enraged mob attacked the building, setting it afire in several places. Before the outbreak ended, about 30 of the deputies had been killed or wounded, and another 150 people were dead.

The massacre at the city hall placed Condé and his followers in temporary control of Paris. The next day a new municipal administration was established headed by the *parlementaire* Broussel. The city then declared its union with the rebellious princes. Later in the month a coerced, truncated Parlement, from which more than a third of the judges had withdrawn, also endorsed the revolt by a small majority and acknowledged the military and political command of Condé and the duke of Orléans.[73]

The insurrection in Paris lacked any organization, ideology, or distinctive social base. It depended on mob action and involved diverse elements of the populace, which the Frondeur magnates exploited for their own profit, but was rooted in nothing solid or durable. Condé himself had no idea of how to follow it up or any wish to sponsor popular radicalism. To him, moreover, the movement brought only momentary advantage and

[73] The events in Paris after Condé's arrival and the massacre at the Hotel de Ville are discussed in Kossmann, *La Fronde*, 217–32. Miscellaneous details may also be found in Moote, *The revolt of the judges*, 337–45; and J. B. Perkins, *France under Mazarin with a review of the administration of Richelieu*, 2 v., New York, 1886, v. 2, 195–200.

beyond that remained only an embarrassment and encumbrance. For the Fronde, its effect was completely negative. What it did was to horrify the magistrates, officials, and bourgeois well-to-do, intensify the desire to end the civil war, and encourage the forces of capitulation.

After July, the Fronde's decline proceeded swiftly. Further rebel military reverses prevented help or relief to Paris. In August, the king, staying at Compiègne, ordered the Parlement of Paris to transfer itself to Pontoise; an increasing number of judges obeyed and formed a rival body. The other sovereign courts presently suspended their sittings. As an act of conciliation, the king now also dismissed Mazarin, who again went into exile. This removed the last obstacle to peace. Delegations from the capital came to negotiate with the king, queen mother, and government, while individual Frondeurs tried to get any terms they could. The insurrectionary municipal regime was dissolved. Finally, following Condé's flight, Louis XIV reentered a defeated Paris on October 21. Hardly more than three months later, in February 1653, he recalled Mazarin, as was always intended, and the cardinal resumed his power as chief minister of the crown.

Besides Paris, other towns too experienced a variety of disturbances and insurrections during the Fronde. Some, like Aix, as we have already seen, were the seat of provincial *parlements* that headed the local movements. One of the biggest such conflicts, however, occurred in Angers, where there was no *parlement* to lead or canalize revolt. Here, a fierce struggle broke out between the Loricards, compacted of lesser bourgeoisie, artisans, and *menu peuple*, and the tight oligarchy of the rich and the officials that governed the city. The decline of the monarchy's authority, which had always stood behind the oligarchy, enabled the Loricards to seize control in 1649. Defeated by royal troops, they renewed their insurgency and captured Angers again in 1651 in alliance with the duke of Rohan, the Frondeur governor of Anjou, who had joined Condé's rebellion. When a royal army expelled Rohan and reconquered Anjou in February 1652, insurrectionary Angers fell too, and the oligarchy was restored to power.[74]

Another insurrection, the sole popular movement in the Fronde to reflect a radical political consciousness, was the Ormée in Bordeaux, which got its name from the platform of elm trees (*ormière*) where its adherents met. In the first part of the Fronde, the Parlement of Bordeaux conducted the battle against Mazarin and Guienne's royalist governor, becoming as a result the dominant power in the city. Subsequent divisions gave birth in 1651–2 to the Ormée, which emerged as popularly based protest against the Parlement and linked to the nobility's Fronde.

[74] For the Loricards (vagabonds, masterless men) at Angers, see Kossmann, *La Fronde*, 137–8, 212–13; and Bonney, *Political change in France under Richelieu and Mazarin*, 296, 319, 335–6.

While Condé was imprisoned in 1650, Condé's wife and friends roused
Bordeaux to resistance on his behalf in opposition to its Parlement, which
wanted peace with the crown. Later, upon launching his own rebellion,
the prince stayed in the city for six months till March 1652. He enjoyed a
considerable following there, which he cultivated personally and through
his family and agents. Meanwhile, the Ormée took shape in gatherings
held at the *ormière* to discuss public affairs. As many as three thousand
people took part in these meetings, which mobilized anti-Mazarinist sentiment and provided a forum for complaints against the Parlement's
maladministration as well as for speeches in favor of liberty and self-
government. Adherents of Condé, in the spring of 1652 the Ormists pressed
their fight against the Parlement and demanded a purge of its members.
The polarization precipitated riots and armed clashes between partisans
of the two sides that were the prelude to a showdown. Condé's sister and
brother, the duchess of Longueville and the prince of Conti, tried to con-
ciliate these differences, but in vain. At the end of June, concurrently with
the insurrection in Paris, the Ormists occupied the Hotel de Ville, and
three thousand men invaded the residential quarter where the *parlementaires* lived. Houses were pillaged and burned, property destroyed, and
fifty to a hundred people killed. After this bloody fight, the Ormée dominated the city. It retained its ascendancy for a year, until Bordeaux capitulated to a royal army in July 1653.

In the vague institutional form it acquired, the Ormée resembled both a
civic political association and a fraternal society. In some articles of union
of 1652, one of its few authentic documents, the Ormée's members refer
to themselves as "bourgeois" and "inhabitants" of the city of Bordeaux.
They pledge obedience to the king, service to their governor (Condé), and
fidelity to their *"patrie,"* that is, their town, for whose franchises and privileges they affirm their readiness to risk life and goods. As part of these
privileges, they particularly declare their determination as "bourgeois" to
insist on a deliberative voice in the general assembly of the city and to
demand a full account of the management of public money. Other pledges,
which invoke the name of Jesus Christ, include brotherly love, peace,
arbitration of disputes among members, and assistance to members vexed
by legal process and fines or afflicted with poverty or illness.[75]

The size of the Ormée's membership is unknown (indeed, a great deal
concerning it is very obscure), but, considering the crowds it mustered in
its cause, its supporters must have been very numerous: according to a
modern student, about a quarter of Bordeaux's population, or 10,000–
12,000 people.[76] The movement naturally gained its following from the

[75] These Ormist articles of union are printed in Bercé, *Histoire des Croquants*, v. 2, 819–20.
[76] S. Westrich, *The Ormée of Bordeaux*, Baltimore, 1972, 4. This work, the fullest account
of the movement, is useful for its numerous facts, on which I have drawn, but fails to

middle and lower sectors of the city: the smaller merchants, modest tradesmen, minor functionaries, artisans, and below. A list of 124 Ormists includes merchants as the largest category plus a variety of petty officials, some independent artisans, a few men of the professions, and eight noblemen.[77] The members of the Ormée who held the status of *bourgeois* of Bordeaux – and this entailed a property qualification – possessed formal citizenship privileges but obviously felt excluded from civic power by an upper group of merchants and officials. The entire Ormist insurrection was a crystallization of social and political antagonism toward both the oligarchy of the city and the Parlement as well as toward royal absolutism, condemned alike for their monopoly and abuse of power, their management of public affairs in their own interest, and their fiscal oppression.

The Ormists followed up their victory by establishing domination of the municipal government. Through election they gained a majority on the Jurade, the city council, and went on to eliminate the influence of the Parlement, which by custom was represented in various civic functions. They also created several new institutions, including a five hundred–member Chamber of the Ormée and a Chamber of Thirty, which became the principal executive authority. To its opponents among the *parlementaires*, wealthy merchants, and officials, it dealt out fines, confiscations, and banishment. The Ormée had to direct Bordeaux's military resistance to the monarchy's troops as well as manage civil affairs. It resorted to requisitions and tried to fix food prices and prevent hoarding. One of its most drastic measures was a decree, promulgated in January 1653 by the prince of Conti, ordering the reduction of rents in the city by a quarter because of the economic adversities due to the civil war.[78]

Along with its political militancy and a degree of social radicalism, the Ormée stood for popular participation in government. In 1651, the English republic sent several emissaries to Guienne to investigate the possibility of an alliance with the Fronde. One of them, Edward Sexby, who was a former Leveller activist, gave Condé's agent a French translation of the Leveller *Agreement of the people*, entitled *L'Accord du peuple*. The agent disapproved it, and, although Sexby remained in Bordeaux for nearly two years, there is no evidence that the document ever became known or had any effect.[79] Such as they were, the Ormée's political ideas stemmed from

recognize the Ormée's political and ideological immaturity and goes wrong in conceiving it as a class struggle. Kossmann's discussion (*La Fronde*, 245–58) provides a nuanced and perceptive treatment.

[77] Westrich (*The Ormée of Bordeaux*, 41–6) examines the social substance of the Ormée.

[78] *Ibid.*, chs. 4, 6. It is unclear why the order reducing rents should have been issued in the name of the prince of Conti (*ibid.*, 110–11).

[79] *L'Accord du peuple* and accompanying matter is printed in O. Lutaud, *Les Niveleurs, Cromwell, et la république*, Paris, 1967, 248–74. See the comments of Bercé, *Histoire des Croquants*, v. 1, 513. This episode and English relations to the Fronde generally are discussed by Knachel, *England and the Fronde*.

its own milieu. Unlike the Levellers, moreover, a much more sophisticated radical movement with a rich body of doctrine, the Ormée made
little use of the press and failed to develop any ideological statement of its
position and program. A few anonymous pamphlets, however, composed
either by members or sympathetic observers, did give expression to some
of its basic beliefs.

These writings stressed the quarrel between the people and tyranny
and affirmed the supremacy of popular assemblies as the proper basis of
government. One tract traced such assemblies back to the practice of the
ancient Gauls, the model, it said, for the Ormée's own meetings under
the trees. It also praised equality as the foundation of unity and peace,
contending that "the actual cause of sedition and political strife is the ex-
cessive wealth of the few." Another pamphleteer asserted that only the
people can achieve the restoration of France, whereas "the great nobles
and magistrates are the accomplices of tyranny." According to this same
author, the Ormée had "established a democratic government" in Bordeaux. Ormist propaganda also denounced the injustices of the Parlement
and called for judicial and other reforms. Several tracts denied the accu-
sation that the Ormée opposed the king. It was dedicated, they said, to
the service of God, the king, Condé, and the well-being of the people.
One of the most radical pamphlets, the *Manifeste des Bordelois* (1652), declared that the people of Bordeaux have shown Frenchmen how to break
their chains and restore to the entire kingdom its original liberties lost in
the course of centuries.[80]

Such principles presumably helped to inspire the Ormée's insurgency.
The movement demonstrated a radical and democratic character in its
opposition to oligarchy and absolutism. In a vague way, it embraced the
conception of popular sovereignty. But it did not achieve a full-fledged
ideology expounding and justifying its convictions, nor did it articulate a
program describing its desired reforms. Moreover, despite an occasional
reference to France, the Ormée's real political horizon was parochial, being
largely limited to Bordeaux and perhaps the province, its *patrie*.

VI

In July 1653, the Ormée's rule collapsed due to demoralization and decline
of support as Bordeaux, encircled by royal troops, prepared to surrender.
The city's ensuing fall concluded the Fronde. Of the main actors in the
revolution, only Condé continued his resistance by entering the service of

---

[80] For this summary and extracts, see Westrich, *The Ormée of Bordeaux*, 48–59, an exposition of Ormist ideas. The main pamphlets cited are *Apologie pour l'Ormée* (n.d.) and *Manifeste
des Bordelois* (1652), the latter published in Paris. Kossmann suggests that the Ormée aroused
great interest in Paris and that its ideas circulated there (*La Fronde*, 230).

Spain. Not till the peace of 1659, which ended the Franco–Spanish war, did he return to France to be pardoned and reconciled with the crown. All the other rebel *grands* submitted to the monarchy for the highest price they could obtain.[81]

The Fronde's upheaval left a trail of troubles and turmoil. On top of the economic misery and natural disasters of the time, the material destruction of the civil war inflicted widespread suffering. Sporadic minor disturbances, moreover, persisted into the later 1650s, among them unauthorized assemblies of the nobility in a dozen provinces that worried the government until finally suppressed in 1659, an agrarian insurrection, the Sabotiers of Sologne, around Orléans and Berry, and violent faction quarrels and outbreaks in the towns of Provence and elsewhere.[82] These were the expiring spasms of the convulsion, lingering effects of a debilitated body politic.

Nevertheless, the defeat and liquidation of the Fronde was decisive as far as the future of royal government was concerned. That defeat was due less to the monarchy's strength in the immediate circumstances than to the revolution's weakness. But the Fronde was followed by a recuperation that made the subsequent reign of Louis XIV the most powerful in French history. After 1660, Bourbon kingship attained an unprecedented supremacy, becoming the model of centralized absolutism, while an aggressive, expansionist France became predominant among the European states.

With the suppression of the Fronde, its reforms were quickly swept away. On October 22, 1652, the day immediately following the king's reentry into Paris, a royal declaration in a *lit de justice* prohibited the Parlement of Paris from interfering in affairs of state and financial matters and annulled its previous intervention in those areas. The Parlement registered this declaration, the badge of its submission. Subsequent royal legislation or disregard did away with other parts of the reforms of 1648. After 1652, the intendants were restored in the provinces, charged with their former responsibility for financial administration and other tasks. What the Chambre Saint Louis had sought to establish as a barrier to absolutism and the fiscal regime was thus undone. Although the Parlement and sovereign courts still continued, of course, to be great institutions of which the government had to take account, they could no longer play a political role or attempt to control the crown. Cardinal Mazarin, too, whom the rebellion had sworn to destroy, remained firmly fixed in office in the post-Fronde years, serving and instructing the king until his death in 1661, after which Louis XIV reigned without a first minister. The ambition of the princes and *grands* to dominate the regime and its policy was also conclusively defeated. They remained no less vital to the

---

[81] See Bonney, *Political change in France under Richelieu and Mazarin*, 297–8, for details.
[82] See *ibid.*, 313–16; Pillorget, *Les Mouvements insurrectionnels de Provence*, bk. 2, ch. 3.

monarchy than before as servants of its rule and in the aftermath of the Fronde received pensions, grants, and governorships. Nonetheless, if they still possessed substantial social and political power over their inferiors, they had largely lost their ability and will to maintain armed resistance against royal sovereignty.[83]

The Fronde was thus a complete failure, and the more so in that it did not leave even a memory, an ideal, or a belief capable of inspiring any future generation. The causes of its failure are obvious enough. For one thing, it was deeply lacking in unity. Bureaucratic officials had too many rivalries to wage a lengthy common struggle, and the Parlement of Paris refused to ally itself with the provincial *parlements*. Similarly, the judges were chary of the nobility and refused to form a coalition with the *grands* and princes. The monarchy was accordingly never forced to fight its opponents as a single front.

Weakness of leadership was another reason for the Fronde's failure. The movement was devoid of outstanding statesmen and strategists. The Parlement of Paris contained some magistrates noted for courage, integrity, and prudence, like its eminent first president Mathieu Molé, whom Cardinal de Retz called "one of the most intrepid men of the century, as great in heart as in mind."[84] But such men belonged to the conservative lawyerly type and had their own personal connections with the government; they were hardly the sort to conduct a fierce, unremitting combat against the monarchical state. As for Condé and his confederates, they were even more lacking in political leadership and vision.

A third cause of the Fronde's failure lay in its ideological indecision and inadequacy. Although it stood for legal limits on the king's sovereign power, it was unable to develop another conception of government as the alternative to absolutism. The Parlement of Paris fought for reforms that have been compared with the constitutional revolution wrought by the English Long Parliament,[85] yet it always avoided a direct ideological confrontation with the absolutist system. In political thought and ideological clarity, the Fronde was far inferior to the contemporary English revolution or to the Huguenot revolt of the sixteenth century, from which, moreover, it took practically nothing. The Fronde never really proclaimed a full-fledged doctrine of rebellion; its defense of the right of resistance remained timid, too, and did not occupy a prominent place in its propa-

---

[83] Bonney (*Political change in France under Richelieu and Mazarin*, 67–9, 420–1) and Moote (*The revolt of the judges*, 350–4) discuss the effects of the Fronde's defeat. Moote underestimates, I think, the extent of the royal triumph.

[84] *Mémoires*, v. 1, 262–4, contains a portrait of Molé, who appears often in this work. Retz noted that as Molé had been nurtured in the legal forms of the Palais de Justice, "everything that was extraordinary was suspect to him." For Molé's own *Mémoires*, see the edition by A. Champollion-Figeac, 4 v., Paris, 1855–7.

[85] Moote, *The revolt of the judges*, 370.

ganda. Its commitment to constitutionalist principles was genuine enough but profoundly wanting in theoretical amplitude and resolution.

The popular movements that appeared in the Fronde displayed similar shortcomings. Mob action and insurgencies among the middle and plebeian strata were an important part of the revolution. They were hardly linked at all, however, with social radicalism and in any case had no clear ideas and goals of their own. For the most part, they were ancillary to the objectives of the elites who dominated the Fronde. Nowhere, not even in the case of the Ormée, did a popular party emancipate itself to a position of independence within the overall constellation of forces. The paradoxical alliance of the Ormée with the princes and Condé, who desired its support but had quite different interests, was a sign of the subordination and immaturity of these movements.

All these observations only confirm Kossmann's percipient comment that the Fronde "turned in a circle, enveloped by an incertitude that paralyzed it."[86] The ultimate explanation for its failure lay in the divided society that produced it. France had developed no national political class to voice its grievances and give it revolutionary leadership. The *grands* with their personal ambitions, the bureaucratic officials of the robe with their professional vested interests, were not such a class. France also lacked a national representative institution to provide a focus and vehicle for revolution. The Estates General had never served this function and was now obsolete. The Parlement of Paris was very good at obstruction, but it was only one of the sovereign courts and was unprepared by its traditions and in too many ways part of the existing system ever to aspire to govern. Provincialism, jurisdictional rivalries, and a confusion of overlapping and countervailing authorities made a common resistance against the monarchy all but impossible. Royal absolutism was fundamentally much tougher, more clear-sighted, and more resilient than any of its adversaries. Only the monarchy and its servitors possessed the political and institutional capacity for national rule. The Fronde's failure to reverse the course of absolutism was thus foreordained. Its defeat helps to suggest the conclusion that nothing less than a movement as great in scope as the subsequent revolution of 1789, with its uncompromising will, its terrible destructive power, its ideological clarity and force, and its impassioned faith in the nation, liberty, and citizenship, could ever have been strong enough to overthrow the political structure of the *ancien régime*.

[86]*La Fronde*, 30.

14

Epilogue

The revolutions we have surveyed were part of a world that was still strongly bound to its traditions and had not yet come to envisage the possibility of fundamental, continuous transformation in the conditions of humanity. After 1660, as the gales of the mid-century revolutions blew themselves out, the states and society of Western Europe entered a more stable phase, which lasted almost to the close of the next century. The crisis of the seventeenth century was overcome, and the succeeding period became a time of renewed economic growth and expansion. Revolts and disturbances continued to occur, of course, but with nothing like the frequency, seriousness, or magnitude of the civil conflicts of the preceding era.

That era, despite all its upheavals, had known only one great foundational revolution, the struggle in the Netherlands that brought forth the Dutch republic. Nearly all the other revolutions of the sixteenth and earlier seventeenth centuries, monumental as some of them were in their combat with absolutism, went down to defeat, unable to survive and found lasting regimes. Following the Netherlands rebellion, it was a hundred years before another significant foundational revolution took place in Europe, that of 1688 in England. This event, already celebrated at the time as the "Glorious Revolution," was brief and very limited in its violence and was justified by its aristocratic makers as restorative, not innovative. Nevertheless, under its conservative guise it wrought a decisive, permanent change in the political order. It enthroned new rulers, William III and Mary, secured subjects' rights and Parliament's supremacy, and provided a moderate installment of civil and religious liberty. Henceforward, the "British constitution" became famed among liberal thinkers and foreigners as the embodiment of political freedom in a Europe that remained dominated by absolute sovereigns and enlightened despots.

The tempo of history continued to move slowly until it was suddenly accelerated by the effects of the revolutions in America and France, which spelled the destruction of the *ancien régime*. The first of these issued in one of the most momentous of foundational acts, the creation of the United States as a federal republic. The new state and nation proclaimed their adherence to the principles of popular freedom, equality, and representative self-government in the Declaration of Independence of 1776 and the federal constitution of 1787. The latter charter opened with words the Levellers might have used, "We the People," thereby defining the ultimate source of authority and laws in the governmental structure it ordained. The great seal of the American republic bore the Virgilian motto, "Novus ordo seclorum," thus identifying the republic's foundation as the commencement of a new age of the world.

Even more pronounced in their foundational ardor and will to break with the old society were the post-1789 revolutionaries in France who swept away the Bourbon monarchy along with so many other relics of the past. In 1793, the French republic abolished the old calendar and instituted a new one that reckoned the Year One from its own inception, a remarkable sign of the futuristic consciousness dominating the greatest revolution that had so far taken place in Europe. The French constitution of 1793 was also the first to announce that the purpose of government is *"le bonheur commun."* It was in hailing this innovation that the youthful Jacobin leader, Saint-Just, made his famous and unforgettable statement, "Happiness is a new idea in Europe."[1]

It was this "sense of a new era," as an American scholar has described it,[2] and of man's ability to build a new world answering to his own rational plan that marked the final point of separation between the revolutions of an earlier time that we have looked at in comparative view and those that followed 1789. The former had equipped themselves with a large body of ideas and principles justifying resistance and revolt; they had given rise to occasional millenarian fervor and utopian hopes; they had invoked religion, God's justice, and the sovereignty of the people on behalf of their aims. But, as a whole, they were more inspired by an image of the past than by a vision of the future. The English revolution of 1640–60 in its more radical manifestations had come closest to the achievement of an ideology welding past and future and looking toward the establishment of a future new order on universal principles of natural rights.

It was only toward the end of the eighteenth century, as a result of the developments in America and France, that the "Prometheanism" of revolution fully emerged. This was the juncture at which the modern faith of revolution, almost like a secular religion, entered the bloodstream of Eu-

[1] See M. Lyons, *France under the Directory*, Cambridge, 1975, 24.
[2] R. R. Palmer, *The age of the democratic revolution*, Princeton, 1959, 239. This work and its successor volume contain a rich and interesting account of the American, French, and other revolutionary movements of the later eighteenth century and their mutual relations.

ropean society. Revolution finally acquired a new meaning as the conscious molding and transformation of history. The apostles of this new faith conceived the French revolution as the divine ancestor of the inevitable and ultimate liberation to come. The revolutionary faith united with the kindred faith in progress. It infused visions of social justice based on the abolition of private property and classes. It began to stir workers and to animate the growing sentiment of nationalism and emancipation among subject peoples. The goals of revolution expanded almost limitlessly, as men came to imagine that they could shape the political, social, and moral order as they willed, in accordance with the laws of universal or of historical-dialectical reason.

The nineteenth and twentieth centuries have seen not only innumerable revolutionary conflicts and movements plus an enormous amount of revolutionary violence but also a larger number of foundational revolutions, alike in Western and non-Western societies, than all the past together. If the last two centuries have increasingly brought changes at an unprecedented rate and on a scale hardly known before, this is due in considerable part to a new dynamic conception of revolution and to the exceptional role for good and ill that revolution as myth and deed has come to assume in human affairs.

Index

absolute power, 64, 144, 195, 196

absolutism, 1, 9, 17, 19, 68, 80, 85–6, 90, 91, 117, 119–20, 127, 138, 142, 144, 185, 190–2, 198, 200, 213, 220, 221, 222

Act of Abjuration, 117, 118, 169

Acton, Lord, 52

Aerschot, duke of, 112

Agreement of the People, 165, 167, 218

Alais, count of, 211

Alpujarras, 14

Alva, duke of, 97, 98, 99, 100, 101, 102, 103, 104, 107

American revolution, 224

Amsterdam, 95, 104, 115, 126

Angers, 216

Anjou, duke of, 75, 76, 119–20, 123

Anne of Austria, 54, 192, 195, 197, 198, 199–200, 201, 207, 208, 214

Antwerp, 88, 95, 96, 111, 116, 121

Apology of William of Orange, 116–18

Aragon, 5, 32–3, 49

Armada, 79, 125

Arminians, 141–2, 148

Aske, Robert, 24–31

Avranches, 11, 12

Bacon, Francis, 32, 49, 58, 127, 181

Baptists, 174

Barcelona, 34, 35, 37

Béarn, 17

Beggars, the, 93, 102, 103, 115

Bekenntnis of Magdeburg, 67

Belgium, 87, 126

Beza, Theodore, 62, 67, 69, 106

Bodin, Jean, 1, 20, 71, 120, 191

Bordeaux, 211, 214, 216–19

Boucher, Jean, 80

Bourbon, house of, 56, 57, 59, 84

bourgeois revolution, 52, 137–8

Braudel, Fernand, 13

Brederode, Baron, 92, 96

Brill, 102, 109

Brisson, Barnabé, 82

Bristol, 155

Broussel, Pierre, 198–9, 215

Bruges, 95, 116

Brussels, 114

Buckingham, duke of, 141

Caen, 11, 12

Calvin, John, 67

Calvinists, 92, 94–6, 99, 104, 105, 108, 111, 114–16, 120, 123

Casimir, John, 73, 113

Castelnaudary, 10

Castile, 3–4

Catalonia, 4, 5, 32, 33–7, 49

Catherine de Medici, 56, 58, 66

Catherine of Aragon, 23

Catholic League, 54, 55, 57, 59, 75–84, 115, 119, 122, 191

Catholicism, and revolution: England, 20–31; France, 54, 55, 56, 57, 66; Ireland, 43, 44, 46, 47, 48; *see also* Catholic League

Cevennes, 18

Chambre Saint Louis, articles, 198, 200, 220

Charles I, 17; and English revolution, 133, 134, 135, 139, 141, 142–3, 144, 145, 146, 147, 150, 151, 152, 153, 160, 161, 162, 166, 167, 168–9, 174; and Irish rebellion, 44, 45, 46, 47; and Scottish rebellion, 38, 39, 48

Charles II, 173, 183, 184, 185

Charles V, 88, 89, 114

Charles IX, 56, 57, 58, 65, 66, 95

Clarendon, earl of, 154

Claris, Pau, 35

Clark, G.N., 90

class and class conflict, 54, 138, 155

227

DATE DUE

░░░░░░░░░░		
BURG NOV 1 2 1988		
░░░░░░░░░░		
		░░░░░░░░
BURG DEC 0 6 1988		
BURG JAN 2 4 1989		░░░░
OFFIC. FEB 8 1990		
BURG MAR 2 8 1991		
201-6503		Printed in USA